ROOSEVELT'S
Thrilling Experiences
IN THE WILDS OF AFRICA
HUNTING BIG GAME

¶ Exciting Adventures hunting the wild and ferocious beasts of the Jungle and Plain and mingling with the Savage People, studying their strange customs, their awful superstitions and weird beliefs, their curious marriage ceremonies and barbarous treatment of young girls and women . . . .

¶ Together with graphic descriptions of the mighty rivers, wonderful cataracts, inland seas, vast lakes, great forests, and the diamond mines of untold wealth . . . .

¶ A vast Treasury of all that is wonderful, marvelous, interesting and instructive in the Dark Continent . . . .
¶ Including the Story-Life of Roosevelt, with his boyhood adventures and strenuous career on a Western Ranch . .

—— BY ——
MARSHALL EVERETT,
The Great Descriptive Writer and Traveler

¶ Illustrated with a large number of Exciting Hunting Scenes and Photographs of the Strange Natives of Darkest Africa

COLONEL ROOSEVELT IN A TIGHT PLACE.

The Colonel's remarkable ability as a hunter and his unerring aim stood him in good stead when confronted by three big lions. He has killed one, hit another which is springing in the air before dropping mortally wounded. He is reloading for a shot at the third, a lioness.

ROOSEVELT IN A SMALL BOAT WITH TWO AFRICAN NATIVES ATTACKS A PARTY OF TWELVE HIPPOPOTAMI AND KILLS THREE BULLS.

THE HERO OF SAN JUAN HILL.
When the news of Dewey's victory reached America, Mr. Roosevelt resigned his position as Assistant Secretary of the Navy. "There is nothing more for me to do here," he said, "I have got to get into the fight myself."

COLONEL ROOSEVELT AND HIS SONS.

The above picture shows Mr. Roosevelt and his four sons, Theodore, Archibald, Quentin and Kermit, sitting in order named, reading from left to right.

MR. ROOSEVELT AS A COWBOY.
In the Colonel's work, "Ranch Life and the Hunting Trail," the author pays the following tribute to the rough rider of the plains: "Brave, hospitable, hardy and adventurous, he is the grim pioneer of our land."

COLONEL ROOSEVELT RIDING ACROSS COUNTRY.

Mr. Roosevelt is an enthusiastic horseman. He is never so happy as when, astride his favorite animal, he sets off for a long ride. He is absolutely fearless in the saddle and does not hesitate to take the highest of rail fences.

THE HAPPY ANTICIPATION OF A FINE FEAST.

They will chew him up with their sharp teeth like the Hyenas down to the marrow of the bones. Such a huge water-buck not often falls prey to their gluttonous stomachs. When it comes to Lion hunting they all prefer staying in Camp. "Shimba" (The Lion) drives the fear of death into their hearts, especially if a Lion breaks the silence of the African night by his dreadful roaring.

THEODORE ROOSEVELT AND HIS FAMILY.

The ex-President has six children, Theodore, Jr., born September 13, 1887; Kermit, born October 10, 1889; Ethel Carow, born August 10, 1891; Archibald Bulloch, born April 9, 1894; Quentin, born November 19, 1897. Alice, who occupies the center of the above group, is the daughter of his first wife.

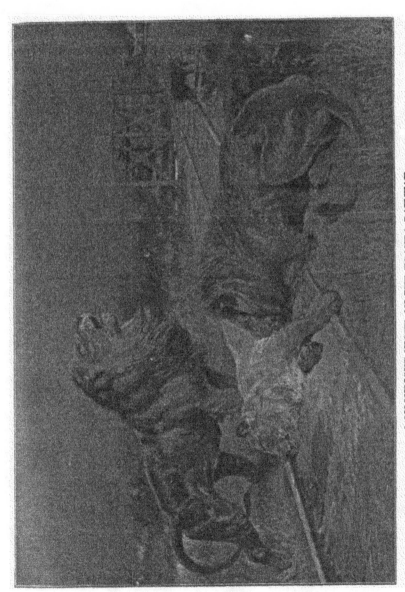

A MOONLIGHT NIGHT ON THE UGANDA RAILWAY.

The lions have discovered the dead bodies and as is their custom they stand beside the dead body and roar in their most terrible manner, sometimes so loud that they can be heard for nearly two miles. The hyena waiting for his prey can be seen to the right. Colonel Roosevelt traveled along this line sitting on the cowcatcher of the engine and saw many thrilling and weird scenes of animal life.

A FINE EAST AFRICAN RHINOCEROS JUST KILLED BY THE HUNTERS.

A WEIRD DANCE BY AFRICAN NATIVES.

On festive occasions this dance is given. The headdress is made of grass fiber, the necklaces are of dogs and other animal teeth, while the anklets are of feathers. The central figure wears an enormous headdress of Bird-of-Paradise plumes surmounted by a gigantic aigrette of parrots' feathers. The dancers wear great bunches of grass behind and carry light wands purely for decorative effect. During these dances old tribal jealousies arise and a man finds opportunity to spear his adversary.

WITH THE FLASHLIGHT CAMERA IN THE WILDS OF AFRICA.
Zebras photographed by flashlight while drinking at night. The zebra advance very cautiously to a drinking place, but the herd feels quite safe under the guidance of a cautious and watchful male leader. Colonel Roosevelt and Kermit secured some perfect specimens of this animal.

NO RACE SUICIDE IN THIS DISTRICT.
Photograph of a South African warrior, his wives and family. Motherhood is regarded by these savage women as the greatest blessing that can come to them.

PREPARING YOUNG AFRICAN GIRLS FOR THE MARRIAGE MARKET.

A BULL HIPPOPOTAMUS IN AN AFRICAN STREAM.

A FALLEN LION IN AN AFRICAN FOREST.

PUBLISHER'S PREFACE

THE publishers of this work deem it fit to impress upon our readers that we have left nothing undone to make it in every respect worthy of its interesting subject and the august personality who plays such an important part in it. The fact that Theodore Roosevelt is the hero of our book is alone enough to secure it an introduction and hearty welcome in every American home. Add to this the unusual environments in which he is placed, the thrilling incidents and narrow escapes he passes through, the tropical natural scenery in which he dwells, the many unknown and strange quadrupeds, bipeds and quadrumana he meets, the fabulous wealth of the African fauna and flora, which baffles his eyes, and you will see enacted before your wondering and admiring eyes a drama so unique, so exceptional and so extraordinary as to surpass anything you have either seen or heard of before.

And, further, consider that this strange and fascinating world is described to you in the most picturesque and vivid language, by an author who is thoroughly familiar with his subject, who has spent years of his life in travels in all parts of the world, and with his own eyes seen many of the localities he depicts—if we did not know that we could offer the American public a work that in its kind has never yet been surpassed, yea, not even equalled, we would not care to send it out with the imprint of our well-known firm. The text is embellished by hundreds of explanatory illustrations, many of them exact representations of photographs or drawings of prominent artists and professional students of nature, and also by maps of some of the localities made world-famous by Roosevelt's exploits.

We need not call the attention of parents, teachers and friends of the young to the high educational value of a work like this. It will place in the hands of our boys and young men a more welcome and needed substitute for the many novels and other story books of a doubtful nature, of which the bookmarket now abounds. It will divert the minds and thoughts of the young to nature, the source of health and happiness, prevent a morbid longing for and brooding on the dark deeds of the slippery dime-novel heroes, and steel the mind for noble and manly feats. Our ex-President, who in so many other respects, has broken new soil and opened new roads for our ambitious youth has also through the achievements related in this fascinating work proven himself a standardbearer of healthy and invigorating ideas, and a wayshower to hitherto untried fields of activity.

But our book will not only serve as an entertainment on leisure hours or an instruction for the young. It also will afford an interesting, useful and profitable reading for the full-grown man or woman, who is seeking a refuge from overwork and business cares. Might it not even be possible, Mr. Businessman, that you will discover in these fascinating pages new fields for your enterprising mind, new fields for American trade and industry? The old world is soon covered by competing concerns—China and Japan will before long be able to supply their own demand and will become less and less dependent on America and Europe. But Africa's virgin soil and barbarian population will for decades and perhaps centuries to come be in need of our products and our commerce. This continent, therefore, deserves our more serious attention—it will no doubt become a source of untold wealth to those who understand to avail themselves of its resources and to supply its demands. From this point of view this irksome work will deserve the attention of the businessman no less than the educator.

We feel confident that no one can read this book without feeling that he has spent his time most agreeably and profitably.

We extend a hearty greeting to all our readers, young or old, and hope that they will join with us in a sincere wish that our work may find a way to every home in our country, where Theodore Roosevelt's name is known and respected and where the flame of love for useful knowledge burns high on the family hearth. THE PUBLISHERS.

AUTHOR'S PREFACE

WHEN Theodore Roosevelt after having swung the big stick over the heads of the evil-doers and dealt out a square deal to everybody for the space of seven years, covered with glory and beloved as no other President had ever been, retired to private life, he did not go to enjoy a well-needed rest in some of the paradises of France or Italy or idle away his leisure hours among the crowned heads of the old world—No, his active and restless spirit was clamoring for a still more strenuous life than before.

From early youth Roosevelt had been deeply interested in hunting, natural history and scientific pursuits. This domineering trait in his character came to prominence already during his college years at Harvard. His early youth, therefore, was divided between bookstudies, athletic sports and hunting expeditions. And were it not for his strong sense of duty to his country and his public-spirited nature it is very likely that he never would have accepted the public offices, which unsought came to him. It therefore was in perfect accord with his previous history when the papers announced that he was going straight from Washington and his beloved Oyster Bay as the head of an expedition undertaken by the Smithsonian Institution, to explore the wilderness of the Dark Continent and enrich our country with new and valuable specimens of the animal world of this wonderful region.

This was the original and unexpected answer Roosevelt gave to the many questions as to what he would do when his term of office had expired. It cannot be said that his enterprise was paved with unanimous approval. Thousands had expected him to spend his time at home and after a few weeks rest again enter the political arena, and voices of warning were heard from near and far. A journey in Africa is something very different from a pleasure trip through Europe or America. Instead of gliding smoothly along in a luxurious parlor car, stopping now and then in large and heartily welcoming cities to listen to flattering eulogies from governors and captains of industry and commerce, the African traveller has to traverse the almost impenetrable jungles and marshes and endless forests of a wild and inhospitable country, where every step might bring disaster, sickness or even death either from disease or beast or the poisoned arrow from some treacherous savage's bow.

But Roosevelt is not a man to balk in the face of difficulties. His iron will never faltered. Declining the flattering invitations that passed over him from all the courts of Europe he boarded the same magnificent steamer of the Hamburg American Line, which once had carried the Kaiser around the Mediterranean, and only 19 days after the expiration of his office term started his now so famous voyage to the land, in whose primeval forests he would have for his daily music the lion's roar, the leopard's grunting, the elephant's shrill trumpet-blasts, the boa-constrictor's hissing or the concert of feathered tribes, to which our orchestras seem tame and commonplace.

This book gives you a vivid and lifelike description of what Roosevelt saw and experienced on this daring journey and tells about his unexampled encounters with the kings of the forest, the majectic lion, it lets all the wonders of the animal and vegetable world of the tropics pass before your eyes. It describes the habits, customs and appearance of unknown beasts, of graceful fishes, varicolored birds and brilliant insects. And last but not least it introduces you to the primitive inhabitants of this mysterious continent, the brown and black savages, to whom civilization is a question mark and culture is as little known as snow in August. It makes you acquainted with the strange habits, superstitious rites and religious ceremonies of these darkhued cousins of the apes and the monkeys, whose only right to bear the human name seems to be their poor and infantile jabbering.

Nothing can indeed be more interesting and fascinating than to read about these strange human beings, their ways, their daily life, their marriage customs, and their adventurous existence. This book tells you all about it and it places it all before your wondering eyes not only in words but also in pictures drawn from life by some of the world's greatest masters.   THE AUTHOR.

TABLE OF CONTENTS

CHAPTER I.

OBJECT OF ROOSEVELT'S AFRICAN EXPEDITION.

Roosevelt's Exciting Encounter with a Lion—A Frightful Spectacle—How the Lion is Traced and Finally Brought at Bay—Roosevelt's Narrow Escape from the Lion's Teeth—His Marvelous Presence of Mind Saves Him.

ROOSEVELT had not been many days on African soil when he had a chance to show his record-breaking skill as a crackshot in the encounter with a lion.

The lion hunt is one of the most exciting and perilous events in an African explorer's experience. The king of the forests had to be found in his jungle bed and driven by mounted natives through grass, underbush and morasses until he was brought at bay. Woe to the man who misses the target or loses his presence of mind when the lion, swifter than a galloping race-horse, darts at him in blind fury.

Three lions had been discovered attacking a buffalo on the open prairie at the edge of a jungle. Two of Roosevelt's companions were trying to drive the beasts in the direction of the other members of the party. Two of the lions, frightened by the sudden attack and instinctively trying to save themselves, bounded off and hid in the high grass, but the third and largest one with a terrific roar, that shook the ground almost like an earthquake, made for the terrified men with a leap through the air swift as lightning, and in one instant they would have been between his jaws—when "Crack!" echoed a rifle over the vast plains and down to earth tumbled Roosevelt's first big African game—and the lives of the men were saved.

The same day another lion was found. One of the frightened bearers fired at the beast but missed. The infuriated animal crouching for a last leap, which would have in a moment sent the bearer into eternity, charged at him with lightning speed, and the horrified man made a wild dash to get under Roosevelt's protection. The Ex-President was on a run, however, and approaching the lion on the right side, where his heart could not be reached. What was to be done? There was no time for long deliberation. A second more and the man would have been

THE KIND OF LIONS ROOSEVELT SHOT IN AFRICA.

killed. With the same coldblooded presence of mind and quick decision, which always had characterized him, whether commanding the American Rough Riders against the Spanish fusillades or swinging the famous Big Stick over the shivering heads of the Trusts or the leaders of despotic labor unions he threw his rifle to his shoulder and, aiming at the only unprotected vulnerable spot, the spine, split it with one ball.

The man's life was saved, and Roosevelt had in less than one day won from the natives the proud title of The Lion Slayer.

Let us now go back to the historical events, which led up to the above described interesting incidents.

PRIMITIVE METHODS OF THE PEOPLE OF AFRICA.

Why did Roosevelt go to Africa? Why did he not stay at home and take an active and influential part in our internal politics even after his official term as President of the greatest and most progressive nation on earth has expired? He no doubt could have followed the example of Prince Bismark who even after his retirement from public life for a number of years continued to be the most influential man in the German Empire. Roosevelt's unequaled popularity certainly would have made him an even greater power in American politics than any office-holder, no matter how high and exalted.

But Roosevelt is not and never was neither an office seeker nor a popularity hunter. He is an independent man of principle, and from early youth he had been a lover of sports and nature. The cowboys in the Rocky Mountains and the ranchmen in the great American wilds can tell many a thrilling story of adventure about the young college-bred huntsman who could run down the grizzly and lasso the wild horse

From the Minneapolis Journal.

MOVING DAY AT THE WHITE HOUSE.

with even more skill than they, who were born and bred among the moving herds of the deserts. But he apparently had already exhausted the American supply of big game. Leaving the popular "Teddy-Bears" to the children as a remembrance of his youthful feats, where else could he go but to Africa, the only continent still remaining so to say in Nature's hands; to Africa where still are found in their natural state the interesting specimens of the animal kingdom, which have not yet been exterminated by our advancing civilization; to Africa, which still teems with millions of savages, many of whom are not far above the wild beasts. And to Africa he went!

AFRICAN LIONS HOWLING ON A MOONLIGHT NIGHT.

Realizing the value of time Roosevelt left New York two weeks after President Taft's inauguration, on March 23, 1909. His destination was British East Africa including a voyage on the great Victoria Nyanza and a journey down the valley of the Nile. Ostensibly he went for a fifteen months' recreation trip, but the real object of his enterprize was not pleasure but rather scientific. For he was the head of an expedition undertaken by the great Smithsonian Institution in active charge of N. J. Cunninghame of Nairobi, the headquarters of the Uganda Railroad Co., one of the most expert of African hunters. Other members of the party were the famous sportsman and author F. C. Selous, and the Ex-President's son, Kermit, a youth, of twenty summers, who was the official photographer of the expedition. A number of newspaper reporters from Europe and America swarmed around the former chief anxious to follow him on his adventurous trip but they were all refused the privilege and the bold warrior even threatened to drive them away by force if they should attempt to intrude upon his privacy.

His departure from New York was one of the most memorable events in his triumphant career. Had he ever entertained any doubts as to his popularity with the American people, they were dispersed like dust before a cyclone when he saw tens of thousands of enthusiastic men and women from all parts of this vast country crowded along the pier anxious to get a glimpse of their former chief and beloved national hero. The crowd was so dense that the ex-President had to be escorted to the landing by mounted police. In fact, he was almost borne on the hands of the people to the waiting steamer. On board the great liner Hamburg, which was ready to take him to his point of destination, he was received and greeted by President Taft's representative and military aide, Captain Archibold W. Butt, of the quartermaster's department of the army, wishing the former chief executive "Good-bye and the best of health," and presenting him with a gold seal inscribed with the name "Theodore Roosevelt," as a symbol of the "Square Deal" he had meted out to everyone. Roosevelt returned his "best wishes to the President," and then sent him the following brief but expressive telegram: "Parting thanks, love and sincere wishes." Men

From the Minneapolis Journal.

THE ROOSEVELT GUARD.

prominent in politics, and influential in finance and business, office-
holders and men in all walks of life, foreign and domestic diplomats,
educators and public men were there to bid the most distinguished
American citizen good-bye. Italian and German marine bands struck

up national airs and all were agreed that they had never witnessed anything to compare with this most hearty and brilliant farewell acclaim.

The steamer Hamburg is one of the most luxuriously equipped and commodious steamers of the Hamburg-American line that cross the Atlantic. A suite of five elegantly furnished rooms—once occupied by the Kaiser on his Mediterranean tour—had been reserved for him. Here he met former Secretary of State, Senator Elihu Root, Senator Lodge, of Massachusetts, and Mrs. Admiral Cowles, of the navy, the ex-President's sister.

Looking out of the door at the crowds gathered before it, he caught sight of his former private secretary, Mr. Loeb. Grasping him by the hand and giving him a pull which brought him past the two police-officers who were guarding the entrance, he cried: "Come, Loeb, come here." A newswriter was greeted with a friendly "Let the muck-raker in." Still more cordial was the reception allowed some Rough Riders. "Let them pass," he cried and saluted them with a hearty grasp of his hand.

INCIDENTS DURING THE VOYAGE FROM NEW YORK TO NAPLES.

The steamship company had made the most exquisite and elaborate provisions for the comfort of its distinguished passenger. The walls in his department were adorned with portraits of Mrs. Roosevelt, President Taft and the Kaiser, picture of the ex-President's home at Oyster Bay, scenery from Europe and Africa, and other pleasing decorations.

When the steamer whistle sounded for all ashore and the majestic steamer slowly backed into the river, the immense crowds on the pier began to cheer, the whistles of every factory and steamer shrieked, the ladies waved their handkerchiefs—and the great chief was off under more boisterous demonstrations than New York had seen for years.

The voyage was not characterized by any remarkable incidents. Like most crossings of the ocean, it was monotonous, every one having to follow the ship's prescribed routine. It was probably to relieve the monotony of the reports that some news agents invented the unfounded story of that an attempt to assassinate the ex-President had been made

**WARRIORS AND TRIBES IN THEIR WONDERFUL COSTUMES WAITING TO
GREET COL. ROOSEVELT.**

The Women and Children are in front and the Warriors at the back. The headgear
of the warriors is most elaborate, being made of wicker work and shells with enormous
ostrich plumes, which, though barbaric, makes a fantastic picture. Note the tail piece
which the women on the right of the picture have on; that is the symbol of marriage
and it is practically all of the clothes most of the women wear. The women and children
nearly all have sticks or gourds in their hands and the warriors their long spears. Col.
Roosevelt was greatly pleased with the reception given him by these native savages.

From Stereograph, Copyright 1909, by Underwood & Underwood.

COL. ROOSEVELT'S GUARD OF HONOR.

These Native Troops are drilled by European officers and are efficient and capable. They act as police in maintaining law and order throughout British East Africa. They met Col. Roosevelt on his arrival and escorted him to the Government House.

From the Minneapolis Journal.

GOODBYE, TEDDY! TAKE GOOD CARE OF YOURSELF.

by a steerage passenger. When Roosevelt heard of this unnatural story, he expressed his regret that such a dastardly lie had been allowed to gain publicity, and to show his confidence in his poor fellow-passengers, he went down to the third-class passengers and shook hands with

4

every one of them. In fact, Roosevelt was the most popular of all the passengers on the Hamburg and no one ever thought of doing him any harm.

All Europe had been anxious to see and welcome our former President. Invitations for him to visit all the capitals of the Old World had been sent out and rejected; but nothing could prevent the Europeans from manifesting their interest in this extraordinary man by extending to him a most cordial and elaborate welcome upon his arrival at Naples. Thousands had gathered there from far and near to greet the former executive. The U. S. Ambassador, Griscom, had come down from Rome, and newspaper men from all the capitals of Europe had hurried to Naples to interview him and to cable their impressions to their respective countries.

He left Naples late at night by the steamer Admiral which was going to take him to the ruins of Messina and to Mombasa—gliding slowly along the beautiful Italian shore through the balmy breezes of southern Europe. He passed close to the Lipari Islands and the volcano Stromboli whose cone rising more than 3,500 feet above the sea sent out a huge column of vapor that enwrapped the whole country in its cloudy veil. About noon they passed through the Strait of Messina, where the ancients believe that the two horrible sea monsters, Scylla and Charybdis who according to the immortal Homer, caused the Trojan hero Ulysses so much trouble, had their abodes. It is not recorded, however, that our national hero had any difficulty in escaping these fabled monsters, and he arrived hale and hearty at Messina, so recently the theatre of one of the most terrible spectacles contemporary annals have registered.

Approaching Messina and armed with a pair of marine glasses, Roosevelt saw at a distance the barren ruins of the wrecked city. Observing them from a distance, he remarked: "There is more standing than I expected." He was greeted by an immense crowd at the landing, and was saluted by the Re Umberto with the King of Italy on board. The King sent Captain Pfeister, the former Italian military attache at Washington and now adjutant to Admiral Mirabello, with his compliments and an invitation to his presence. Roosevelt with his son Kermit and Ambassador Griscom at once set out for the battleship

From the Minneapolis Journal.

WISHING ROOSEVELT A WARM RECEPTION IN AFRICA.

and were met by the King at the gangway and greeted by a most cordial handshake. The King was anxious to meet so distinguished a personage and thank him for the assistance his country had extended to Italy in her affliction. Replying Roosevelt emphasized that the Ameri-

HE'S COMING BOYS—LET'S SKIDDOO.

can people did not want any thanks and had simply done its duty. The King wished him a successful hunting trip and expressed the hope that he would meet the Count of Turin who had just gone on an expedition in Africa. Before they left a photograph was taken of a group consisting of Roosevelt and his party and the King.

Immediately at the close of the reception, Roosevelt and his party went ashore to inspect the ruins of the once beautiful city. Signor Trincheri, the prefect of Messina, who under orders from Premier Gialitti, was their guide, took them into the interior of the gigantic heap of waste and rubbish, which a few weeks before had been Messina. The desolation was appalling. Ruins of palaces, blocks of stone and antique pillars caused them much trouble in making their way through the city and a heavy rain, which soon began to fall, increased their difficulties, the mud being almost knee-deep. The people emulated in showing him their appreciation and gratefulness. Many women kissed their hands to him, while the children threw roses in his path and the men cheered. This spontaneous expression of sympathy moved him to emotion, and turning to one of his party, he said: "I am glad and proud as an American citizen that my country could do something to help this immense disaster, for which even all the assistance in the world would be insufficient."

FROM MESSINA TO MOMBASA.

The three days voyage across the always storm tossed Mediterranean brought our ex-President in touch with passengers, most of whom were officials or residents of the Dark Continent. The majority of them were of mixed English, German and Portuguese descent, and the stories wherewith they regaled our ex-President were certainly not lacking in spiciness or dramatic flavor.

An old fellow, whose respect for the truth certainly was not surpassed by his hatred for the tame and commonplace, told of the dog-headed monkeys he had seen in Nairobi, who had heads and claws like dogs and barked like them. Another old hunter spoke about a people who are wondrous swift though they progress by hopping on one leg. At midday, he said, when unable to find a forest shade, they lie down upon the back and hold their foot aloft, which is so large that it serves the purpose of a shade umbrella in protecting their bodies from the sun. There were also, another of his fellow-passengers affirmed, a headless people, whose heads and mouths were situated on their breasts, but who had neither ears nor nose.

From the Minneapolis Journal.

HOORAH! HE'S GONE! LET'S CELEBRATE.

THROUGH THE SUEZ CANAL.

In Port Said, the northern entrance to the Suez Canal, Roosevelt first set foot on African soil. While the steamer was coaling there, he had a good opportunity to observe the half naked, jabbering and perspiring natives and to see their huts and primitive dwellings, as well as the public buildings, the canal offices and the modern hotels. Black and Nubians, Sudanese of every tribe and color, Arabs and Egyptians from the desert and mountainous regions of the Holy Land, all wearing their mani-colored Oriental apparel, were so blended in this meeting place of the East, the West and the Tropics as to make the whole one of the most varied and wild places ever witnessed by a stranger. In fine, everything in Port Said, whether white, black or yellow had gathered round the pier to get a glimpse of the most famous man in the world.

The trip through the Suez Canal was no doubt Roosevelt's most interesting experience so far. Standing on the bridge of the vessel during the entire trip he evinced most intense interest in that great waterway from end to end. It no doubt reminded him of the Panama Canal, which he had personally inspected, and one of the greatest enterprises commenced during his administration. He scanned the channel minutely on either side and plied Ambassador Juserand with volleys of questions concerning the cost, construction, operation and profits, while the steamer slowly and solemnly glided through the narrow waterway between low and level shores stretching as far as the eye could reach over sandy wastes and barren plains to the distant horizon, where the towering pink and bluish mountain chains of the Holy Land like a ghostly vision on the eastern sky only added to the lonely desolation of the landscape.

As the Admiral entered Bitter Dakes Roosevelt was greeted with hearty cheers from passengers on the Indian liner City of Paris. A huge Teddy Bear on the liner's bridge amused him and he waved his sombrero in acknowledgment. The cheers were heartily participated in by the natives, some on camels, some on mules and some on sandaled feet who traveled with the steamer or were going northward. At short intervals little Arab settlements, rising like dust-covered spectres out of the sand on either side came to view and relieved the hopeless monotony of the desert. As the ship passed some of the neatly kept canal stations, which now and then reminded the traveler of a more advanced civilization than the surrounding country can boast, Kermit, Dr. Mearns and other hunters who disembarked at Ismalia returned to the ship here having bagged a few quail.

The Suez Canal passes through the hottest places on earth, with not a bit of vegetation. There is practically no rainfall except once a year, and the water is collected in great dams in the rocky gorges back of the towns and supplied to the public in barrels, hauled by donkeys, camels and big Indian humped oxen, as well as carried in goat skins on the backs of men. Beyond Suez, the southern terminal point of the canal, the traveler is reminded of the passage of the Israelites through the Red Sea, while towards the east might be seen the shadowy peaks of Mount Sinai, where Moses received the Ten Commandments from the Lord's hands under lightning and thunder.

There is no relief from the scourging heat as the steamer gets into the Red Sea, along whose shores the sun of the tropics has dried up every blade of grass and where not even a lonely lion breaks the mute monotony of those fierce solitudes.

As you approach Aden some barren, bleak and red islands rise and fade away, and other red peaks frown over the desert city as the ship anchors in the green water. The noisy throng of natives who swarm about the steamer in their little boats offering sandalwood, ivory, sea-shells, ostrich feathers and other queer products of Africa do not prevent you from enjoying the brilliant spectacle of the exquisite tropical sunrise that greets you. While the steamer is coaling you disembark and go to take in the city. You drive to Solomon's Wells, said to have been built by this illustrious monarch.

The Oriental features of Aden represent nothing attractive to an American. The dirt and filth can not but be disgusting to one who comes from a land, where "cleanliness is next to godliness," and the lean and emaciated, long-limbed, black-skinned and woolly specimens of humanity who carry coal in baskets to the ship or throng the narrow lanes as you take a drive in one of the little, ramshackle phaetons, while the poor, unfed horses threaten to collapse before getting half the way, are not calculated to inspire you with any high ideas of Oriental civilization.

Soaking in the hot sunshine in the square stands a beautiful marble statue of Queen Victoria looking down upon this varied scenery of poverty, brutality, and Oriental laziness, while ships from Australia, India and China are coaling in the harbor and a few English officials pass from building to building indifferent to both natives and strangers.

In other parts of this mongrel city are seen black-curled Jewish merchants, turbaned Arabs or Hindus, tall and proud Persian princes on long-tailed Arab steeds or in queer carts drawn by donkeys or camels, while native Africans of various tribes and colors pass to and fro.

CHAPTER II.

FROM MOMBASA TO THE WILDERNESS.

Old and New Mombasa—Its Romantic History—Enthusiastic Reception to Roosevelt—Tropical Scenery—The Desert and the Jungle—The Railroad from Mombasa to Nairobi, the Chicago of East Africa.

W HEN Roosevelt first landed on African soil he did not come to a new country. Old Mombasa, where he arrived April 31, is over 400 years old. He found it inhabited by over 60,000 people, half of whom African natives, lithe, dignified worshippers of the prophet of Mecca, stout Soudanese, calm and dusky Hindoos, alert and

WARFARE OF THE NATIVES ALONG THE UGANDA ROAD.

warlike Somalis. The city well deserves its name, "The Battle City," for it has for centuries been the bone of contention between the Portuguese, the Arabs and the English on account of its great commercial importance as a depot of the trade in rubber, skins, ivory, and slaves, until its final capture by the Imperial British East African Company, in 1887, made an end of the old feuds.

The new city is located nearer the ocean than the old. It has many attractive features, two or three comfortable hotels and an excellent clubhouse frequented by Americans, Englishmen and commercial travelers, and extends a hearty welcome to white visitors. The East India Bank is also located in the new city. One of its characteristic novelties is the many street car lines, which not only take care of the communication along the main thoroughfares but also branch off into every private house, the little cars which transport the wealthy European residents to and from their offices being pushed along by native coolies. Roosevelt found this commodious and novel transportation very convenient in this tropical climate. Unfortunately the new city has no harbor, but two miles to the southeast is the port of Kilindinis, with anchorage for ships of the largest tonnage, which therefore first receives the important passengers and valuable cargoes destined for British East Africa and Mombasa, and no doubt in a not far distant future will become the headquarters both of the government, railroads and commerce. It was here Roosevelt and his party landed, and notwithstanding a tropical rain, pouring down in torrents, the shores were crowded with Afro-Europeans, Arabs, Hindoos and natives, and a military band struck up "The Star Spangled Banner," and under the constant cheer of this mongrel population the Ex-President was conducted by the Commissioner of the province to the government house.

PREPARATIONS FOR THE GREAT HUNT.

With the eagerness and enthusiasm of the genuine sportsman and true American he did not stay here long, however, but at once started to make preparations for entering the wilds.

You might imagine that anyone can go hunting in the wilds of Africa without government permission. Not so, however. You have to take out a license ranging from $85 for an elephant to $25 for a giraffe or rhinoceros and $15 for an antelope, and the killing is limted to two

FIGHT BETWEEN ELEPHANT AND RHINOCEROS.

elephants, rhinoceri, hippopotomi and zebras, which animals as well as buffaloes and ostriches are classified and protected as Royal Game. The British authorities courteously offered to dispense with these formalities but in true democratic spirit Roosevelt refused to receive special privileges and insisted, as he always has done in America, that the law should be enforced. Lions and leopards are classed as pests and vermin condemned to extermination and, therefore, may be killed without a license.

To a complete equipment of an African hunting expedition also belongs the indispensable native help, which is usually figured at thirty

From the Minneapolis Journal.   THE AMERICAN DANIEL IN THE LION'S DEN.

bearers for each white person and his baggage weighing about sixty pounds. They are paid from $4.50 to $25 per month, besides board, consisting of cereals and fresh meat, of which they devour enormous quantities every day, not only picking the bones clean but also extracting the marrow. A medium-sized party will consume two elands and waterbucks, animals as big as our common ox, every day, if they can get it, and if they don't they will be sure to grumble.

Among Roosevelt's best and most reliable helpers were the Somali or Shikaris. They are absolutely fearless in the face of death, being fatalists as all Mohammedans, scrupulously clean and as temperate as our most immaculate teetotalers—their religion absolutely prohibiting the use of intoxicants. They are most faithful servants and as ready to die for their master as other natives are to desert him. The records of African Hunting Grounds are full of stories of the bravery of these sons of the wilderness. A Somali will for instance follow the fresh track of a lion to the mouth of its dark cave, the small opening of which will admit only two men. Without a moment's hesitation they enter the cave one armed with a rifle the other with nothing but a butcher's knife. Cheerily they proceed in the darkness chanting their "God willing we come back." Or a lion charges a white hunter and his Somali gun bearer. It crushes him to the ground, but swift as lightning the Somali circles around, springs upon the back of the infuriated beast, cuts his teeth deep into his neck, pulls its ears and pounds his eyes so ferociously that the beast turns upon him, and gives the white hunter an opportunity to pull his rifle free and chase a bullet through the lion's brains.

A leader, a headsman, a gunbearer, a cook, a mess-boy and a tent-boy, twenty to twenty-five native bearers, tents, beds and provisions were attached to the expedition in Mombasa, and Roosevelt's famous Safari, or hunting party, was ready to start out for the African jungles.

ROOSEVELT'S AMMUNITION IN HIS AFRICAN HUNT.

Roosevelt inaugurated a novelty in big game hunting when he left Mombasa in pursuit of elephant and rhinoceros, armed with an American repeating rifle of far lighter bore than the weapons with which

British sportsmen pursue the same animals, although the rhino is considered about as dangerous game as can be found on the Dark Continent, due to his habit of blindly charging at top speed any object he deems hostile. The former President will use a rifle of only 405 caliber in the chase.

From the Minneapolis Journal.

THE TEDDY BEAR IN AFRICA.

This rifle is better known by the American term of "forty" caliber, and it would have been considered little short of suicide fifteen years ago to attempt the hunting of such big game with such a caliber. Improvements in high pressure, smokeless powder and the development of the steel-jacketed bullet have increased the efficiency of the arm many times since then, however. The steel bullet was intended for the African buffalo, which is a far more dangerous customer than his American namesake used to be.

This same gun with soft-pointed bullets may be used on such game as lions. It has terific "smashing" power, as it has tremendous velocity, and the bullet spreads or mushrooms on impact, thus tearing a hole through soft tissue and the lighter bones through which the hand could be thrust. To penetrate the tough hide of a rhino, however, the steel bullet was used.

For lighter game such as the African species of deer, and for long range shooting Roosevelt carried two 303 caliber repeaters, popularly known as "thirties."

For feathered game he had two twelve gauge repeating shotguns and two twenty-two caliber automatic rifles for small game and for amusement around camp. His shotgun ammunition was specially loaded for him and was in brass shells. The wads had been carefully waterproofed and instead of the shell being merely crimped over the wad at the end, it had been cut into small flanges and bent over. To prevent swelling in the moist climate, which might affect paper shells, the wad had been covered with wax.

HEARTY WELCOME FOR OUR EX-PRESIDENT.

A guard of honor, comprised of marines and blue jackets from the Pandora, was at the railroad station when the Roosevelt party arrived at Mombasa and was inspected by Roosevelt. A number of officials and civilians also were present, and the station building was decorated with flags. Roosevelt passed the morning at government house, where he was the guest of Mr. Jackson. Kermit and other members of the party occupied the time up to the departure of the train in driving about the city.

From Mombasa Roosevelt dispatched a cablegram to the Kaiser expressing his appreciation of his treatment on board the German steamer Admiral and admiration of the astounding growth of German colonization in Africa. At a dinner party given in his honor by members of the Mombasa Club Governor Jackson read the following telegram to Roosevelt from King Edward:

"I bid you a hearty welcome to British East Africa and I trust that you will have a pleasant time and meet with every success."

Continuing Governor Jackson said Mr. Roosevelt had left the "Big Stick" at home, and, after seven strenuous years as President of the United States had come out to Africa to make use of the rifle. He promised the noted visitor an immense variety of game and good sport.

When Roosevelt arose to reply he was enthusiastically received with full highland musical honors. He began with a tribute to the British people for their energy and genius in civilizing the uncivilized places of the earth. He said he was surprised at what he had heard of the progress of British East Africa, but he warned his hearers that they could not expect to achieve in a short time what it had taken America several hundred years to accomplish. He then emphasized the necessity of leaving local questions to be solved by the authorities on the spot and commented on the fact that the people at home knew little of affairs abroad. In this connection he cited the United States and the Philippine Islands.

Mr. Roosevelt expressed his great pleasure at the welcome given to him by the British cruiser Pandora, whose rails and masts were manned by cheering sailors when the Admiral came into the harbor. He said he believed in peace, but considered that strength meant peace and he hoped that all the great nations would provide themselves with this means to the end. In conclusion, Mr. Roosevelt referred briefly to his future plans and gave some of his first impressions of the country.

Before departing Roosevelt telegraphed to King Edward, thanking him for the message of greeting read at the dinner.

COLONEL ROOSEVELT AND GENERAL SLATIN OFF TO VISIT THE SIGHTS AT "KERRERI."

Although the Colonel has ridden Bucking Bronchos during his life on the Western Plains in America, he went through a new experience in Egypt.—Like the game sportsman that he is, he mounted the camel and soon was at his ease. They are on their way to visit a famous battlefield.

COLONEL ROOSEVELT'S RETURN FROM THE AFRICAN JUNGLE.

The Colonel's first appearance in civilisation after spending almost a whole year in the wilds of Africa. The picture shows him landing at the palace, Khartoum, Egypt, from the steamer sent to meet him on the Blue Nile. He is accompanied by General Slatin and followed by his son, Kermit.

OFF FROM MOMBASA FOR RANCH.

Theodore Roosevelt and the members of his party left Mombasa at 2:30 P. M. April 22, on a special train for Kapiti Plains station, whence they were conveyed to the ranch of Sir Alfred Pease on the Athi river. Sir Alfred was already there, awaiting the coming of the guests. The party remained at the ranch for one week, making it the base for shooting expeditions and then moved on for Nairobi. Acting Governor Jackson, of the protectorate accompanied the party.

The train ran upward and westward all day over ridge and valley and through broken ground, deep, rugged gorges and glades of palms and climbing plants. After Makindu station the train passed over immense green pastures, watered by streams wooded by dense shrubbery and dark fir-looking trees. Looking out from the windows of his comfortable car, the American traveler could see a whole zoological garden of wild animals crowding the plains. Zebras, antelopes and gazelles in herds of from 300 to 600 gaze in mute astonishment at the speeding train or scamper shyly away while the steam-whistle fills the wilderness with its chrill and awe-inspiring noise. With his field glass the ex-President could see at a distance long lines of black wildebeests or gnus, wild ostriches and many kinds of smaller game.

The Kapiti Plains are entirely bare of trees and covered with short bushy grass, while the numerous ravines are filled with weeds, reed and thorn, with here and there a water pool—favorite haunts for lions and rhinoceros. A famous hunter, Colonel G. E. Smith, Chief of the Anglo-German Boundary Survey, who has spent almost half a lifetime in the wildest places in Eastern Africa, killed in these same places seventeen rhinos in one day. Here Sir Alfred Pease has built a new house for the reception of Roosevelt. It is a genuine one-story African bungalow of five rooms, located on the high south end of the Machakos range, nearly seven thousand feet above the level of the sea. From its broad veranda Roosevelt will have a splendid view over the surrounding olive-clad hills and the endless Kapiti Plains to where, at a distance of 120 miles, the gigantic Mount Kilimanjaro towers 20,000 feet above the horizon.

Arrived at Simba station we are at "The Place of the Lions"; and sometimes two or three or even half a dozen of these marauders are seen skulking across the plain, while smaller game is keeping at a respectful distance, or brooding in silence in the shoulder-high jungle. Farther away on the more remote plains, where the grass grows high from the fertile volcanic ground, we find the rhinoceros in his open pastures.

A famous traveler who recently spent several weeks hunting in these regions describes his first encounter with one of these beasts as something overwhelmingly exciting and impressive. A black shadow in the middle of the sunlit plain this gigantic survivor from a past age was grazing calmly and leisurely, while the hoary domes of the surrounding mountain peaks formed a fitting background to the striking picture. The hunters walked up to the beast as near as possible, protected by the shoulder of a hill, and the thud of the first bullet which struck his bony skull with an impact of a ton and a quarter piercing through hide, flesh and bone, re-echoed like distant thunder. The beast started, looked around, and then came bearing in upon the hunters in a clumsy trot like a great steam engine, indifferent to fear or pain. A few seconds more and he would have crushed us under his feet. As he was swerving to the right across our front we all fired a broadside into his huge body, and down he tumbled with a groan that shook the ground.

It was while in Kapiti Plains that the news of the bitter attack on him for refusing to admit British reporters to his safari reached Roosevelt as told in another chapter.

During his three weeks' stay in Kapiti Plains Roosevelt killed four lions, two rhinoceros, two giraffes, two wildebeests and one Thompson gazelle. Kermit during the same time dispatched two lions, one cheetah, a species of leopard, one giraffe and one wildebeest. All the lions were killed in the Mau Hills, where the camp was pitched. Roosevelt's mighty gun brought three of them to earth, each on the first shot. Thus one of the former President's fondest ambitions has been realized, and he is proud, too, that the fourth of the jungle kings fell before the rifle of his son Kermit, who, however, took three shots to kill his quarry.

JOY IN FIRST LION HUNT.

Both father and son were jubilant. It was their first lion hunt and so magnificent a kill was far beyond their expectations, but lions had been plentiful in the hills for the last month, and the English hunter, F. C. Selous, had been out for several days laying plans for their extinction. How well he succeeded can be seen from the results of the chase.

Mr. Selous accompanied the former President, who also was attended by the usual retinue of beaters. As a rule the beaters go into the jungle with considerable trepidation, but as Mr Roosevelt's reputation as a hunter had reached there long before he arrived in person the beaters on this occasion were exceptionally enthusiastic. They seemed ever eager to play a part in the first hunt of the distinguished American.

The caravan started early Thursday morning from the ranch of Sir Alfred Pease on the Athi River and proceeded slowly to the Mau Hills. This range is open for wide areas, but in places is covered with dense growths, where game is plentiful.

The first night in camp was without especial incident, no attempt being made to go after lions, although their call was heard now and then during the night, but at dawn the camp was astir and the drive speedily organized.

TEN KINDS OF GAME BAGGED.

The native beaters set out in all directions under the instruction of the "head man," armed with all sorts of noisemaking devices, which could not but arouse any game within earshot. Some of the beats proved blanks, but by nightfall no less than ten kinds of game had been bagged.

Kermit during the greater part of the day did more effective work with his camera than he did with his gun, he and the other members of the party allowing Mr. Roosevelt the much prized shots.

Details of the actual shooting were not brought down to Nairobi at once from the camp, but it was declared that in each case a single bullet from the ex-President's rifle sufficed to bring down his lion. From this it is regarded that Mr. Roosevelt is living up to the reputation which he has gained in Africa of being a crack shot. All the lions were of normal size, and after the natives had dragged them together in the grass they executed the usual dances around the trophies.

In the beginning of our first chapter you find a detailed account of this lion hunt.

While the Roosevelt expedition was in camp on the ranch of Sir Alfred Pease, at a point near Machakos, some cases of smallpox were discovered among the natives. All the members of the party were well. May 4 Roosevelt bagged his fifth lion. His host, Sir Alfred Pease, made an effective sketch of him shooting his first lion over the shoulder of a native gun bearer at a distance of sixty yards. There was a perfect pest of ticks at Kapiti Plains. While all the members of the expedition were bitten, none showed any signs of the dreaded fever. Roosevelt was boyishly exhuberant over the result of his lion hunt. The party's bag for the first six days of real hunting was twenty-seven head of game, representing ten species.

The dreaded fever, better known as the sleeping sickness is the scourge of Africa, and medical science has not yet succeeded in finding an effective remedy for its poisonous ravages. It is known to have its origin in the bite of a venemous insect, the tsetse fly, and its name is derived from a curious resemblance to sleep, which characterizes the last stages of the disease. The actual sting of the insect is not poisonous but serves as an agent depositing a death-carrying parasite. The victim first becomes extremely excitable and nervous, then lapses into a doze at certain intervals, the attacks becoming more and more violent. At last the glands all over the body begin to swell and the pitiable sufferer sinks into a lethargy, from which he never awakes. The patient may sleep for a year or two—and there is no relief but death. Two hundred thousand natives are known to have died from the disease and at present about a quarter of a hundred thousand are affected.

KERMIT LOST IN NIGHT.

One day when out on a hunting expedition Kermit lost his way from his father's camp near Machakos and passed an entire night alone on horseback, riding through a region unknown to him. Finally he turned up at Kiu, a station on the railway forty miles below

Nairobi and thirty or forty miles southeast of Machakos. He had been following an old cart road from Machakos to Kiu, where the country was sparsely inhabited by natives of the Wakamba tribe, a peaceful people engaged chiefly in agriculture.

From Kapiti our hunters moved next to the JaJa ranch as the guests of an American, William McMillan, and from there Roosevelt undertook several hunting expeditions. He went out one day and bagged a female rhinoceros. The first shot wounded her in the shoulder and the animal fled to the bushes. Roosevelt followed on horseback and six more shots were required to bring her down. The head and skin weighed 532 pounds. He also the same day added a hippopotamus to his big game bag. The animal was killed a short distance from the Jaja ranch.

Speeding over the rolling and almost seamless surface of the Athi river district the train took our hunters in a few hours to Nairobi, the headquarters of the Uganda Railroad, and also a military depot and political centre. The city is well supplied with telgraph and telephone connections, its streets glitter with electric lights and automobiles run in every direction. It also is the headquarters for hunting expeditions and caravan parties, which arrive and depart daily, while parties loaded with trophies of the chase, and European and Hindu merchants are conspicuous everywhere.

The American hunting expedition, of which Roosevelt is the head, selected Nairobi for its headquarters and from there made trips all over that part of the continent, and here most of the hunting and collecting was done. Space does not permit us to relate all the adventures of our ex-President. Neither would it interest our readers for it would simply be a repetition of what we have already told. August 23 Roosevelt killed his first elephant—and he did it all by himself too. The animal was a bull of moderate proportions as elephants go, and the skin was taken care of by the skilled taxidermists who follow the expedition.

THE PRONGHORN ANTELOPE SEEN BY ROOSEVELT.

CHAPTER III.

LIFE OF THEODORE ROOSEVELT.

His Ancestors and Boyhood Days—College Studies—His Brilliant Political Career—On a Western Ranch—The Rough Rider—Stories and Anecdotes.

THEODORE ROOSEVELT, twenty-sixth President of the United States, was born in New York City, October 27, 1858; son of Theodore (1831-78) and Martha (Bulloch) Roosevelt, grandson of Cornelius Van Schaack and Margaret (Barnhill) Roosevelt, great-grandson of James (or Jacobus) John and Mary (Van Schaack) Roosevelt, and is descended in a direct line from Claes Martensoon and Jannetje (Thomas) Van Rosevelt, who came to New Amsterdam from Holland about 1651.

He attended for a short time the McMullen School, New York City, but was so frail in health that he was unable to continue, and was then placed under private instructors at his home. He was tutored for college by Mr. Cutler, subsequently the founder of the Cutler School, and was graduated from Harvard in 1880.

Was married September 23, 1880, to Alice, daughter of George Cabot and Caroline (Haskell) Lee of Boston, Mass. She died in 1883, leaving one daughter, Alice Lee.

He became a student in the New York law school; was a Republican member of the New York assembly 1882, 1883 and 1884; was candidate of his party for speaker of the assembly in 1884; chairman of the committee on cities and of a special committee known as the Roosevelt Investigating Committee. As a supporter of the civil service reform, he introduced bills which became laws affecting the government of New York City, and especially the patronage exercised by the sheriff, county clerk and register, which greatly reformed the conduct of their respective offices.

He was a delegate to the Republican State Convention of 1884; dele-

gate-at-large from New York and chairman of the New York delegation
to the Republican National Convention that met at Chicago, June 3,
1884; purchased the Elkhorn and the Chimney Butte ranches at Medora
on the Little Missouri River in North Dakota, where he lived, 1884-86.

He was a member of the New York State Militia, 1884-88, serving in

From the Minneapolis Journal.

"I FOOLED YOU THIS TIME"—TEDDY.

the Eighth Regiment, N. G. S. N. Y., as lieutenant, and for three years as captain.

He was married secondly, December 2, 1886, to Edith Kermit, daughter of Charles and Gertrude Elizabeth (Tyler) Carow of New York City.

He was the unsuccessful Republican candidate for mayor of New York City in 1886, when Abram S. Hewitt was elected; was in May, 1889, appointed on the U. S. Civil Service Commission in Washington, D. C., by President Harrison, and served as president of the commission. He was continued in office by President Cleveland, but resigned in May, 1895, to accept the position of police commissioner of New York City in the administration of Mayor Strong, and he was president of the bi-partisan board, 1895-97.

He was appointed assistant secretary of the U. S. Navy in April, 1897, by President McKinley, and on the declaration of the war with Spain in April, 1898, he resigned to recruit the first U. S. V. Cavalry, a regiment of "Rough Riders" made up mostly of his acquaintances on the Western plains, including cowboys and miners, with some members of the college athletic clubs of New York and Boston—men who could ride, shoot and live in the open. He was commissioned lieutenant-colonel, May 6, 1898, and was promoted to the rank of colonel after the battle of La Quassina, San Juan, when Col. Leonard Wood was promoted to brigadier-general and assigned to the governorship of Santiago.

When the war closed, the Republican party of his native State nominated him their candidate for governor, and he was elected over Van Wyck, Democrat, Kline, Prohibitionist, Hanford, Social Labor, and Bacon, Citizens' ticket, by a plurality of 17,786 votes in a total vote of 1,343,968. He served as governor of New York, 1899-1900. His administration as governor was conspicuous in his thorough work in reforming the canal boards; instituting an improved system of civil service, including the adoption of the merit system in county offices, and in calling an extra session of the legislature to secure the passage of a bill he had recommended at the general session, taking as real estate the value of railroads and other franchises to use public streets, in spite of the protests of corporations and Republican leaders.

He was nominated Vice-President of the United States by the Republican National Convention that met at Philadelphia, June, 1900, where he was forced by the demands of the Western delegates, to accept the nomination, with William McKinley for President, and he was elected November 6, 1900. He was sworn into office as the twenty-sixth President of the United States, September 14, 1901, by reason of the assassination of President McKinley; Roosevelt being, at the time, less than forty-three years old, the youngest man in the history of the United States to have attained the chief magistracy of the government. He served to the end of the presidential term, which expired March 4, 1905.

At the following election he was re-elected with the greatest majority any presidential candidate had attained so far, and his administration during the four years of his last term was characterized by the same honesty, fearlessness and diplomacy, which had already made him so dear to the American people. To the last he was faithful to the trust imposed upon him and when he retired to private life the general verdict of friend and foe was that he had lived up to his motto and given everybody a square deal.

CHAPTER IV.

STORIES AND ANECDOTES ABOUT ROOSEVELT.

How He Looked when a Boy—Was a Born Leader—The Old Dutch Reformed Church—How He Strengthened His Delicate Frame—First Love.

THEODORE ROOSEVELT was born in that old, aristocratic portion of New York known as Gramercy Park. The family residence was in East Twentieth Street, just beyond Fifth Avenue, the number being 28. Many of the people in that neighborhood remember most vividly the childhood days of "Little Teddy." One of the neighbors, in speaking of his infancy and boyhood days, has said:

"As a young boy he was thin-shanked, pale and delicate, giving little promise of the amazing vigor of his late life. To avoid the rough treatment of the public school, he was tutored at home, also attended a private school for a time—Cutler's, one of the most famous of its day. Most of his summers, and in fact two-thirds of the year, he spent at the Roosevelt farm near Oyster Bay, then almost as distant in time from New York as the Adirondacks now are.

"For many years he was slow to learn and not strong enough to join in the play of other boys; but as he grew older he saw that if he ever amounted to anything he must acquire vigor of body. With characteristic energy he set about developing himself.

"He swam, he rowed, he ran, he tramped the hills back of the Bay, for pastimes, studying and cataloguing the birds native to his neighborhood, and thus he laid the foundation of that incomparable physical vigor from which rose his future prowess as a ranchman and hunter."

President Roosevelt's father was wise enough to patronize the public schools by sending his children through them. Here they learned the American lesson of mixing with their neighbors' children and of taking the place their abilities entitled them to in the classes.

The children were given the best educational advantages to be obtained. They attended private institutions, as did most of the children whose parents were wealthy and belonged to the same set. The family lived right in an atmosphere of the old Dutch stock, which had advanced to a high premium years before Theodore was born. The spirit of his family, however, was for sterling quality, merit and high character in their children rather than an exclusiveness from those around them who happened to be less fortunate. They were intent upon preserving close and intimate relations with the world as they found it. This is certainly the true American spirit and is reflected in our President to-day in the highest possible degree. Theodore Roosevelt is a striking illustration of what early training will do for a man.

A SYSTEMATIC CHURCH-GOER.

The Roosevelts were strict church people. They belonged to the Dutch Reformed Church. All of the children were devoted to their church and attended it and worked with it with all their heart and soul. The church-going of the Roosevelts was not a mere perfunctory matter. The sermons that young Theodore listened to, because of their length, would try the patience of too many of our boys in this day. There was too masterful a hand and heart back of Theodore Roosevelt's church-going to permit or desire his escaping any of the services. Through all his busy life, Mr. Roosevelt has followed closely the habits of church-going that he formed in his childhood and boyhood days. He still retains the traditions of his ancestors in their idea regarding the Sabbath and religious services for the whole family.

OVERCAME THE IMPEDIMENT OF A DELICATE FRAME.

The high straight-backed seats of his old church in New York are something of a memory to him, for new and more modern pews have taken their place. But the relation which he began with that old family church continues to this day.

The fact of Theodore's delicate physique was a matter of deep concern for his parents. He possessed the robust spirit of his ancestors and with it presented a more volatile quality than is usually found in the Hollander with his phlegmatic temperament. Young Theodore had the energy and ambition, but did not possess the physical force to back up his desires and his purposes. His lack of muscular powers caused him to suffer throughout his boyhood days, in comparison with his school-mates and companions.

With the will power that has carried him over so many obstacles, Theodore resolved to overcome his impediment of a delicate frame. He turned his effort and time to developing the strength which Nature had denied him and which he so much desired. He went about this task systematically. He was out of doors in the open air continually. He exercised by means of walking and horseback riding, and other physical exercises. We have in this robust man to-day an example of what deter-mination and a systematic course of physical culture will do for a deli-cate young person.

· At school Theodore Roosevelt was from the first a good student and a model scholar. We have read of many great men who were dullards at school. It is recorded that General Grant, who graduated in the class of '44, was almost at its foot, and that Walter Scott, the great novelist, was most stupid at school. Neither could apply himself to a book. They developed great talent, however, later in life. They began to be great men at about the age that Theodore Roosevelt was when he entered the White House as the nation's Chief Executive. Theodore Roosevelt, however, was a bookworm from his earliest days, and his devotion to study was inspiring for his fellow students.

A LOVE STORY.

'An interesting romance is told of Theodore's early life. He became acquainted with Edith Carow, a girl of his own age. She was a fellow student at school and belonged to the same social set. A most charming romance continued between the two from the time they were mere chil-dren until he entered upon college life at Harvard. They had been constantly together during their earlier school days, and in those old days they had spent many hours together over their games in Union Park. Her home was in Fourteenth Street, very near Union Square. This was in a very aristocratic part of the city in those days, a strictly residential district, and the great business blocks that now surround Union Square had not begun to appear in that day.

Young Theodore and Edith met at the same birthday parties and went over their lessons together in the same school. This was sufficient reason for their intimacy. Later, Edith was placed in a fashionable boarding school. Miss Comstock's School, where Edith attended, had on its roll many young ladies at that time who were great friends of Edith's, and to this day vividly recall her romance with young Theodore. It is unnecessary to say that they all enjoy relating it.

Edith's father was a business man, and her mother was, by birth, Miss Gertrude Tyler of Connecticut. Her father was General Tyler. Her family was one of wealth and social position. Theodore occupied a similar position in society, and his father was a lawyer and judge and had been in turn an alderman, a member of the Legislature at Albany, and a representative in Congress.

SHE LIKED TEDDY ROOSEVELT.

Edith Kermit Carow has said, in the happy, established days since her marriage, that she had "liked Teddy Roosevelt in those distant times because he could do so much more than she could." And yet he was a delicate stripling of a boy, while she was possessed of all the vigor of a healthy girlhood. But Theodore Roosevelt had strong will power, determination, independence and sincerity, and this was enough for Edith.

Theodore's brother testifies to the fact that Theodore never permitted himself nor Edith to be imposed upon. He was ready to champion her cause at all times, and this meant everything to Edith. Later in life Theodore discovered more than a friend of his childhood days in the girl companion of his leisure hours. He had found one who sympathized with him and his work. Moreover, she had faith in him and encouraged him. When mature years came, after sorrow had visited him, he found in her the one to share his home, to increase his fortune, and to exalt and make sacred his success.

LAYING THE FOUNDATION.

Theodore, after a thorough preparation, entered Harvard University, determined to take the full college course. Here he spent four years. He proved at Harvard that he was well equipped for the work before him. He had taken the greatest delight in history and civil government as studies. Mathematics was something of a task, but he had made himself master of his inclinations and desires. This explains why he could apply himself to mathematics with success. He was imaginative, and mathematics in any of the branches never was attractive to an imaginative man. He loved books of adventure. He was thoroughly familiar with the story of his own country. He was also well informed regarding modern Europe. He had been an incessant reader and student of history. This was easy for him, but he made up his mind to devote himself to studies less attractive for him. He realized that this was necessary to give him a well-rounded and perfectly-balanced education. The mental training he secured in following out his determination must be in large part responsible for the close-knit intellectual fiber which his manhood has revealed. It was the substantial structure upon which his later fancy could build, just as his acquired physical strength formed a magazine from which his tireless energy might draw without fear of exhausting it.

During the last McKinley campaign it was said that "Theodore Roosevelt was born with a gold spoon in his mouth." But the charge is unfair. He was an ordinary boy as to mental attainments, and considerably under the average in physical strength. Whatever success has come to him is his from an inherent will that would not brook defeat in any line rather than from peculiar advantages which he inherited.

He was born with many social advantages and with wealth. But these have failed to bring success to thousands of men. We ourselves can cite instances where wealth and social position have more often been a stumbling-block to young men rather than a help in gaining for them success and position. Certainly Theodore Roosevelt is one of the most striking examples in America of a young man who has advanced simply because of his own merit.

He is a type of American manhood that of which we are all proud.

The following characteristic story from his boyhood is told by a close friend of the Roosevelt family:

At the age of eleven years, young Roosevelt made a voyage across the Atlantic with his father. A boyhood friend, by name George Cromwell, tells several amusing incidents of the European voyage. It was a great event in 1869 to cross the Atlantic, particularly for youngsters, all of them under eleven years of age.

"As I remember Theodore," recalls Mr. Cromwell, "he was a tall, thin lad, with bright eyes and legs like pipe-stems.

"One of the first things I remember about him on that voyage was, that after the ship had got out of sight of land he remarked, half to himself, as he glanced at the water, 'I guess there ought to be a good many fish here.' Then an idea suddenly struck him, and turnig to me he said: 'George, go get me a small rope from somewhere, and we'll play a fishing game.' I don't know why I went at once in search of that line, without asking why he didn't go himself; but I went, and it never occurred to me to put the question. He had told me to go, and in such a determined way that it settled the matter.

A MASTERLY LEADER FROM BOYHOOD.

"Even then he was a leader—a masterful, commanding little fellow—who seemed to have a peculiar quality of his own of making his playmates obey him, not at all because we were afraid, but because we wanted to, and somehow felt sure we would have a good time and get lots of fun if we did as he said.

"Well, I went after the line and brought it to him. While I was gone on the errand he had thought out all the details of the fishing game, and had climbed on top of a coiled cable; for, of course, he was to be the fisherman.

" 'Now,' he said, as I handed him the line, 'all you fellows lie down flat on the deck here, and make believe to swim around like fishes. I'll throw one end of the line down to you, and the first fellow that catches hold of it is a fish that has bit my hook. He must just pull as hard as he can, and if he pulls me down off this coil of rope, why then he will be the fisherman and I will be a fish. But if he lets go, or if I pull him up here off the deck, why I will still be the fisherman. The game is to see how many fish each of us can land up here. The one who catches the most fish wins.' "

"The rest of us lay down flat on our stomachs," Mr. Cromwell says, in continuation of his narrative, "and made believe to swim; and, Theo-

DRAGGED FROM VICTORIA NYANZA LAKE BY 120 MEN AND WOMEN.
This huge Hippopotamus which weighed over two tons was dragged ashore with six bullets in its massive head. Three hundred natives gathered around and fell upon it like Vultures cutting and slashing the carcass. Only men eat Hippopotamus meat, the women being afraid to eat it for fear of being childless.

THEY ARE TOO EAGER FOR THE MEAT TO NOTICE THE CAMERA.
The Eland is one of the rarer types of Antelope and its meat is excellent eating. Some of Col. Roosevelt's boys have killed one and were snapped by the photographer in the act of skinning it.

AFRICAN NATIVES DEFYING THE LIGHTNING.

Among the curious superstitions of African natives are that of making rain, and the one depicted in this scene of defying the lightning.

dore, standing above us on the coiled cable, threw down one end of his line—a thin but strong rope. If I remember correctly my brother was the first fish to grasp the line—and then commenced a mighty struggle. It seemed to be much easier for the fish to pull the fisherman down than for the fisherman to haul up the dead weight of a pretty heavy boy lying flat on the deck below him—and I tell you it was a pretty hard struggle. My brother held onto the line with both hands and wrapped his legs around it, grapevine fashion. Theodore braced his feet on the coiled cable, stiffened his back, shut his teeth hard, and wound his end of the line around his waist. At first he tried by sheer muscle to pull the fish up—but he soon found it was hard work to lift up a boy about as heavy as himself.

THE FISH CAUGHT BY STRATEGY.

"Then another bright idea struck him. He pulled less and less, and at last ceased trying to pull at all. Of course the fish thought the fisherman was tired out, and he commenced to pull, hoping to get Theodore down on deck. He didn't succeed at first, and pulled all the harder. He rolled over on his back, then on his side, then sat up, all the time pulling and twisting and yanking at the line in every possible way; and that was just what Theodore hoped the fish would do. You see, all this time, while my brother was using his strength, Theodore simply stood still, braced like steel, and let him tire himself out.

"Before very long the fish was so out of breath that he couldn't pull any longer. Besides, the thin rope had cut his hands and made them sore. Then the fisherman commenced slowly and steadily to pull on the line, and in a very few minutes he had my brother hauled up alongside of him on the coil of cable."

The elder Roosevelt was a firm believer in hard work, and made this a part of the science he knew so well—the science of bringing up a boy. Although a man of wealth and position he taught his children—the four of them, two boys and two girls—the virtue of labor, and pointed with the finger of scorn to the despicable thing called man who lived in idleness. With such teachings at home, it is no wonder that Theodore was moved to declare:

"I was determined as a boy to make a man of myself."

GIRAFFES GALLOPING OFF WITH HUNTERS IN HOT PURSUIT.

CHAPTER V.

BIG GAME WHICH ROOSEVELT HUNTED IN BRITISH EAST AFRICA.

The Lion and Other Beasts of Prey—The Elephant and Other Huge Thick-Skinned Animals—The Rhinoceros and Hippopotamus—The Royal Game—The Buffalo, the Giraffe, the Camel and the African Antelope—Monkeys, Crocodiles, Birds, Snakes and Other Venomous Reptiles.

FOREMOST among the wild beasts of the African wilderness stands the lion, the King of the forests and jungles. He is exquisitely formed by nature for the predatory habits which he is destined to pursue. Though considerably under four feet in height, he is enabled, by means of the tremendous machinery wherewith nature has gifted him, to dash to the grave and overcome almost every beast of the forest, no matter how superior to him in weight and stature. The powerful buffalo and the gigantic elephant not excepted.

The full-grown male lion is adorned with a rank and shaggy mane almost reaching to the ground and of a dark or golden yellow color. The females have no mane, being covered with a glossy coat of tawny hair. The color of his fur makes it almost impossible to discover him in the dark, where his eyes, which glisten in the night like balls of fire, are almost the only signs of his stealthy and silent approach. His habits are nocturnal. During the day he lies resting in the thickets or in some inaccessible cave, and not until the sun sets does he start out on his search for prey. It is then his loud, deep-toned, solemn roars, repeated five of six times in quick succession, and increasing in loudness to the third or fourth, when it dies away in a low, deep moaning, or in five or six muffled sounds resembling a distant thunder, startles the forest and warns its denizens of the approaching danger.

Next to the lion the leopard or panther and the hunting leopard is the most formidable beast of prey in the Dark Continent. His spotted

coat, playful manners and wild, graceful springs, as he is romping around
and sporting with his cubs, or even with lions, reminds one of his feline
relation, our domestic cat.   He is, however, much larger, measuring in
length nearly five feet, not inclusive of three feet of tail.

In its habits it differs essentially from the lion, being thoroughly at
home in trees, running up a straight-stemmed and smooth-barked trunk

AFRICAN PANTHERS.

with the speed and agility of a monkey. Moreover the leopard is a much
more active animal than the lion, frequently taking tremendous leaps
and springs.

From their habit of lurking in the vicinity of the habitations of man,
to prey upon cattle, ponies, donkeys, sheep, goats and dogs, leopards
are frequently brought into collision with the natives, and a leopard being
mobbed in a thicket, from which he will charge several times, and bite
and claw half a dozen, before he is despatched or makes his escape, is

no uncommon occurrence in Africa. It is but seldom that the leopard takes to man-eating, though in some instances it has occurred. His distribution is more extensive than that of the lion, embracing, besides Africa, nearly the whole of Asia, from Persia to Japan, but not extending as far north as Siberia.

Notwithstanding his ferocious nature the leopard has often been tamed, and, indeed, almost domesticated, being permitted to range the house at will, greatly to the consternation of strange visitors. This complete state of docility can, however, only take place in an animal which has either been born in captivity, or taken at so early an age that its savage properties have never had time to expand. Even in this case the disposition of the creature must be naturally good, or it remains proof against kindness and attention, never losing a surliness of temper that makes its liberation too perilous an experiment.

If the lion is majestic and the leopard ferocious and bloodthirsty, the African hyena is, by common consent of hunters, travelers and naturalists, classed as the most skulking, cowardly, cruel and treacherous of all beasts of prey, and it would be difficult to find even one who would defend it.

The hyena is remarkable for its predatory, ferocious and cowardly habits. The African spotted hyena is much larger and more powerful than the striped and shaggy, rough-coated one, which is found in Syria and Palestine, but the habits of all are very similar. The hyenas, although very repulsive in appearance, are yet very useful, as they prowl in search of dead animals, especially of the larger kinds, and will devour them even when putrid, so that they act the same part among beasts that the vultures do among birds. They not unfrequently dig up recently interred corpses and voraciously devour all carcasses they can find. Their jaws and teeth are exceedingly powerful, as they can crush the thigh-bone of an ox with apparently little effort.

The favorite haunts of the hyena are holes and caves in the rocks or a hole dug by itself on the side of a hill or ravine. The call of the hyena is a very disagreeable, unearthly cry, and dogs are often tempted out by it when near, and fall a victim to the stealthy marauder. On one occasion a small dog belonging to a farmer was taken off by a hyena very

early in the morning. The den of this beast was known to be not far off
in some sandstone cliffs, and some natives went after it, entered the cave,
killed the hyena, and returned the dog alive, with but little damage done
to it.   A hyena, though it does not appear to move very fast, goes over
rough ground in a wonderful manner, and it takes a good long run to

HUNTING THE BUFFALO IN AFRICA.

overtake it on horseback, unless in most favorable ground. A stray hyena
is now and then met with by a party of sportsmen, followed and speared;
but sometimes not till after a run of three or four miles, if the ground is
broken by ravines. It is a cowardly animal, and shows but little fight
when brought to bay. The young are very tamable and show great signs
of attachment to their owner, in spite of all that has been written about
the untamable ferocity of the hyena.

The striped hyena's food is mainly carrion or carcasses killed by
other animals; and in inhabited districts the animal is much dreaded on
account of its grave-robbing propensities. Portions of such carcasses as

it finds arc eaten on the spot, while other parts are dragged off to its den, the situation of which is generally indicated by the fragments of bones around the entrance. These hyenas will also feast on skeletons that have been picked down to the bone by jackals and vultures; the bone-

THE SACRED BABOON.

cracking power of the hyena's jaws rendering such relics acceptable, if not favorite, food.

The striped hyena—probably on account of its "body-snatching" propensities—is cordially detested by the natives of all the countries it inhabits. When a hyena is killed, the body is treated with every mark of indignity, and finally burnt. On one occasion, says a traveler, I came across a party of natives cruelly ill-treating a nearly full-grown hyena, which had been rendered helpless by its jaws being muzzled and its feet broken. I soon ended the sufferings of the poor brute by a bullet.

Although, owing to their nocturnal habits, hyenas are seldom seen, yet in some parts of Africa, from the multitude of their tracks, they must be very common.

The African spotted hyena is much larger and more powerful than the striped species. It inhabits the greater part of Africa at the present day. Formerly the geographical range of this hyena was far more extensive than it is at present, as is proved by the vast quantities of its remains found in the caves of various parts of Europe, from Gibraltar in the south, to Yorkshire in the north. It was formerly considered, indeed, that the so-called "cave-hyena" indicated a distinct species from the living one; but zoologists are now generally in accord in regarding the two as specifically identical, although the fossil European hyenas were generally of larger dimensions than the existing African form.

Other wild animals of the African jungles, many of whom have fallen for our ex-President's swift bullets, are the Black Rhinoceros, who from his dark hiding-places, tearing through whole caravans of tourists, in blind fury charges and slays his victims; then there is the hereditary foe of the lion, the Buffalo, the favored meat for the King of Beasts; the great dog killer, the Sable Antelope, who mercilessly drives his spear-like horns through the hunter's body; the Haartbeasts and Gnus, stronger and swifter than the horse; and last, but not least, the huge elephant, whose gigantic tusks are one of the most valuable articles of export from Africa.

No sooner were the skins of the animals properly prepared than they were sent in casks to the Smithsonian Institution in Washington, where the work of stuffing them was undertaken. The first consignment of boxes arrived Sept. 1. Scientists of the institution expressed themselves as having never seen a more interesting and well preserved collection of mammals and birds. There were also valuable species of rats, rabbits, moles, mice and other small mammals. What the scientists considered a great prize was the warty rat. It is slightly larger than the ordinary rat and has two warts on its lower lip and has never before been seen in this country.

CHAPTER VI.

ROOSEVELT'S HUNTING GROUNDS.

British East Africa—The Chicago of East Africa—Tropical Scenery—Primeval Forests, Rocky Mountains and Running Streams—Wonders of the Animal and Vegetable Kingdoms—Pheasants, Doves, Monkeys—Flowers in all the Colors of the Rainbow—Man's Cruelty Marring the Beauty of Nature.

BRITISH East Africa, which was penetrated by Roosevelt on his famous hunting expedition, is located south of Egyptian Soudan, Abyssinia and Italian Somaliland, and north of German East Africa. It stretches as far west as to the Congo State and on the east is bordered by the Indian Ocean. The Equator passes right through it

RHINOCEROS BULL.

between Nairobi and Port Florence and it, therefore, has all the characteristics of the Tropics.

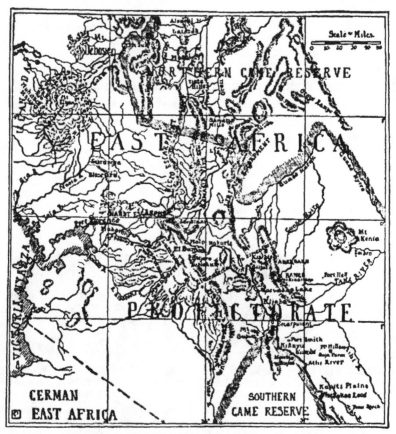

ROOSEVELT HUNTING GROUNDS.

It is, however, not an entirely barbarian country. The British have opened up its vast resources to civilization by establishing a government, building cities, furthering trade and commerce and last, but not least, by the construction of the great Uganda Railroad, which connects Mombasa and the coast with Lake Victoria Nyanza, one of the largest inland lakes in the world. This road, which passes through one of the most wonderful regions and is 600 miles long, has cost thousands of lives and about $50,000,000, but this immense sacrifice seems small compared to the great benefits that have accrued from it to civilization. It has begun the transformation of Equatorial Africa from a wilderness into a Garden of Eden; it has made a wonderful country and a land full of charming attractions for the painter and the artist accessible to the scientific explorer and to industry and commerce; it has opened up the way for the Christian missionaries and prepared the way for the entrance of civilization into the interior of Africa, and last but not least, made it possible for our Teddy to reach his hunting grounds with full strength of body and keenness of mind to the strenuous work before him. It enables him to make a journey of about 600 miles, which by caravan could not be accomplished in less than three months' time and at the expenditure of a small fortune in cash, in less than forty-eight hours at a cost of from six to fifty dollars, according to the class of accommodation.

Through wilds, forests, craggy mountains and pestiferous jungles this gigantic work went on for six years. Neither poisonous insects, deadly disease, venomous reptiles, warlike native tribes, ferocious wild beasts, or the fearful ravages of the red hot blasts from the never-resting furnaces of a tropical climate, before which both imported and native laborers fell like soldiers swept away by the Gatling gun, could stop the work and when the line in 1903 was accomplished everyone felt that one of the most important milestones in the development of Equatorial East Africa was reached.

Famous travelers who have recently made trips along this road, give pictorial descriptions of the scenery, now so much more interesting to us as the theatre of our popular ex-President's latest achievements.

The Uganda Railroad runs sharply upward and westward to the highlands of Nairobi through undulating ground covered with luxuriant tropical vegetation until 150 miles from the coast it reaches its extreme elevation of 8,500 feet above the level of the sea. Various and surprising is the panorama that passes before the traveler's eyes. Many colored birds and gorgeous butterflies flutter in the rich foliage of the tropical trees or among the flowers, that glitter in all the colors of the rainbow. Deep ravines, filled by rushing streams and foaming cataracts open up below through glades of palms and vine-clad trees.

Here and there along the route the traveler sees African plantations, with neat cottages and villages and other works of advancing civilization. The rubber, fibre and cotton raised on these productive farms will in the future supply the yet unmeasured demand of Europe and America

GIRAFFES SEEN BY ROOSEVELT ALONG THE UGANDA RAILROAD.

and become an inexhaustible source of wealth to this yet unbroken soil.

About one hundred miles further west the train enters the barren waste known as the Taru desert. It is here where Roosevelt from his commodious palace cars saw the prowling hyena, or the lion and the leopard seeking their prey among the herds of gazelles and antelopes that still remind the traveler of animal life.

As the train has been climbing higher and higher the country loses its tropical aspect. Instead of the impenetrable jungle luxuriant forests please the eye, the palm gives place to the olive, the dark fir to the mangoes, and endless fields of green grass watered by streams and broken by bold uptowering bluffs and ridges.

Upon reaching Voi, one of the many little stations the traveler meets every few miles along the road, our ex-President availed himself of the facilities the government had provided the tourists for seeing one of the most magnificent sights in the Dark Continent, the snow-clad, Kilimanjaro, whose shimmering summit shrouded in the blaze of clouds rises 19,700 feet above the level of the sea, and is known as the highest mountain peak in Africa. A good road leads to the very foot of the "Mountain of the Spirit Ajax," as it is called by the superstitious natives, but the climbing in a heat of over 100 degrees through thickets of bamboo and rocks is a feat that has only been accomplished two or three times, and is more dangerous than pleasant.

Along the railroad may be seen scattering villages of the generally agricultural, but sometimes dangerous Wangtka tribe, and also the Wakamba, the largest tribe of East Africa and the only one to hold its own against the war-like and hunting Masui. The naked natives around Victoria Nyanza are bronze models of physical perfection and moral and peaceable habits, while the Nandi tribe are known for stealing telegraph wire for bracelets and earrings and railroad bolts for spear heads. The native Kingdom of Uganda is a well organized state under British protection. The country is fertile and abounds in cotton, cocoa, coffee, oranges, lemons, pineapples, and the people are eager for knowledge. From Naimbi to Florence the train passes through a region of farms and plantations, and then we enter upon the scenic section of the Uganda railway, which rises 2,000 feet, the first 24 miles pitching over cliffs, volcanic hills, craters, escarpments and abrupt land pitches. Lake Naivasha, with its many lovely islands and bright blossoms, hides under its blue waves a submerged crater. Thousands of water fowls cover its surface, while big game and great herds of sheep and goats surround its shores. In this vicinity is a breeding farm for zebras, where the government tries to solve the horse problem for Africa by producing a hybrid once. Near the charming salt lake of Nakura, you cross the Mou escarpment on twenty-seven huge viaducts built by American engineers. The last section of the railroad runs through a swampy but fertile country, and the approach to Port Florence, a transfer station on Lake Victoria Nyanza, is anything but inviting. Across the lake lies Entebbe, the British capital of the Uganda Protectorate. In this carefully planned city, charmingly located on shores of lake blazing with color and dotted with gemlike islands, Roosevelt and his party were splendidly entertained by Judge George Ennis and his lovely wife, who is a native of Chicago, and the only American in the city.

Mrs. Ennis was formerly Miss Ethel Kirkland, daughter of Mrs. Joseph Kirkland of Rush street, Chicago. Her husband's (Judge Ennis) position is second only to that of the governor of Uganda, and Mrs. Ennis, who is the only American in the Colony, is regarded as the foremost hostess in Entebbe. All noted people who visit Central Africa enjoy the hospitality of the Ennis home, and among those who have stayed under its roof are the Duke d'Abruzzi, the famous Dr. Koch and others.

The house or bungalow, where Roosevelt was received, is a rambling one, gray in color, with a sloping roof of red corrugated iron. It is set in a large garden, sweet with frangipani, bright with crimson hibiscus and yellow accacia and numberless varieties of roses. The side verandas are covered with vines and the garden is fenced with plaited branches of the elephant plant, which shields it from curious persons passing on the red road beyond. The servants' quarters are apart from the house.

This is the lovely picture that greeted Roosevelt when he reached Entebbe, 3,700 feet above the level of the sea, and when he looked out of his window he could see Lake Victoria Nyanza.

Roosevelt's hostess holds a unique position in her adopted home. In the heart of Africa, she is surrounded by all the formality of high life in London. Judge Ennis has a retinue of native servants, of various tribes, quick to do the bidding of their young mistress. The only white one is the nurse for the small son and heir.

After the strenuous time which Roosevelt had spent in and around Nairobi he and his son enjoyed immensely the social relaxation of Entebbe and the comparative quiet of their surroundings.

CHAPTER VII.

ROOSEVELT'S LIFE IN THE WEST.

Exciting Adventures—A Mistaken Ruffian—A Western Episode—The Pleasures of the
Chase—Shoots His First Buffalo—Kills Two Deer at Four Hundred Yards—An Exciting
Elk Hunt—Hunting Dangerous Game—Stands Off a Band of Indians—Tribute to the
Rough Riders.

M R. ROOSEVELT has told the story of his Western life in several
exceedingly interesting volumes. Although full of exciting adventures and thrilling experiences, these captivating tales are modest
to a fault. He seems to take as much delight in telling of the shots he

MOUNTAIN WOLF.

missed as of those which reached the mark. He never boasts, and while
he must have participated in many adventures on the frontier, those
which might suggest any display of heroism on his part are either omitted
or else lightly touched upon.

Although Mr. Roosevelt was undoubtedly looked upon as more or
less of a "tenderfoot" by the indigenous Westerner with whom he was
thrown into daily contact, he asserts that he was always treated with

the utmost courtesy, whether on the roundup or in camp, and the few real desperadoes he met were scrupulously polite. To use his own words:

MR. ROOSEVELT MAKES GOOD.

"I never was shot at maliciously but once. This was on an occasion when I had to pass the night in a little frontier hotel where the bar-room occupied the whole floor, and was, in consequence, the place where every one, drunk or sober, had to sit. My assailant was neither a cowboy nor a *bona fide* 'bad man,' but a broad-hatted ruffian of cheap and commonplace type, who had for the moment terrorized the other men in the bar-room, these being mostly sheep herders and small grangers. The fact that I wore glasses, together with my evident desire to avoid a fight, apparently gave him the impression—a mistaken one— that I would not resent an injury."

"Beware of entrance in a quarrel; but being in, bear thyself that the opposer may beware of thee," is the precept laid down by Shakespeare. How Mr. Roosevelt bore himself on this occasion he leaves to the imagination, but an eye-witness to the encounter states that after a short but decisive tussle he took the "bad man's" gun away from him and then proceeded to give him a practical illustration of the "strenuous life," by kicking him unceremoniously from the room. To say that this act made him popular with the cowboys would be putting it mildly. To use a familiar Western expression, Mr. Roosevelt "made good."

HE DANCED DOWN THE MIDDLE.

The following incident will serve to explain in a measure his popularity with his companions of the plains. In one of his books he tells of a deadly affray that took place in a town not very far distant from his ranch. It seems that a Scotchman and a Minnesota man had become involved in a dispute. Both were desperadoes, and after a bitter quarrel the former, mounted on his broncho, rode to the door of his enemy's house, "looking for trouble," but before he could open fire was promptly shot down by the American. Mr. Roosevelt, in relating the occurrence, described how, a few days later, he opened a cowboy's ball, with the wife of the victor of his contest, he himself dancing opposite the husband. "It was the lanciers," says the narrator, "and he knew all

IMAGINE COL. ROOSEVELT CAPTURING THIS MONSTER CROCODILE.

This Crocodile was caught asleep on shore and its back broken by a shot from a high power Winchester rifle. It is being dragged back into the water where it will be devoured by its own kind. The Natives at the headwaters of the Nile, and along the shores of Lake Victoria Nyanza live in mortal terror of Crocodiles and whenever possible they kill them with poisoned spears. Among some of the tribes no young man is considered a real warrior unless he has speared a Crocodile; all of the belles of the tribe worship him then for his courage and wish him for a husband.

A FINE LION SHOT BY A HUNTER JUST BEFORE ROOSEVELT'S ARRIVAL.

the steps far better than I did. He could have danced a minuet very well with a little practice. The scene reminded one of the ball where Bret Harte's heroine danced down the middle with the man who shot Sandy Magee "

AMERICAN BISON KILLED BY ROOSEVELT IN THE ROCKY MOUNTAINS.

THE DELIGHTS OF THE CHASE.

Mr. Roosevelt devoted much of his time to hunting among the mountains and on the plains, both as a pastime and to procure hides, meat, and robes for use on the ranch; and it was his good luck to kill all the various kinds of large game that can properly be considered as belonging to temperate North America. What a stirring description of the delights of the chase, which he calls the best of all national pastimes, is to be found in the following taken from his book, "The Wilderness Hunter":

"No one but he who has partaken thereof can understand the keen delight of hunting in lonely lands. For his is the joy of the horse well ridden and the rifle well held; for him the long days of toil and hardship. resolutely endured, and crowned at the end with triumph. In after years prairies shimmering in the bright sun; of vast snow-clad wastes lying desolate under gray skies; of the melancholy marshes; of the rush of mighty rivers; of the breath of ice-armored pines at the touch of the winds of winter; of cataracts roaring between hoary mountain masses; of all the innumerable sights and sounds of the wilderness; of its immensity and mystery; and of the silences that brood in its still depths."

A BUFFALO HUNT.

On one of his first hunting trips, some twenty years ago, Mr. Roosevelt decided to go on a buffalo hunt. Leaving camp early in the morning, he set out with one companion across a tract of the Bad Lands, and late in the afternoon came across three male buffalo. After picketing their ponies the two men began to creep on hands and knees toward the animals, and at length succeeded in getting within shooting distance. This was the first time Mr. Roosevelt had ever shot at a buffalo and, deceived by the size and shape of the animal, he made the mistake of aiming too far back, with the result that, although he hit the beast, he only succeeded in wounding him, and to his chagrin the three animals disappeared in a cloud of dust. Mounting their horses, they dashed after the fleeing buffalo, and for several miles rode at a rapid gait and soon had the satisfaction of seeing the three stop and begin to graze. As the two men galloped toward them they again dashed away. The ponies they had been riding were completely jaded, but they finally succeeded in getting within a few yards of the wounded buffalo. Meanwhile the moon had risen, and, what with the uncertain light and the rough ground over which they were riding, it was almost impossible to get a good shot. Nevertheless, the future President of the United States fired, and, to his disappointment, missed. He not only missed, but to his surprise, the infuriated animal, with a loud bellow, charged him with lowered horns. His pony bolted and the rifle was knocked against his forehead, cutting a terrible gash. The buffalo then turned his attention to Mr. Roosevelt's companion, who made off on his tired horse, shooting at the pursuing animal as he went. None of the shots produced any effect, however, and wearying of the sport, the buffalo disappeared in the darkness and they saw him no more.

Several days later he was more successful. Shortly after noon, as the two hunters were entering a ravine, their ponies suddenly threw up their heads and sniffed the air.

KILLS A BISON.

"Feeling sure that they had smelt some wild beast," says the hero of the adventure, "I slipped off my pony and ran quickly, but cautiously, up along the valley. Before I had gone a hundred yards I noticed in the soft soil, at the bottom, the round prints of a bison's hoofs; and immediately afterwards got a glimpse of the animal himself, as he fed slowly up the course of the ravine, some distance ahead of me. The wind was just right, and no ground could have been better for stalking. Hardly needing to bend down, I walked up behind a small sharp-crested hillock, and peeping over, there below me, not fifty yards off, was a great bison bull. He was walking along, grazing as he walked. His glossy fall coat was in fine trim, and shone in the rays of the sun; while his pride of bearing showed him to be in the lusty vigor of his prime. As I rose above the crest of the hill, he held up his head and cocked his tail in the air. Before he could go off I put a bullet in behind his shoulder. The wound was an almost immediately fatal one, yet with surprising agility for so large and heavy an animal, he bounded up the opposite side of the ravine, heedless of two more balls, both of which went into his flank and ranged forward, and disappeared over the ridge at a lumbering gallop, the blood pouring from his mouth and nostrils.

"We knew he could not go far, and trotted leisurely along on his bloody trail; and in the next gully we found him stark dead, lying almost on his back, having pitched over the side when he tried to go down it."

A LONG SHOT.

Upon one occasion, while sitting on his veranda, he heard a splashing sound in the river some distance away, and glancing in that direction saw three deer, which had emerged from the thicket of the trees on the opposite bank, slaking their thirst in the stream. Entering the house

he picked up his rifle and, using the pillar of the porch as a rest, fired
at the largest of the animals, a magnificent buck. It was a long shot, and
fully 250 yards, but he brought down the deer. The best shot he ever
made, and, as he apologetically puts it, just such a shot as any one occasionally will make if he takes a good many chances and fires often at
ranges where the odds are greatly against his hitting, was at a black-
tailed deer. Coming across three of these animals, when about 200 yards
distant he fired, but missed, the bullet striking low. Holding his rifle
high he made a second shot, above and ahead of them, which only succeeded in turning the deer, which quickly vanished behind the shelter
of a bluff. Elevating the sight of the gun to 400 yards, he waited for
them to reappear, and had the satisfaction, a few minutes later, of seeing one of them standing broadside toward him. As he was about to fire,
another deer appeared, and, thinking it would be a good plan to have as
large a mark as possible to shoot at, he waited and when the second
animal came to a stop abreast of the first, he aimed carefully and fired.
The next instant, to his surprise, he observed the two deer struggling
upon the ground, and hurrying to the spot, discovered that the bullet
had broken their backs. Measuring the distance from where the animals
lay to the point where he had stood when firing the shot, to his wonder and
delight he found that it was over 400 yards.

AN EXCITING ELK HUNT.

In 1891, Mr. Roosevelt made an elk hunt in northwestern Wyoming
among the Shoshone Mountains, and his description of the trip makes the
reader tingle with excitement as he follows every step of the chase from
the moment the call of the bull elk echoes through the woodland until
the proud giant of the forest falls beneath the unerring shot of the hunter.

"It was very exciting," says Mr. Roosevelt in telling of one adventure, "as we crept toward the great bull, and the challenge sounded
nearer and nearer. While we were still at some distance the pealing
notes were like those of a bugle, delivered in two bars, first rising, then
abruptly falling; as we drew nearer they took on a harsh, squealing
sound. Each call made our veins thrill; it sounded like the cry of some
huge beast of prey. At last we heard the roar of the challenge not
eighty yards off. Stealing forward three or four yards, I saw the tips

of the horns through a mass of dead timber and young growth, and I slipped to one side to get a clean shot. Seeing us, but not making out what we were, and full of fierce and insolent excitement, the wapiti bull stepped boldly toward us with a stately swinging gait. Then he stood motionless, facing us, barely fifty yards away, his handsome twelve-tined antlers tossed aloft; as he held his head with the lordly grace of his kind, I fired into his chest, and as he turned I raced forward and shot him in the flank; but the second bullet was not needed, for the first wound was mortal, and he fell before going fifty yards.

"The dead elk lay among the young evergreens. The huge, shapely body was set on legs that were as strong as steel rods, and yet slender, clean and smooth; they were in color a beautiful dark brown, contrasting well with the yellowish hue of the body. The neck and throat were garnished with a mane of long hair; the symmetry of the great horns set off the fine, delicate lines of the noble head."

EASY TO SHOOT STRAIGHT IF YOU ARE CLOSE.

Speaking of shooting dangerous game, Mr. Roosevelt believes that steadiness is more needed than good shooting; that no game is dangerous unless a man is close up, and if a man is close it is easy enough for him to shoot straight, if he does not lose his head. In recounting several exciting episodes in connection with the hunting of grizzlies, he utters this characteristic maxim: "A bear's brain is about the size of a pint bottle, and any one can hit a pint bottle offhand at thirty or forty feet. I have had two shots at bears at close quarters, and each time I fired into the brain, the bullet going in between the eye and ear. A novice at this kind of sport will find it best and safest to keep in mind the old Norse viking's advice in reference to a long sword: 'If you go in close enough your sword will be long enough.' If a poor shot goes in close enough you will find that he shoots straight enough." Once he came into contact with far more dangerous game than grizzlies—Indians—and it was his steadiness that brought him out of the encounter unscathed—but we will let him tell the story hims

"One morning I had been traveling along the edge of the prairie, and about noon I rode Manitou up a slight rise and came out on a plateau

that was perhaps half a mile broad. When near the middle, four or five Indians suddenly came up over the edge, directly in front of me.

AN INDIAN CHARGE.

"The second they saw me they whipped their guns out of their slings, started their horses into a run, and came on at full tilt, whooping and brandishing their weapons. I instantly reined up and dismounted. The level plain where we were was of all places the one on which such an onslaught could best be met. In any broken country, or where there is much cover, a white man is at a great disadvantage if pitted against such adepts in the art of hiding as Indians; while, on the other hand, the latter will rarely rush in on a foe who, even if overpowered in the end, will probably inflict severe loss on his assailants. The fury of an Indian charge, and the whoops by which it is accompanied, often scare horses so as to stampede them; but in Manitou I had perfect trust, and the old fellow stood as steady as a rock, merely cocking his ears and looking round at the noise. I waited until the Indians were a hundred yards off, and then threw up my rifle and drew a bead on the foremost. The effect was like magic.

SCATTERED LIKE DUCKS.

"The whole party scattered out as wild pigeons or teal ducks sometimes do when shot at, and doubled back on their tracks, the men bending over alongside their horses. When some distance off they halted and gathered together to consult, and after a minute one came forward alone, ostentatiously dropping his rifle and waving a blanket over his head. When he came to within fifty yards I stopped him, and he pulled out a piece of paper—all Indians, when absent from their reservations, are supposed to carry passes—and called out, 'How! Me good Indian.' I answered, 'How,' and assured him most sincerely I was very glad he was a good Indian, but I would not let him come closer; and when his companions began to draw near, I covered him with the rifle and made him move off, which he did with a sudden lapse into the most canonical Anglo-Saxon profanity. I then started to lead my horse out to the prairie; and after hovering round a short time they rode off, while I followed suit, but in the opposite direction. It had all passed too quickly .

for me to have time to get frightened; but during the rest of my ride I was exceedingly uneasy, and pushed tough, speedy old Manitou along at a rapid rate, keeping well out on the level. However, I never saw the Indians again. They may not have intended any mischief beyond giving me a fright; but I did not dare to let them come to close quarters, for they would have probably taken my horse and rifle, and not impossibly my scalp as well."

THE ROUGH RIDER.

But there is something more interesting in Mr. Roosevelt's books than his wonderful stories of the chase. From them the reader will obtain a correct idea of the West as it was twenty years ago and as it is today. In his work entitled "Ranch Life and the Hunting Trail," from which the foregoing extract is taken, one is brought face to face with the Western cattle country—the excitement and danger of "riding herd," the mysteries of the round-up, the terrors of "broncho busting," and all the interesting details that go to make up the life of a cowboy or ranchman. In one of the most interesting chapters in the book, Mr. Roosevelt pays the following tribute to the wild rough rider of the plains: "Brave, hospitable, hardy and adventurous, he is the grim pioneer of our land; he prepares the way for the civilization from before whose face he must himself disappear. Hard and dangerous though his existence, it has yet a wild attraction which plainly draws to it his bold, free spirit."

This close familiarity with the rough life of these hardy sons of the Western Wilds explains to a certain extent the unexampled enthusiasm wherewith Roosevelt was greeted when during the last Presidential campiagn he traveled from 10,000 to 15,000 miles through the Western States and Territories where he spent so many years of his early youth, for everywhere he was greeted as a friend and an old acquaintance. It also explains how he could stand making from ten to twenty vigorous campaign speeches a day, visiting over two hundred towns and cities and keeping up the strain for eight consecutive weeks—for among the cowboys and ranchmen of the Western plains did he lay the foundation of the unexampled physical vigor that has served him so well during his strenuous life.

CHAPTER VIII.

NATIVES OF AFRICA.

What Specimens of Humanity Roosevelt Met in Africa—Black and White—Arabs, Negroes and Other Races—Hottentots and Bushmen—Speke's and Burton's Discoveries.

WHEN Roosevelt threw himself into the midst of the Dark Continent he found himself among a variety of races entirely different from all the many nationalities he had governed in his own native land. Most advanced in civilization are the Arabs, who belong to the Semitic stock, and form the main portion of the population of Egypt, Algeria, Tunis and part of Abyssinia, but owing to their commercial instincts are found in smaller or larger settlements all over the

AFRICAN KRAALS OR ROUND HUTS.

country. The black races are represented in northern, eastern and central Africa and in Soudan, while in southern Africa we find Negroes, Kaffirs, Bechuanas, Suahelis, and other dark-hued races. To the southwest of these are the Hottentots and the Bushmen, while Madagascar is in-

SAVAGES BURNING VILLAGES AS THEY TRAVEL.

habited by a Malayan stock, the Nile countries by the Nubians and the Niger valleys by the Tulahs.

The following incident from the famous expedition undertaken by R. F. Burton and J. H. Speke, two captains in the British army, through the same territory now traversed by Roosevelt give a vivid idea of the habits and nature of the natives. Says Captain Burton:

"On the wayside appeared for the first time the Khambi, or substantial kraals, which give evidence of unsafe traveling and of the unwillingness of caravans to bivouac in the villages. In this country they assumed the form of round huts, and long sheds or booths of straw or grass supported by a framework of rough sticks firmly planted in the ground and lashed together with bark strips. The whole was surrounded with a deep circle of thorns, which—the entrance or entrances being carefully closed at night-fall, not to re-open until dawn—formed a complete defense against bare feet and naked legs."

TRAINING BOYS TO FIGHT.

The tribe through whose territory they first passed was the Waza-ramo, a people that dress their hair by means of a pomatum of clay, moistened with castor oil. When this preparation is nearly dry, the hair is pulled out into numerous wiry twists, which point in all directions. They levy heavy taxes upon all the merchants and others who pass through the territory of their tribe, which amount to positive plunder. Their nearness to the coast, has changed them in many respects, from their natural state; they wore more clothes than are the fashion among most of the tribes of Africa; while their houses are superior, in point of "modern conveniences," to the huts of their neighbors.

The travelers arrived at the foot of the mountain near the end of July. They both suffered much from malaria, common to the coast and were so ill that they could scarcely sit up as they rode. On the way up the mountains they saw many skeletons of those who had perished

NATIVES IN THEIR CANOES ON THE TANGANYIKA LAKE.

on the road, the bones picked clean by the birds of prey. As they ascended, the purer air of the mountains banished their malaria, and they recovered, to some degree, from their wasting fevers.

As they traversed a plain between two ranges of mountains, they came upon a sight which spoke more eloquently than anything else could (where human figures were lacking) of the horrors of one great African traffic. A village was completely destroyed, the houses battered or burned down, and every evidence of human habitation defaced. There were many signs of struggling, such as the earth and neighboring trees could tell; though there was no blood. The village had been attacked by slavers, and the inhabitants carried off. Two negroes lurked in the neighboring jungle, but when the travelers would have invited them to closer quarters, fled in terror. Both Burton and Speke felt the tragedy of which they beheld the scene; but not so their native attendants. To them it was a mere matter of course; they spent the night in singing and dancing, and helping themselves to whatever they could find in the ruins.

AFRICAN BOYS PLAYING GAMES.

The climate of the country through which they were now passing is described as "a furnace by day and a refrigerator by night." They reached "Windy Pass," at the foot of the third range of the Usagara mountains, early in September. In spite of all that they had had to endure from the heat of the sun and the lack of water, the most difficult part of the journey was still to some. From their camp in the valley, the explorers could see the almost perpendicular face of the mountain, and wonder how they, weak and sick (for they were again troubled with ague) could ascend it. But they did not despair. The asses stumbled at almost every step, while the men were endeavoring to mount a precipice where almost every foot dislodged a rolling stone. The ascent required six hours; and Captain Speke suffered so severely from it that two days of violent delirium intervened before he was able to continue the journey, even in a hammock.

Through countries where each tribe seemed more intent on plunder (they called it presents to the chief) than the last had been, the travelers came at length to Unyamwezi, the Land of the Moon. Their approach to Tura Nullah, the first town of this country, created a sensation—literally "astonished the natives:"

"We reached a large expanse of pillar-stones, where the van had halted, in order that the caravan might make its first appearance with dignity. Then ensued a clearing, studded with large stockaded villages, peering over tall hedges of dark-green milk-bush, fields of maize and millet, manioc, gourds, and water-melons, and showing numerous flocks and herds, clustering around the shallow pits. The people swarmed from their abodes, young and old hustling one another for a better stare, the man forsook his loom and the girl her hoe, and for the remainder of the march we were escorted by a tail of screaming boys and shouting adults; the males almost nude, the women bare to the waist, and clothed only knee-deep in kilts, accompanied us, puffing pipes the while, striking their hoes with stones, crying 'beads, beads!' and ejaculating their wonder in strident expressions of 'Hi! hi!' and 'Hiu! ih!' and 'Ha! a!a!'"

The porters took possession of a considerable assemblage of vacant huts, and the two white men were assigned to a wall-less roof, bounded on one side by the village palisade. Here the mob came to behold the strangers, and from morning till night there was no cessation of their staring; when one had gazed his fill, another at once took his place.

From this point onward, we find the progress of the party even less rapid than it had been heretofore; so greatly were they delayed by sickness. Before they had passed into the country which lies nearest to Lake Tanganyika, they were obliged to dismiss those servants who had been hired for a term of six months; and it was nearly seven months after their departure that they resumed their march without these persons. It was to occupy almost two months, before they came upon the lake which it was their intention to explore. We quote again from Burton:

"On the 13th of February we resumed our travel through screens of lofty grass, which thinned out into a straggling forest. After about an hour's march, as we entered a small savannah, I saw the fundi running

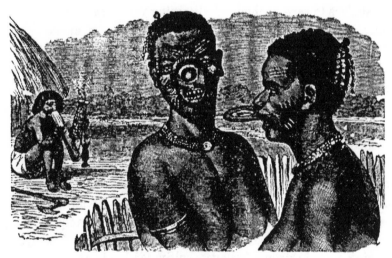

AFRICANS DEFORMING THEMSELVES FOR STYLE.

forward and changing the direction of the caravan. Without supposing that he had taken upon himself this responsibility, I followed him. Presently he breasted a steep and stony hill, sparsely clad with thorny trees. Arrived with toil, for our fagged beasts now refused to proceed, we halted for a few minutes upon the summit. 'What is that streak of light which lies below?' I inquired of Seedy Bombay. 'I am of opinion,' quoth Bombay, 'that that is the water.' I gazed in dismay; the remains of my blindness, the veil of trees, and a broad ray of sunshine illuminating but one reach of the lake bend, shrunk its fair proportions. Somewhat prematurely, I began to lament my folly in having risked life and lost breath for so poor a prize, to curse Arab exaggeration, and to propose an immediate return, with the view of exploring Nyanza, a northern lake. Advancing, however, a few yards, the whole scene burst upon my view, filling me with admiration, wonder and delight.

"Nothing could be more picturesque than this first view of the Tanganyika lake, as it lay in the lap of the mountains, basking in the gorgeous tropical sunshine. Below and beyond a short foreground of rugged and precipitous hill-fold, down which the foot-path zig-zags painfully, a narrow strip of emerald green, never sere, and marvelously fertile, shelves toward a ribbon of glistening yellow sand, here bordered by sedgy rushes, there cleanly and clearly cut by the breaking wavelets. Farther in front stretch the waters—an expanse of the lightest and softest blue—in breadth varying from thirty to thirty-five miles, and sprinkled by the crisp east wind with tiny crescents of snowy foam. The background in front is a high and broken wall of steel-colored mountain, here flecked and capped with pearly mist, there standing sharply penciled against the azure air; its yawning chasms, marked by a deeper plum-color, fall toward dwarf hills of mound-like proportions, which apparently dip their feet in the wave. To the south, and opposite the long low point behind which the Malagarazi river discharges the red loam suspended in its violent stream, lie the bluff headlands and capes of 'Aguhha, and as the eye dilates, it falls upon a cluster of out-lying islets specking a sea-horizon. Villages, cultivated lands, the frequent canoes of the fishermen on the waters, and on a nearer approach, the murmurs of the waves breaking upon the shore, give something of a variety of movement, of life to the landscape, which, like all the fairest prospects in these regions, wants but a little of the neatness and finish of art—mosques and kiosks, palaces and villas, gardens and orchards—contrasting with the profuse lavishness and magnificence of nature, and diversifying the coup d'œil unbroken of excessive vegetation, to rival. if not to excel, the most admired scenery of the classic regions, the riant shores of this vast crevasse appeared doubly beautiful to me after the silent and spectral mangrove creeks on the East African sea-board, and the melancholy, monotonous experience of desert and jungle scenery,

From Underwood & Underwood, N. Y. COLONEL ROOSEVELT IN VENICE,

Seated in one of the famous gondolas from which the famous American traveler viewed the canals and palaces of this celebrated city.

COL. ROOSEVELT IN THE HUNTER'S PARADISE.
Arrival at Kapiti Plains, a station near the ranch of Sir Alfred Pease.

tawny rock and sun-parched plain, or rank herbage and flats of black mire. Truly it was a revel for soul and sight.''

Proceeding at once to Kawele, which may be considered as the port of Ujiji, the explorers endeavored to procure a boat for the navigation of the lake; but this was no easy matter. Despairing of procuring a vessel at Kawele, Captain Speke went in a canoe, with twenty men, to Ukaranga, for the purpose of hiring a dhow from the Arab merchant there who was the possessor of the sole vessel of this kind upon the

NATIVES REFUSE TO PROCEED.

lake. The Arab detained him there by evasive answers for several days, and at last agreed to let him have it at the end of three months.

The natives had told them of a river by means of which the waters of the lake were emptied—a great river, flowing toward the west; and their eager interest was too thoroughly aroused to permit them to wait all this time inactive. They hired two canoes for an exorbitant sum, one sixty feet by four, the other about forty feet long. In such vessels, they proposed to navigate the lake which they believed to be the recipient and absorbent of the entire river system—the heart from which the great rivers, like arteries, drew their floods, and to which the vein-like smaller streams brought their constant contributions. For fifteen days they kept onward; nine days they remained at the point so reached, Uvira, and in nine days more they returned to their starting-place. Of the difficulties of the journey, Captain Burton says:

"The boating was rather a severe trial. We had no means of resting the back; the holds of the canoes, besides being knee-deep in water, were disgracefully crowded. They had been appropriated to us and our four servants by Kannena, but by degrees he introduced, in addition to the stores, spars, broken vases, pots and gourds, a goat, two or three small boys, one or two sick sailors, the little slave girl, and the large sheep. The canoes were top-heavy with the number of their crew, and the shipping of many seas spoiled our tents, and, besides, wetted our salt and soddened our grain and flour; the gunpowder was damaged, and the guns were honeycombed with rust. Besides the splashing of the paddles and the dashing of the waves, heavy showers fell almost every day and night, and the intervals were bursts of burning sunshine."

It should be remembered, in explanation of what is said above of the leaking of the canoes, that these vessels are hollowed out of logs, which soon shrink and crack; for want of caulking, they become leaky at once; and it is a regular part of the proceedings during any trip by water to bale out the boats. Narrow seats are placed across the vessel, and on each of these sit two men, managing the clumsy paddles which are their substitutes for the oars. A clear space in the middle about six feet long constitutes the hold in which, according to Captain Burton's account, so many and such various articles were stowed away. Nor was this all; from morning till night, or as long as they were engaged in paddling, the men whom they had hired for this work kept up a long, monotonous howl, varied by yells and shouts, and accompanied by the bray of horns, tomtoms, shamms, and whatever other instruments of noise are known to them; so that it was simply impossible to make calculations, to take observations, or do anything else to further the scientific objects of the expedition. Superstition forbade the boatmen to tolerate any questions, or to permit the lead to be hove; nor could the captain who had been engaged to control them dissuade them from stopping where they pleased, or from going on from a point where they did not wish to stop.

As above stated, they proceeded only fifteen days' journey along the shores of the lake; the reasons why they did not go any farther was that the captain and sailors refused to do so, although they had been hired for the whole trip. Persuasions were useless, and so were threats; they

TYPES OF DIFFERENT AFRICAN RACES.

had made up their minds that they would go no farther, and the Englishmen who had suffered so much in the journey thither were compelled to turn back by the whim of a set of ignorant savages.

Burton and Speke remained at Ujiji for three months and a half; and being unable to accomplish anything more, set out on their return journey as soon as a caravan with the needful supplies had reached the lake. Their departure was taken May 26, 1858; and nearly a month later, they arrived at Kazeh, two hundred and sixty-five miles distant. Here it was determined that they should separate for a time; for they were desirous of exploring a great lake, which the natives told them, lay some fifteen or sixteen marches toward the north. This, of course, was no other than the Victoria Nyanza, as it was named by its discoverer. Hitherto, Tanganyika and the Nyanzas, judged by the native accounts which had reached European ears, had been confused, just as at an earlier date, the Niger and Congo had been confused. Both Burton and Speke now, however, grasped the situation; all discrepancies were explained, if this hitherto unknown basin should be proved to have an actual existence. Captain Burton was so reduced by fever that he was compelled to forego the enterprise, and Captain Speke accordingly left him at Kazeh, and pressed forward without a white companion.

After a journey of twenty days, he saw, on the 30th of July, 1858, the vast inland sea stretching before him. It was the long-sought source of the Nile, he believed; and to the lake which no white man had ever before looked upon, he gave its native name, coupled with that of the sovereign to whose service he was sworn—the Victoria Nyanza.

Returning in all haste, he reached his companion on the 25th of August, and they together set out for Zanzibar; whence they set sail, arriving in England February 9, 1859.

The two explorers were received with much enthusiasm by the Royal Geographical Society, and presented each with a gold medal, as a reward (or rather recognition) of their services. In Captain Burton's response to the speech of Sir Roderick Murchison, the President of the Society, we find the summing up of what part each had taken in the expedition:

"You have alluded, sir, to the success of the last expedition. Justice compels me to state the circumstances under which it attained that success. To Captain Speke are due those geographical results to which you have alluded in such flattering terms. While I undertook the history and ethnography, the languages and peculiarity of the people, to Captain Speke fell the arduous task of delineating an exact topography, and of laying down our positions by astronomical observations—a labor to which, at times, even the undaunted Livingstone found himself unequal.''

Captain Burton's health had been so seriously affected by the African climate, and by the hardships endured on this journey, that he felt himself unequal, for the time at least, to farther efforts of this nature. Captain Speke, however, was ready to undertake the venture; and he says that this expedition ''may be said to have commenced on the 9th of May, 1859, the first day after my return to England from my second expedition, when, at the invitation of Sir R. I. Murchison, I called at his house to show him my map for the information of the Royal Geographical Society. Sir Roderick, I need only say, at once accepted my views; and knowing my ardent desire to prove to the world, by actual inspection of the exit, that the Victoria Nyanza was the source of the Nile, seized the enlightened view that such a discovery should not be lost to the glory of England and the society of which he was president; and said to me: ''Speke, we must send you there again.''

The expedition, thus informally projected, was afterward discussed in good earnest; Captain Speke requesting that five thousand pounds be given him for the purpose. The Society thought his demand too large, however, and he finally accepted half the sum named, saying that he would pay from his own pocket whatever else was needed. It was his plan to send forward a quantity of supplies by caravans, to be lodged in certain towns awaiting his arrival; so that he should not have to travel through a thievish country with such great stores; but this intention, owing to the delays which ''red tapeism'' interposed, could not be wholly carried out.

Captain Grant, an old friend and fellow-sportsman, hearing of the projected expedition, requested to be allowed to accompany it; and he was formally detailed as Captain Speke's companion. The route by which they were to go was at first a matter of some doubt. Many persons said, if they wished to find the source of the Nile, the natural plan would be for them to ascend the river until they came to the head-waters; but Captain Speke urged against this that several travelers had tried it, and from some unexplained reason had failed; he preferred to proceed to Zanzibar, thence strike across the country, and, having reached the lake, explore its coasts until he came to the stream issuing from it which might be supposed to be the Nile, and descend that far enough to verify his conclusions. The nature of the return journey would have to be determined by the circumstances then encountered.

TWO-HORNED RHINOCEROS.

October 2, 1860, the march inland from Zanzibar began. The caravan consisted of about two hundred persons; but eleven deserted before starting. Go they must, however, because one desertion would be sure to lead to another; and go they did. The route as far as Zungemero was the same as that traversed on the previous expedition, and was followed without special incident until they reached the last district in Ugogo, Khoko. Near this point Captain Speke met with a hunting adventure which is well worth repeating. Ninety-six men of his caravan had deserted, and it was necessary to halt while Sheikh Said found new recruits, laid in provisions of grain to last them eight days in the wilderness, and settled for their maintenance with the chief whose hospitality they were then experiencing.

"For this triple business I allowed three days, during which time, always eager to shoot something, either for science or the pot, I killed a bicornis rhinoceros, at a distance of five paces only, * * * as the beast stood quietly feeding in the bush; and I also shot a bitch-fox, * * * whose ill-omened cry often alarms the natives by forewarning them of danger. This was rather tame sport; but next day I had better fun.

"Starting in the early morning, accompanied by two of Sheikh Said's boys, Suliman and Faraj, each carrying a rifle, while I carried a shot-gun, we followed a foot-path to the westward in the wilderness of Mgunda Mkhali. There, after walking a short while in the bush, as I heard the grunt of a buffalo close on my left, I took 'Blissett' in hand, and walked to where I soon espied a large herd quietly feeding. They were quite unconscious of my approach, so I took a shot at a cow, and wounded her; then, after reloading, put a ball in a bull, and staggered him also. This caused great confusion among them; but, as none of the animals knew where the shots came from, they simply shifted about in a fidgety manner, allowing me to kill the first cow, and even to fire a fourth shot, which sickened the great bull, and induced him to walk off, leaving the herd to their fate, who, considerably puzzled, began moving off also.

"I now called up the boys, and determined on following the herd down before either skinning the dead cow or following the bull, who, I knew, could not go far. Their footprints being well defined in the moist sandy soil, we soon found the herd again; but, as they now knew they were pursued, they kept moving on in short runs at a time, when occasionally gaining glimpses of their large dark bodies as they forced through the bush, I repeated my shots and struck a good number, some more and some less severely. This was very provoking; for all of them being stern shots were not likely to kill; and the jungle was so thick I could not get a front view of them. Presently, however, one of them with her hind leg broken pulled up on a white-ant hill, and tossing her horns, came down with a charge the instant I showed myself close to her. One crack of the rifle rolled her over, and gave me free scope to improve the bag, which was very soon done; for on following the spoors, the traces of blood led us up to another one as lame as the last. He then got a second bullet in the flank, and, after hobbling a little, evaded our sight and threw himself into a bush, where we no sooner arrived than he plunged headlong at us from his ambush, just, and only just, giving me time to present my small 40-gauge Lancaster.

"It was a most ridiculous scene. Suliman by my side, with the instinct of a monkey, made a violent spring and swung himself by a bough immediately over the beast, while Faraj bolted away and left me single-gunned to polish him off. There was only one course to pursue; for in one instant more he would have been into me; so, quick as thought I fired the gun, and, as luck would have it, my bullet, after passing through the edge of one of his horns, stuck in the spine of his neck, and rolled him over at my feet dead as a rabbit. Now, having cut the beast's throat to make him 'hilal,' according to the Mussulman usage, and thinking we had done enough if I could only return to the first wounded bull and settle him too, we commenced retracing our steps, and by accident came on Grant. He was passing by from another quarter, and became amused by the glowing description of my boys, who never omitted to narrate their own cowardice as an excellent tale. He begged us to go on in our course, while he would go back and send us some porters to carry home the game.

"Now, tracking back again to the first point of attack, we followed the blood of the first bull, till at length I found him standing like a stuck pig in some bushes, looking as if he would have liked to be put out of his miseries. Taking compassion, I leveled my Blisset; but as bad luck would have it, a bough intercepted the flight of the bullet, and it went pinging into the air, while the big bull went off at a gallop. To follow on was no difficulty, the spoor was so good; and in ten minutes more, as I opened on a small clearance, Blissett in hand, the great beast, from a thicket on the opposite side, charged down like a mad bull, full of ferocity —as ugly an antagonist as I ever saw, for the front of his head was all shielded with horn. A small mound fortunately stood between us, and as he rounded it, I jumped to one side and let fly at his flank, but without the effect of stopping him; for, as quick as thought, the huge monster was at my feet, battling with the impalpable smoke of my gun, which fortunately hung so thick on the ground at the height of his head that he could not see me, though I was so close that I might, had I been possessed of a hatchet, have chopped off his head. This was a predicament that looked very ugly, for my boys had both bolted, taking with them my guns; but suddenly the beast, evidently regarding the smoke as a phantom which could not be mastered, turned round in a bustle, to my intense relief, and galloped off at full speed, as if scared by some terrible apparition.

"Oh what would I not then have given for a gun, the chance was such a good one! Still, angry as I was, I could not help laughing as the dastardly boys came into the clearance full of their mimicry, and joked over the scene they had witnessed in security, while my life was in jeopardy because they were too frightened to give me my gun. But now came the worst part of the day; for though rain was falling, I had not the heart to relinquish my game. Tracking on through the bush, I thought every minute I should come up with the brute; but his wounds ceased to bleed, and in the confusion of the numerous tracks which scored all the forest we lost our own."

The boys were no more reliable as guides than they had been as hunting companions; for insisting that they were following the right track, they passed that which their own feet had really made, and wandered about in the pathless forest for hours. Nor was their judgment regarding the points of the compass to be relied upon; but after a night spent on the rain-soaked earth, Captain Speke could only convince them that east was not west by pointing to the rising sun.

Their absence had naturally created alarm at the camp, and volleys had been fired throughout the night. Some echoes of these had indeed reached their ears, but had been confounded with rolls of distant thunder, of which there had also been many.

Speke was surprised, on reaching the bounds of Unyanyembe, to find that changes had taken place since his previous visit; the Arabs, who had then been simple merchants, carrying on commerce between the natives and the coast, had engaged in a deadly war with the negroes, and, being victorious, lived as lords of the soil. The war was not yet over; and, in addition to its horrors, the explorers learned that a famine was here raging. These circumstances detained them for several months at Kazeh, for it was literally impossible to procure porters for the transportation of their baggage.

They improved the time by a careful study of the Wagandas. It should be remembered that the languages of this part of Africa agree in denoting, by prefixes, the variations of geographical terms. For instance, Uganda is the country, Waganda denotes the people inhabiting it; Miganda is the designation of an individual of the Waganda; and Kiganda is the language which he speaks. It should further be noted that Nyanza, more properly written N'yanza, is a general term applied to any great body of water, either river or lake. The earliest explorers of this section of the continent made the mistake of supposing it to be a proper name, and hence arose a confusion of ideas.

It must not be supposed that they were wholly inactive during this period; they progressed somewhat, but very slowly; sickness having its due influence in hindering their advance, as well as the external circumstances which have been mentioned. They entered the rich flat district of Mininga late in March, and took up their quarters in a hut belonging to Sirboko, a broken-down ivory merchant, and the greatest man of the district. He advised them to remain there for a time; and after consultation with the chief of their own followers, they resolved to accept the advice.

Their host had lost all his property by the burning of a village in which it had been stored; and come hither, in order to avoid his creditors on the coast. He had engaged in agriculture, his operations being confined chiefly to rice, because the natives do not like it well enough to steal it.

Here they had the opportunity or doing a humane act; for one of Sirboko's slaves, recognizing Speke, told him that he had been in a

fight at Ujiji, speared all over and left for dead, but then seized by the returning enemy and sold to the Arabs. His touching appeal could not be
withstood, and the explorer interceded with his master to grant him
freedom. The release was effected; the freedman was newly named Far-
han (Joy) and duly enrolled in Speke's service.

The two white men frequently separated for a few days at the time,
Captain Speke most often making short excursions into the surrounding country, while Captain Grant remained with the caravan, recruiting
his health, which had been much affected by the climate, and enjoying
himself dancing with the native women.

Late in November, 1861, they reached the palace of King Rumanika,
situated on the shores of a beautiful lake in the bosom of the hills, to
which the discoverers gave the name of Little Windermere. Rumanika
received them with cordiality, and even requested that they would take
two of his sons with them when they returned to their own country, that
they might be taught the white men's learning. He was the best native
prince that they had yet encountered; and they were not a little pleased
with his generous and eager mind.

This king sent a messenger to Mtesa, the king of Uganda, to announce
the approach of the party. This embassador returned January 10, 1862,
accompanied by an escort of smartly dressed men, women, and boys, to
conduct the white men to the capital of Uganda. Captain Grant was
unable to travel; but leaving him to follow later on, Captain Speke set
out the next day with this retinue.

They crossed the equator February 7; and shortly after passing the
line, they were met by some pages who came as messengers from Mtesa,
to say that the king had made a vow that he would neither eat nor drink
until the white men should have come to him. Speke says:

"One march more, and we came in sight of the king's kibuga, or
palace, in the province of Bandawarogo, north latitude twenty-one minutes, nineteen seconds, and east longitude thirty-two degrees, forty-four
minutes, thirty seconds. It was a magnificent sight. A whole hill was
covered with gigantic huts, such as I had never seen in Africa before. I
wished to go up to the palace at once, but the officers said: No, that would
be considered indecent in Uganda; you must draw up your men and fire

your guns off, to let the king know that you are here; we will then show you your residence, and tomorrow you will doubtless be sent for, as the king could not now hold a levee while it is raining.' I made the men fire, and then was shown into a lot of dirty huts, which, they said, were built expressly for the king's visitors. The Arabs, when they came on their visits, always put up here, and I must do the same. At first I stuck out my claims as a foreign prince, whose royal blood could not stand such an indignity. The palace was my sphere; and unless I could get a hut there, I would return without seeing the king.

"In a terrible fright at my blustering, Nyamgundu fell at my feet and implored me not to be hasty. * * * I gave way to this good man's appeal, and cleaned my hut by firing it to the ground; for, like all the huts in this dog country, it was full of fleas. Once ensconced there, the king's pages darted in to see me, bearing a message from their master, who said he was sorry the rain prevented him from holding a levee that day, but the next he would be delighted to see me."

The next day, word was duly sent that the stranger was awaited at court; and costuming himself for the occasion, and preparing his presents for presentation, Speke gave the signal that he was ready to proceed. * * * Arrived at the ante-reception court, he found it necessary to assert his dignity in no measured terms.

"By the chief officers in waiting, who thought fit to treat us like Arab merchants, I was requested to sit on the ground outside in the sun with my servants. Now I had made up my mind never to sit on the ground as the natives and Arabs are obliged to do, nor to make my obeisance in any other manner than is customary in England, though the Arabs had told me that from fear they had always complied with the manners of the court. I felt that if I did not stand up for my social position at once, I should be treated with contempt during the remainder of my visit, and thus lose the vantage-ground I had assumed of appearing as a prince, rather than as a trader, for the purpose of better gaining the confidence of the king. To avert over-hastiness, however,—for my servants began to be alarmed as I demurred against doing as I was bid— I allowed five minutes to the court to give me a proper reception, saying if it were not conceded I would then walk away.

"Nothing, however, was done. * * * The affair ended by my walking straight away home."

The Waganda stood "still as posts," unable to understand such temerity; Speke's own servants were greatly troubled for their master, not knowing what would be the consequence of his deed. Meantime Mtesa

THE KING WAS SEATED ON HIS THRONE.

had been told of his action; and sent messengers in hot haste to beg him to return. Speke coolly shook his head and patted his heart, and walked on a little faster. Shortly after he arrived at his hut, other messengers came to say that if he would but return, he might bring with him a chair to sit upon—an unparalleled concession, since no one in Uganda but the king is allowed the dignity of such a seat. Having drank a cup of coffee and smoked a pipe, the angry prince (?) leisurely returned to the court of King Mtesa.

King Mtesa was seated on his throne to receive the guest, who, on being told to halt and sit in the burning sun, coolly put on his hat and raised his umbrella. For upwards of an hour he and the king sat silently regarding each other; Speke mute, but Mtesa pointing and re-marking with those around him on the novelty of the visitor's guard and general appearance, and even requiring to see his hat lifted, the umbrella opened and shut, and the guards face about and show their red cloaks—for such wonders had never been seen in Uganda.

Then, inquiring by means of an interpreter if Speke had seen him, and receiving an affirmative reply, the chief arose and walked away, in what was intended to be a very majestic gait. "It was the traditional walk of his race, founded on the step of the lion; but the outward sweep of the legs intended to represent the stride of this noble beast, appeared to me only to realize a very ludicrous kind of waddle, which made me ask Bombay if anything serious was the matter with the royal person."

Speke stayed long enough in Uganda to become thoroughly well ac-quainted with the customs of the people. Under date of March 25, 1862, he says:

"I have now been for some time within the court precincts, and have consequently had an opportunity of witnessing court customs. Among these, nearly every day since I have changed my residence, incredible as it may appear to be, I have seen one, two, or three of the wretched palace women led away to execution, tied by the hand, and dragged along by one of the body-guard, crying out, as she went to premature death, '*Hai minange!*' (Oh, my lord!) '*Kbakka!*' (My king!) '*Hai n'yawo!*' (My mother!) at the top of her voice, in the utmost despair and lamentation; and yet there was not a soul who dared lift his hand to save any of them, though many might be heard privately commenting on their beauty."

On the arrival of Captain Grant, the queen-dewager, with whom Cap-tain Speke was already very well acquainted, desired that the new-comer should be presented to her. Speke complied with this demand, repre-senting Grant as his brother. Her majesty persistently ignored his claim that they were of one house, but finally gave up her attempt to extort a separate present from Grant.

For more than four months after Speke's first arrival at the capital of Uganda, Mtesa had resisted every argument and inducement to permit him to continue his journey northward. Finally, however, he became intensely jealous of Rumanika, and declared that he would show his rival that all the supplies for Uganda need not come through his country. If another route were opened, these mighty strangers would come direct to

THE VICTORIA NILE.

him; and he therefore promised these travelers that he would furnish them with guides to Unyore and with boats for a voyage on the Nile.

The promise was accepted without delay, and the king was resolutely held to it. Setting out from the capital, they determined to separate, Grant going forward with the main body of the caravan to King Kamrasi's capital, while Speke skirted the borders of the lake until he should come upon the Nile, flowing out of it. This latter intention was realized two days after their separation, July 19, 1862.

"Here at last I stood on the brink of the Nile! Most beautiful was the scene, nothing could surpass it. It was the very perfection of the effect aimed at in a highly kept park with a magnificent stream."

MEETING OF STANLEY AND EMIN PASHA AT KAVALLI, ON LAKE ALBERT NYANZA.

NATIVE WIZARD.

This may be the most powerful man in his tribe, whom even the chief may fear. He knows too much, he knows the meanings of his bones and the secret spells by which disease and disaster may be hurled against the foe. He can "smell out" criminals, who are generally enemies of the chief or himself and who are done to death at his word. He deals in drugs and poisons. In some tribes only the wizard and doctor is allowed to wear the skins of certain animals.

CHARGED BY A LION.

Col. Roosevelt had several experiences similar to this one, and in one instance his life was in danger, but his cool nerve and splendid aim saved him. The picture is exceptionally fine, showing the charging lion emerging from the tall grass, the gunbearers running for the nearest tree. A good idea of the country through which the ex-President hunted can also be obtained.

CHAPTER IX.

ROOSEVELT—THE ROUGH RIDER.

Organizing the Regiment—A Composite Lot—College Athletes and Cowboys—The Officers—Orders to March—The Landing at Daiquiri—The First Skirmish—Death of Sergeant Fish and Captain Capron—The La Quassina Fight—The Baptism of Fire—San Juan Hill—The Surrender of Santiago—The Celebrated "Round Robin."

WHEN the news of Dewey's victory reached this country, Mr. Roosevelt resigned his position as Assistant Secretary of the Navy. "There is nothing more for me to do here," he said, "I've got to get into the fight myself." And again to a friend of his, "I have been a jingo all my life, now I am going to take my own medicine." He first endeavored to get a staff appointment, but finally, when there began to be talk of a regiment of "rough riders," he felt that his opportunity had come.

ROOSEVELT IS OFFERED THE COMMAND.

While Assistant Secretary of the Navy he had met Dr. Leonard Wood, and a friendship had at once sprung up between them. Dr. Wood had previously served in General Miles' campaign against the Apaches, where he had won a medal of honor for remarkable bravery. When the war broke out, they discovered a mutual desire to go to the front, and when Congress authorized the raising of three Western cavalry regiments, both expressed a desire to serve in the same command. Secretary Alger offered Roosevelt the command of one of these regiments, but he replied that while he believed he could learn to command a regiment in a month, that this was just the very month that he could not afford to spare and that, therefore, he would be quite content to go as lieutenant-colonel if he would make his friend Wood colonel.

"This was satisfactory to both the President and Secretary of War," said Mr. Roosevelt, "and accordingly Wood and I were speedily commissioned as colonel and lieutenant-colonel of the First United States Volunteer Cavalry. This was the official title of the regiment, but for some reason or other, the public promptly christened us the 'Rough Riders.' At first we fought against the use of the term, but to no purpose, and when finally the generals of division and brigade began to write in formal communications about our regiment as the 'Rough Riders,' we adopted the term ourselves.''

DELUGED WITH APPLICATIONS.

The mustering places for the regiment were mainly New Mexico, Arizona, Oklahoma and Indian Territory, and the main difficulty encountered was not in selecting, but in rejecting men. From every section of the United States applications began to pour in, and when, finally, the roster was complete, as Mr. Riis has expressed it, ''the Rough Riders were the most composite lot ever gathered under a regimental standard, but they were at the same time singularly typical of the spirit that conquered a continent in three generations, eminently American. Probably such another will never be gotten together again; in no other country on earth could it have been mustered to-day. The cowboy, the Indian trailer, the Indian himself, the packer and the hunter who had sought and killed the grizzly in his mountain fastness, touched elbows with the New York policeman who, for love of adventure, had followed his once chief to the war, with the college athlete, the football player and the oarsman, the dare-devil mountaineer of Georgia, fresh from hunting moonshiners as a revenue officer, and with the society man, the child of luxury and wealth from the East, bent upon proving that a life of ease had dulled neither his manhood nor his sense of our common citizenship.''

INVARIABLY DECLINED COMMISSIONS.

Harvard being Mr. Roosevelt's own college, he naturally received a great many applications from that institution, but what particularly pleased him was that not only the applicants from his Alma Mater, but also the Yale and Princeton men, invariably declined commissions. And so it came to pass that Dudley Dean, the celebrated quarter-back; Wrenn and Larned, the champion tennis players; Waller, the high jumper; Garrison, Girard, Devereaux and Channing, the football players; Wadsworth, the steeple-chase rider; Joe Stevens, the polo player; Hamilton

Fish, ex-captain of the Columbia crew, and others, all entered the Rough Riders and accepted the hard work and rough fare as though they had been accustomed to nothing else. There were recruits from clubs like the Somerset of Boston and the Knickerbocker of New York, and, as Mr. Roosevelt expressed it, it seemed as though every friend that he had in every State had some one acquaintance who was bound to go with the Rough Riders and for whom he had to make a place.

NOT A MAN BACKED OUT.

"Before allowing them to be sworn in," says Mr. Roosevelt, "I gathered them together and explained that if they went in they must be prepared not merely to fight, but to perform the weary, monotonous labor incident to the ordinary routine of the soldier's life; that they must be ready to face fever exactly as they were to face bullets; that they were to obey unquestioningly, and to do their duty as readily if called upon to garrison a fort as if sent to the front. I warned them that work that was merely irksome and disagreeable must be faced as readily as work that was dangerous, and that no complaint of any kind must be made; and I told them that they were entirely at liberty not to go, but that after they had once signed there could then be no backing out. Not a man of them backed out; not one of them failed to do his whole duty."

But these men formed but a small portion of the regiment, the bulk of which came from the Territories. Magnificent specimens of humanity, inured to hardship, unerring shots, ideal horsemen, accustomed to outdoor life, the freedom of the frontier and the rude discipline of the ranch or mining camp; they were difficult men to handle, save by leaders who had demonstrated their ability in that direction.

HOW THE REGIMENT WAS OFFICERED.

Thus it was that the officers of the regiment were men who had either fought against the Indians, or had taken the field against the more desperate white outlaws of the plains. The captain of Troop A was Bucky O'Neill, the mayor of Prescott, Arizona; then there was Captain Llewellyn of New Mexico, one of the most celebrated peace officers of the country; Lieutenant Ballard, who broke up the notorious Black Jack gang; Captain Curry, a New Mexican sheriff, and a sprinkling of men who had been sheriffs, marshals, deputy sheriffs and deputy marshals. Three of the higher officers in the regiment had served in the regular army. One was Major Alexander Brodie, from Arizona, who afterwards became Lieutenant-Colonel; Captain, afterwards Major, Jenkins, and the gallant Captain Allyn Capron, whom Mr. Roosevelt considered the best soldier in the regiment. But whether Easterner, Westerner, Northerner, or Southerner, officer or man, cowboy or college graduate, each "possessed in common the trait of hardihood and the thirst for adventure—they were to a man born adventurers in every sense of the word."

To Wood and Roosevelt fell the task of teaching these men the duties of a soldier and of molding them together into a uniform body of disciplined fighters, and it was owing to their patience and industry that when the time came for the regiment to sail for Cuba these raw recruits had mastered all the intricacies of foot and mounted drill and bore every appearance of regular troops.

On Sunday, May 29th, the regiment broke camp at San Antonio, which had been the recruiting station, and took the cars for Tampa. With the first three sections went Colonel Wood, Colonel Roosevelt following with the remaining four; and several days later they arrived at Tampa. Here for several days the regiment worked with great perseverance in perfecting itself in skirmish and mounted drill. On the evening of June 7th orders were received that the expedition was to start from Port Tampa, nine miles distant, at daybreak the following morning, and if the men were not on board their transports by that time they would not be allowed to go. It was not, however, until five days later that the fleet weighed anchor and steamed to the southwest, and on the morning of June 22d landed at Daiquiri, the village having first been shelled by the smaller gunboats. The afternoon of the following day the Rough Riders received orders to march.

Just before leaving Tampa the Rough Riders had been brigaded with the First (white) and the Tenth (colored) Regular Cavalry under Brigadier-General Young, as the Second Brigade. The First Brigade consisted of the Third and Sixth (white) and the Ninth (colored) Regular

Cavalry under Brigadier-General Sumner. These two brigades were under the command of General Joseph Wheeler, the celebrated Confederate leader.

ON CUBAN SOIL.

After landing at Daiquiri, the Rough Riders marched about a mile inland and camped. In the meantime General Lawton, who afterwards lost his life in the Philippines, had taken the advance and established outposts, and General Wheeler, who had made a reconnoisance and located the position of the enemy, directed General Young to take the Second Brigade and push forward.

The march began about the middle of the afternoon, and about dark, after a weary tramp beneath a scorching tropical sun, the troops arrived at the town of Siboney. At sunrise the next morning, General Young, acting under General Wheeler's orders, with four troops of the Tenth and four of the First Cavalry, began the march along the valley road which led to Santiago, while Colonel Wood led the Rough Riders along a hill trail to the left, which joined the main road about four miles farther on, at a point where it went over the mountain.

THE BATTLE OF LA QUASSINA.

This place, where the two trails met, was known as La Quassina, and it was at this point that the Spanish had taken up their position. The Spanish fortification consisted of breastworks flanked by block-houses, and after General Young had arrived and made a careful examination of the Spanish position, he placed his battery in concealment about a thousand yards from the Spanish line, deployed the white regulars with the colored regulars in support, and after he had given time for Colonel Wood to arrive, opened the battle. The jungle was extremely dense, and as the Spaniards used smokeless powder, it was almost impossible to locate them, but the advance was pushed forward rapidly, and in the face of heavy firing the American troops climbed the ridges and drove the Spaniards from their intrenchments. In the meantime, Colonel Roosevelt and his Rough Riders had commenced their advance. The way lay up a very steep hill, and numbers of the men, exhausted from their march of the day before, had either dropped their bundles or fallen out of line, so that less than 500 men went into action.

MADE NO OUTCRY WHEN HIT.

"We could hear the Hotchkiss guns and the reply of two Spanish guns, and the Mauser bullets were singing through the trees over our heads, making a noise like the humming of telephone wires, but exactly where they came from we could not tell," said the Colonel of the Rough Riders in describing the fight. "The Spaniards were firing high and for the most part by volleys, and their shooting was not very good. Gradually, however, they began to get the range, and occasionally one of our men would crumple up. In no case did the men make an outcry when hit, seeming to take it as a matter of course; at the outside making only such a remark as, 'Well, I got it that time.'"

Capron's troop took the lead, closely followed by Wood and Roosevelt at the head of the other three troops of the Third Squadron, and then came Brodie at the head of his squadron. After the Spaniards had been driven from their position on the right, the firing slackened somewhat until the enemy's outposts were located near the advance guard, when a brisk skirmish ensued, with the result that the enemy disappeared through the jungle to their main line in the rear.

DEATH OF FISH AND CAPRON.

"Here," says Mr. Roosevelt, "at the very outset of our active service, we suffered the loss of two as gallant men as ever wore uniforms. Sergeant Hamilton Fish, at the extreme front, while holding the point to its work and firing back where the Spanish advance guard lay, was shot and instantly killed; three of the men with him were likewise hit. Captain Capron, leading the advance guard in person, and displaying equal courage and coolness in the way that he handled them, was also struck, and died a few minutes afterwards. While I had led the troop back to the trail, I ran ahead of them, passing the dead and wounded men of L Troop.

A HAIL OF BULLETS.

"When I came to the front I found the men spread out in a very thin skirmish line, advancing through comparatively open ground, each man taking advantage of what cover he could, while Wood strode about leading his horse, Brodie being close at hand. How Wood escaped being hit I do not see, and still less how his horse escaped. I had left mine at the beginning of the action, and was only regretting that I had not left my sword with it, as it kept getting between my legs as I was making my way through the jungle. Very soon after I reached the front, Brodie was hit, the bullet shattering one arm and whirling him round as he stood. Thereupon Wood directed me to take charge of the left wing in Brodie's place and bring it forward. A perfect hail of bullets was sweeping over us as we advanced. Once I got a glimpse of some Spaniards, apparently retreating far to the front and to our right, and we fired a couple of rounds after them. Then I became convinced, after much anxious study, that we were being fired at from some large red-tiled buildings, part of a ranch on our front. Smokeless powder and a thin cover in our front continued to puzzle us, and I more than once consulted anxiously the officers as to the exact whereabouts of our opponents. I took a rifle from a wounded man and began to try shooting with it myself. It was very hot and the men were getting exhausted, though at this particular time we were not suffering heavily from bullets, the Spaniards' fire going too high.

EMPTY CARTRIDGE SHELLS AND TWO DEAD SPANIARDS.

"As we advanced the cover became a little thicker and I lost sight of the main body under Wood; soon I halted and we fired industriously at the ranch buildings ahead of us, some 500 yards off. Then we heard repeating rifles on the right, and I supposed that this meant a battle on the part of Wood's men, so I sprang up and ordered the men to rush the buildings ahead of us; they came forward with a will. There was a moment of heavy firing from the Spaniards, which all went over our heads, and then ceased entirely. When we arrived at the buildings, panting and out of breath, they contained nothing but heaps of empty cartridge shells and two Spaniards shot through the head."

THE KILLED AND WOUNDED.

The Rough Riders lost eight men killed and thirty-four wounded in the last La Quassina fight. The First Cavalry lost seven men killed and eight wounded. The Tenth Cavalry, one man killed and ten wounded. After the charge the regiment moved on a few miles and went into camp. The same day General Young was attacked by a fever and General Wood took charge of the brigade; this left Colonel Roosevelt in charge of the regiment. On June 30th, the Rough Riders received orders to march against Santiago, and at once struck camp and, led by the First and Tenth Cavalry, began to move toward the Spanish city. After marching until about eight o'clock Colonel Roosevelt's men went into camp on El Paso Hill. No orders had been given except to the effect that the infantry under General Lawton was to capture El Caney, while Colonel Roosevelt's force was merely to make a diversion mainly with the artillery. Finding that his force was directly in line of the Spanish fire, which was made very evident by shells which began to burst in their midst, General Wood formed his brigade and, with the Rough Riders in front, ordered Colonel Roosevelt to follow behind the First Brigade, which was just then moving off the ground. Colonel Roosevelt was then ordered to cross the ford of the San Juan River, march half a mile to the right and then halt and await further orders. Meantime the battle was on and the Spaniards on the hills were firing in volleys.

THE SPANIARDS' FIRE PRACTICALLY UNAIMED.

Colonel Roosevelt says that while his troops were lying in reserve they suffered nearly as much as afterwards when they charged. In his opinion the bulk of the Spaniards' fire was practically unaimed, or at least not aimed at any particular man, and only occasionally at a particular body of men; but they swept the whole field of battle up to the edge of the river, and man after man in his ranks fell dead or wounded, although he had his troops scattered far about, taking advantage of every scrap of cover. Finally Colonel Roosevelt received orders to move forward and support the regulars in the assault on the hills in front.

HIS CROWDED HOUR BEGAN.

"The instant I received the order," says Colonel Roosevelt, "I sprang on my horse and then my crowded hour began. Guerrillas had been shooting at us from the hedges and from their perches in the leafy trees and as they used smokeless powder it was almost impossible to see them, though a few of my men had from time to time responded. They had also moved from the hill on the right, which was held chiefly by guerrillas, although there were also some Spanish regulars with them, for we found them dead. I formed my men in columns of troops, each troop extended in open skirmishing order, the right resting on the wire fences which bore on the sunken land. The Ninth and First Regiments went up Kettle Hill with the Rough Riders, and General Sumner giving the Tenth the order to charge, the Third Regiment went forward, keeping up a heavy fire.''

Colonel Roosevelt then adressed the captain in command of the rear platoon, saying that he had been ordered to support the regulars in the attack upon the hills, and that in his judgment they could not take these hills by firing on them; that they must rush them. The officer answered that his orders were to keep his men lying where they were and that he could not charge without orders. He asked where the Colonel was, and as he was not in sight, Colonel Roosevelt said: ''I am the ranking officer here, and I give the order to charge,'' for he did not want to keep the men longer in the open, suffering under a fire that they could not return. The officer again hesitated, but Colonel Roosevelt rode on through the lines, followed by his Rough Riders. This proved too much for the regulars, and they followed after.

GAVE THE ORDER TO CHARGE.

When the Rough Riders came to where the head of the left wing of the Ninth was lying, Colonel Roosevelt gave the order to charge the hill on his right front, and the line, tired of waiting, obeyed the command with alacrity at once. Immediately after the hill was covered by American troops, consisting of Rough Riders and the colored troops of the Ninth, together with some men of the First; but no sooner had they captured the position than the Spaniards opened a heavy fire upon them with rifles, while several pieces of artillery threw shells with considerable effect into their midst. From this vantage ground Colonel Roosevelt could observe the charge on the San Juan block-house on his left, and he decided to gather his men together and start them volley-firing against the Spaniards in the block-house and in the trenches around it.

"The infantry got nearer and nearer the crest of the hill," says Mr. Roosevelt, in his account of the battle. "At last we could see the Spaniards running from the rifle-pits as the Americans came on in their final rush. Then I stopped my men for fear they should injure their comrades, and called to them to charge the next line of trenches, on the hills in our front, from which we had been undergoing a good deal of punishment. Thinking that the men would all come, I jumped over the wire fence in front of us and started at the double; but, as a matter of fact, the troopers were so excited, what with shooting and being shot, and shouting and cheering, that they did not hear, or did not heed me; and after running about a hundred yards I found I had only five men along with me.

A MISUNDERSTOOD ORDER.

"Bullets were ripping the grass all around us, and one of the men, Clay Green, was mortally wounded; another, Winslow Clark, a Harvard man, was shot first in the leg and then through the body. He made not the slightest murmur, only asking me to put his water canteen where he could get at it, which I did; he ultimately recovered. There was no use going on with the remaining three men, and I bade them stay where they were while I went back and brought up the rest of the brigade. This was a decidedly cool request, for there was really no possible point in letting them stay there while I went back, but at the moment it seemed perfectly natural to me, and apparently so to them, for they cheerfully nodded, and sat down in the grass, firing back at the line of trenches from which the Spaniards were shooting at them.

"LEAD ON, WE'LL FOLLOW YOU."

"Meanwhile, I ran back, jumped over the wire fence, and went over the crest of the hill, filled with anger against the troopers, and especially those of my own regiment, for not having accompanied me. They, of course, were quite innocent of wrong-doing, and even while I taunted them bitterly for not having followed me, it was all I could do not to smile at the look of inquiry and surprise that came over their faces; while they cried out, 'We didn't hear you, we didn't see you go, Colonel; lead on now, we'll sure follow you.' I wanted the other regiments to come, too; so I ran down to where General Sumner was and asked him if I might make the charge, and he told me to go and that he would see that the men followed.

"By this time everybody had his attention attracted, and when I leaped over the fence again, with Major Jenkins beside me, the men of the various regiments which were already on the hill came with a rush, and we started across the wide valley which lay between us and the Spanish intrenchments. Captain Dimmick, now in command of the Ninth, was bringing it forward; Captain McBlain had a number of Rough Riders mixed in with his troop, and led them all together; Captain Taylor had been severely wounded. The long-legged men like Greenway, Goodrich, sharpshooter Proffit, and others, outstripped the rest of us, as we had a considerable distance to go. Long before we got near them the Spaniards ran, save a few here and there, who either surrendered or were shot down. When we reached the trenches we found them filled with dead bodies in the light blue and white uniform of the Spanish regular army. There were very few wounded. Most of the fallen had little holes in their heads, from which their brains were oozing; for they were covered from the neck down by the trenches.

KILLS A SPANIARD.

"It was at this place that Major Wessels, of the Third Cavalry, was shot in the back of the head. It was a severe wound, but after having it bound up he again came to the front in command of his regiment. Among the men who were foremost was Lieutenant Milton E. Davis of the First Cavalry. He had been joined by three men of the Seventy-first New York, who ran up, and saluting, said, 'Lieutenant, we want to go with you, our officers won't lead us.' One of the brave fellows was soon afterwards shot in the face. Lieutenant Davis' first sergeant, Clarence Gould, killed a Spanish soldier with his revolver, just as the Spaniard was aiming at one of my Rough Riders.

"At about the same time I also shot one. I was with Henry Bardshar, running up at the double, and two Spaniards leaped from the trenches and fired at us, not ten yards away. As they turned to run I closed in and fired twice, missing the first and killing the second. My revolver was from the sunken battleship Maine, and had been given me by my brother-

in-law, Captain W. S. Cowles, of the Navy. At the time I did not know
of Gould's exploit, and supposed my feat to be unique; and although
Gould had killed his Spaniard in the trenches, not very far from me, I
never learned of it until weeks after. It is astonishing what a limited
area of vision and experience one has in the hurly-burly of a battle.

BLACK AND WHITE SOLDIERS MIXED.

"There was very great confusion at this time, the different regiments
being completely intermingled—white regulars, colored regulars, and
Rough Riders. General Sumner had kept a considerable force in reserve
on Kettle Hill, under Major Jackson, of the Third Cavalry. We were still
under a heavy fire, and I got together a mixed lot of men and pushed on
from the trenches and ranch-houses which we had just taken, driving the
Spaniards through a line of palm trees and over the crests of a chain
of hills.

OVERLOOKED SANTIAGO.

"When we reached these crests we found ourselves overlooking Santiago. Some of the men, including Jenkins, Greenway, and Goodrich,
pushed on almost by themselves far ahead. Lieutenant Hugh Berkely,
of the First, with a sergeant and two troopers, reached the extreme front.
He was, at the time, ahead of every one; the sergeant was killed and one
trooper wounded; but the lieutenant and the remaining trooper stuck to
their post for the rest of the afternoon, until our line was gradually extended to include them.

"While I was re-forming the troops on the chain of hills, one of General Sumner's aides came up with orders to me to halt where I was, not
advancing farther, but to hold the hill at all hazards."

Colonel Roosevelt says that in the attack on the San Juan hills his
regiment lost eighty-nine killed and wounded; the loss of the entire
American forces being 1,071 killed and wounded. "I think we suffered
more heavily than the Spaniards did in the killed and wounded," says
Colonel Roosevelt. "It would have been very extraordinary if the re-
verse was the case."

THE SURRENDER OF SANTIAGO.

Every one is familiar with the events following the charge up San Juan Hill and preceding the capture of Santiago—the suffering in the crowded trenches, the hours of weary waiting and desultory fighting, in all of which the Rough Riders did their part with the precision of regulars. On the 17th of July, the city of Santiago formally surrendered, after which the cavalry was marched back to the foot of the hill west of El Caney, and there went to camp.

Many of the Rough Riders had already been stricken down with fever, and in the new camp matters grew worse in a very short time. Over 50 per cent were unfit for any kind of work; all their clothing was in rags; even the officers were without stockings and underwear. Yellow fever then broke out, but chiefly among the Cubans, and, owing to the panic caused by the dread of this disease, the authorities at Washington hesitated to order the army to return to the United States, fearing that it might introduce the plague into the country. General Shafter then summoned a council of officers, hoping by united action to induce the government to take some active step toward relieving the army at Santiago from destruction.

THE CELEBRATED ROUND ROBIN.

Finally the "Round Robin," signed by Colonel Roosevelt and all the other officers, was made public. As Mr. Riis says, this celebrated communication "startled the American people and caused measures of instant relief to be set on foot, the fearful truth that the army was perishing from privation and fever was not known. The cry it sent up was, 'Take us home. We will fight for the flag to the last man if need be. But now our fighting is done, we will not be left here to die.' It was significant that the duty of making the unwelcome disclosure fell to the Colonel of the Rough Riders. Of all the officers who signed it he was the youngest; but from no one could the warning have come with greater force. The Colonel of the Rough Riders, at the head of his men on San Juan Hill, much as I like the picture, is not half so heroic a figure to me as Roosevelt in this hour of danger and doubt, shouldering the blame for the step he knew to be right.

From the Minneapolis Journal.

A JUNGLE CONCERT.

CHAPTER X.

A BIT OF AFRICAN HISTORY.

Early Discoveries and Explorations—An Incredible Statement Proved True—Mohammedan Conquests—In the Congo Country—On the Eastern Coast—First English Expeditions—Ascent of the Senegal—French Explorations.

A LTHOUGH the country through which Roosevelt undertook his famous hunting expedition was the seat of the earliest civilization known to the world, Africa has long been, above all others, the continent of mystery. Egypt had solved engineering problems which are not far within the capacity of the nineteenth century, before Greece and Rome had learned the rudiments of art or science; and Greece and Rome were the teachers of all Europe; yet every nook and corner of Europe has been thoroughly explored, while there are still vast wildernesses in Africa where the white man's foot has never trod. Less than a century ago, even the great rivers had not been followed to their sources; the Nile itself came from a region of mystery, and no man had fathomed the secret of those annual overflows which had enriched Egypt since the days of the first Pharaohs.

The interest in the exploration of Africa, however, the desire to know more of this great tract which lies so directly under the equator, is not altogether of modern growth. The Father of History himself, Herodotus, who lived in the fifth century before our era, endeavored to obtain accurate information regarding Africa. For this purpose, he visited Egypt in person; but the Egyptians could not tell him much. They knew only a portion of the northern coast, besides their own country. The region nearest to them was well known, and we find full accounts of the temple of Jupiter Ammon and the wonderful spring in its vicinity; but as we follow the account of the historian, in his description of the peoples living farther toward the West, we find them less satisfactory. For some distance beyond Carthage, indeed, the character of the soil and the nature

143

of the inhabitants are accurately described; but soon we find fact mingled with fable, and at last we come to the long and lofty range of Atlas, which is the pillar of heaven, and beyond which the historian does not think of going.

But even before the days of Herodotus, the Carthaginians, those adventurous mariners of antiquity, who without chart or compass had come even to Cornwall, had coasted beyond the Pillars of Hercules, as the rocks on either side of the Strait of Gibraltar were called, and traded with the natives. Just how far down the western coast of Africa they went, modern authorities have not agreed among themselves. A naval expedition set out from Carthage about the year 570 B. C., under Hanno as commander, which passed far beyond the entrance to the Mediterranean. Gosselin says that they reached the point where the Sahara begins; Rennell considers that they succeeded in passing this barren coast, and finished their expedition about the point where Free Town now stands; while Bougainville believes them to have been still more adventurous, and to have gone as far as Cape Three Points, which is about the middle of the southern coast of Guinea. This last theory has not been accepted by many authorities; and the question really is, did they pass the desert coast or not? One answer supposes a run of six hundred miles; the other, a voyage five times as long. Hanno had a fleet of sixty vessels, with thirty thousand souls on board; it hardly seems credible that so vast a number could have carried with them, in the comparatively small vessels of the times, a sufficient stock of food and water to serve them during their slow and uncertain passage along the coast of Sahara; and the account which has come down to us distinctly tells us that they were forced to turn back, because of the sterile and inhospitable nature of the coast.

It is not until after the destruction of Carthage that Eudoxus, a native of the city of Cyzicus, comes upon the scene as an African explorer; and there is no other, of any note, until his day. Alexandria was then the center of naval enterprise, and her Greek rulers the most zealous patrons of all undertakings of the kind. To Ptolemy Euergetes the adventurer appealed, and the question of exploring the Nile to its sources was seriously discussed. But the arrival of a native of India, whom some Alexan-

AN EAST AFRICAN TUSKER KILLED BY THE HUNTERS.

THE HEAD OF AN EAST AFRICAN RHINOCEROS ON ITS WAY TO THE

AFRICAN LADIES' RECEPTION.

The ladies love to ornament and their ideas vary as to the style which suits individual tastes and features. They eat from one dish, which is the pot in which the food has been cooked.

drian sailors had rescued from shipwreck, turned their attention to India; and for a while the subject of African exploration was permitted to rest. Eudoxus made one voyage to India, and set out upon a second; but was driven by a storm upon the coast of Africa, shortly after emerging from the Red Sea. The coast line here extends toward the southwest; and Eudoxus was inspired with the idea that the circuit of Africa, from the entrance to the Red Sea to that of the Mediterranean, was to be made by a determined navigator. From that time forth he was possessed by one ambition, to be the circumnavigator of Africa.

Whether he succeeded or not, is not clear; in the strict sense of the words, he did not succeed, for he did not make the whole circuit. It may be that he coasted along all that portion of the seaboard which had not been previously explored; but certainly his voyage did not extend from the Straits of Bab-el-mandeb to that of Gibraltar. One observation which he records led the geographers of antiquity to believe that he was fabling; it proves to us that he told the truth: he narrates that when he had passed a certain point on his voyage, the sun shone to the northward of his vessel. The ancients, unacquainted with the southern hemisphere, could not credit this; they believed the assertion to be on a par with his accounts of peoples without tongues, and of those who having no mouth, received all their food through the nose. To us, on the other hand, this observation of a phenomenon previously unknown is proof positive that he passed the equator. From a careful examination of his assertions, it appears probable that he did not accomplish his great object, even if we take the limited meaning of the term circumnavigation above stated; but sailed as far south along the eastern coast as Cape Delgado, about ten degrees south of the equator.

The explorations of Eudoxus were made about the year 130 B. C.; and so little credence did his theory that Africa was bounded on all sides by the ocean obtain, that Ptolemy the geographer, who lived during the second century of our era, represented the Indian Ocean as an inland sea, bounded on the south by Africa, which extended easterly and then northerly until it reached the coast of China. His delineation of the northern coast of this continent was, in the main, correct; but he believed the western coast to be nearly a straight north and south line, instead of inclining nearly fifteen degrees of longitude from the Straits of Gibraltar to Cape Verde, as more modern surveys prove. He draws the eastern coast nearly correct, as far south as the equator; and for more than a thousand years, there was but very little more than this known of the Dark Continent.

We are accustomed to consider Mohammedanism as the foe of all progress; but the case was different during the middle ages. When the faith of Islam was first firmly established, the Saracen princes became the patrons of art and science; and their schools became famous seats of learning. Their conquests had extended far to the West, and they had obtained a foothold even in Europe itself, in the domains of the most Catholic King. Across the Mediterranean, they had established themselves in Morocco and other Barbary States; here they early introduced the camel, useful to their native Arabian deserts, and soon to become indispensable in Africa. By the aid of the ship of the desert, they crossed the vast wastes which had hitherto been impassable, and founded states along its southern boundary; their object being mainly commercial, since they wished to obtain gold and slaves from the natives.

Many of the names recorded by the Arabian chroniclers are retained in a spelling but slightly varied at the present day. Their Ghana has become Kano, Tocrur is Takror, and Bornou is unchanged.

Their account of western Africa is confused and vague, showing that their explorations and settlements were confined to the district about the Niger. Of the northern part of the eastern coast, they knew but little; for Nubia and Abyssinia were both Christian countries, and the races of differing faiths were jealous of each other's explorations and investigations. South of Abyssinia, they had explored the coast pretty thoroughly as far south as Madagascar, and had formed settlements at various points along the coast of Mozambique, which were in their possession when the earliest Portuguese navigators ventured around the Cape of Good Hope and reached the eastern coast from the south.

Rome, as the representative of western civilization, had, from the earliest times, made many efforts to extend her empire toward the

East; but had been steadily resisted by the Semitic races. These efforts were not relaxed, even after western civilization had found other representatives. Toward the end of the fifteenth century, however, the fall of Constantinople and the expulsion of the Moors from Spain seemed to establish the boundaries of the Aryan empire and of the Semitic; and

A MAGICIAN AT WORK.

the people of the former race, no longer struggling vainly for a foothold in the East, sought new worlds to conquer in the West. Even before these events had actually come to pass, the results of the movement had begun to be felt. The same spirit which sent Columbus westward to find India, sent the Portuguese southward to explore the coast of Africa.

The local position of Portugal, and its constant wars with Morocco, were the circumstances which seem to have directed the minds of the

people to the exploration and settlement of Africa. Prince Henry, the
younger son of John I., seems to have been the first man of any influence
to undertake the work. Rapid progress was made along the shore of
the Sahara, and before long the Portuguese navigators had reached
that fertile country which we now call Senegambia.

There were many material advantages to be hoped for from a constant intercourse with this part of the world; but the Portuguese were
not content with looking for those things which they were sure existed.
Some early travelers in eastern Asia had told of a mysterious personage whom they called Prester John; probably some Nestorian bishop,
possessed of a degree of temporal power. The Portuguese had heard
vague rumors of the Christian king of Abyssinia, and forthwith concluded that he was Prester John. The dominions of this ruler, it was
reported, reached far inland; and the adventurous spirits who had
embarked upon this series of undertakings decided that it would be comparatively easy to reach his capital by an overland journey from the
Gulf of Guinea.

Their anticipations of the results of such success seem to have been
as vague and uncertain as their knowledge; but whatever they expected
to be the consequence of having reached the court of Prester John, they
spared no pains in the effort to do so. They penetrated into the interior
as far as Timbuctoo, and must have gained a fairly accurate knowledge
of that portion of the continent. Unfortunately, the information so
acquired was either lost, or sedulously kept from the world at large,
until modern discoveries had made their jealous secrecy useless.

They continued to prosecute their discoveries along the coast, and
in 1471 reached the coast of Guinea, where they built Elmina, the Mine,
so called because of its position on the Gold Coast. The Pope gave them
a title to all lands which should be discovered in this part of the world,
and the king of Portugal assumed the title of Lord of Guinea. Hitherto,
the progress of the discoverers had been marked by wooden crosses; but
the king now gave orders that they were to erect stone pillars, twice the
height of a man, surmounted by leaden crucifixes. In 1484, Diego Cam
sailed from Lisbon, and erected such a pillar at what was then the most
southerly limit of Portuguese discovery—the mouth of the Congo, a

river which, from this circumstance, has frequently been called "The River of the Pillar" by the Portuguese writers.

The Congo did not long remain the boundary, however. A number of the natives had been taken to Portugal by Cam, and an expedition to reconvey these to their native country set out in 1490. Many missionaries accompanied the fleet, and strenuous efforts were made to Christianize the country. The natives, at first, willingly received the new faith; but when the missionaries discovered that they had not renounced polygamy, and had no intention of doing so, it was found that the efforts had not been so successful as they at first appeared. Other failures to renounce their former practices became apparent, and the missionaries became despondent; one of them, it is said, died from the effects of the disappointment.

How long they struggled against the persistency of paganism, we do not know; we only know what were the results of their self-sacrificing work in their voluntary exile. When Europeans again reached the mouth of the Congo, there was neither trace nor tradition of the Portuguese missionaries.

Before the date of this second expedition to the Congo, which ended so disastrously for those who remained after the vessels had returned to Portugal, Bartolommeo Diaz had sailed southward, and approaching land when in about twenty-six degrees of south latitude, had followed the coast-line closely until he had almost reached the southern extremity. Here he was buffeted about by contrary winds; but at last cast anchor in Algoa Bay, having rounded the Cape of Good Hope without knowing it. Being rejoined by his companion vessel, from which the storm had separated him, he set out on his return; and then noted his discovery. The cape was at first called "Cape of All the Storms;" but on his return, the king gave it the more auspicious name which it now bears. Diaz was greeted with much enthusiasm; but for some reason, was soon cast into the shade by Vasco de Gama, who was made his superior in the expedition of 1497.

While Diaz was the discoverer of the Cape of Good Hope, Gama was the first to make any use of the discovery. In the year above named, he sailed around the southern point of the continent, touched at various

points on the eastern coast, which had hitherto been wholly unknown to
Europeans, and securing the services of an intelligent Arab pilot, struck
boldly across the Indian Ocean for India. A second expedition, in

KAFFIR MAN AND WOMAN.

1502, saw the founding of the Portuguese colonies of Mozambique and
Sefala, on the eastern coast of Africa.

The Portuguese supremacy over Guinea was ended when the mother
country became involved in wars with the Dutch, which resulted favor-
ably for Holland. Following close in the footsteps of the men of the

Low Countries, came the French and English, lured by the hope of obtaining many slaves, and then by the expectation of finding in Africa another and a richer Peru.

The first English expedition, which was dispatched in 1618, was under the command of Richard Thompson. It was formed for the purpose of exploring the Gambia, and reached the mouth of that river in December of that year. The Englishmen met with fierce resistance from the Portuguese, of whom there were still many in this region; but maintained their station on the river, and sent home for re-inforcements. Most of the men upon the second expedition fell victims to disease; the commander of the third party heard, shortly before reaching his destination, that Thompson had fallen by the hands of his own men.

The fate of this first of English explorers of Africa has never been fully investigated. The history of the times is full of perilous adventures in which the spirit of the leader was more daring than that of his men; possibly Thompson, like Columbus, would have urged his followers onward on an unknown path; but, unlike Columbus, met with no favoring signs at the critical moment. In the way of positive testimony, we have only the representations of the crew, that their leader was oppressive and intolerable—interested evidence.

The leader of this third expedition, intended for the relief of the first, of which Thompson was the chief, was Richard Jobson, who has given us the first satisfactory account of the great river districts of western Africa. Jobson was the first white man who obtained any accurate information regarding the manners and customs of the interior African tribes, and recorded such knowledge in a form readily accessible.

The Portuguese professed entire ignorance of the misfortunes which had befallen Thompson's command, although the first English expedition had, on one occasion at least, suffered severely at the hands of these earlier settlers. Taking their protestations for what they were worth, Jobson pushed on in the ascent of the Gambia, and soon reached the farthest point which had been attained by his predecessor. The advent of a trading-vessel was a great event in the eyes of the natives, who eagerly pressed toward the river, to exchange the products of the country for the commodities of the strangers.

Jobson expected to reach Timbuctoo, by a comparatively short journey; for Europeans generally had no good idea of the dimensions of Africa. He succeeded in getting to Penda, where he was presented at the primitive court of the king by a merchant who had acted as guide; and then set out upon his return. His whole progress, he bitterly complains, had been much hindered by the merchants who formed a part of his company, and who were utterly indifferent to everything except their own profit. His return was further delayed by the condition of the river; the dry season was now far advanced, and it was difficult to descend such a shallow stream.

For the next forty years, the political condition of England was such as to forbid much foreign enterprise on the part of her people. But when the civil dissensions were ended and Charles II. was recognized as king, new moves were made toward exploring this country, which promised so rich a reward. In 1665, an expedition was fitted out by private enterprise, for the exploration of the Gambia, with a view to finding the sources whence the natives derived their stores of gold. All appliances for extracting gold from the mixtures in which it is found were carried with them; but their expectations were not wholly fulfilled. At one place by twenty days' labor, they succeeded in extracting twelve pounds; and the leader declared, subsequently, that he had found the mouth of the mine; but as he never made any use of the knowledge, it is probable that his assertion was unfounded.

Another expedition was sent out in 1720 by the African Company, of which the Duke of Chandos was then director. Of this expedition, Capt. Bartholomew Stibbs was the leader. It was with difficulty that he could persuade his guides to accompany him above the Falls of Barraconda, a point which they declared was the end of the world, and beyond which there were only the rudest and fiercest savages. He at length succeeded in persuading them, however, and ascended the river for some distance above the falls, though not as far as Tenda, which Jobson had reached. The expedition of Stibbs is of importance, because of its effect upon the spirits of English explorers of Africa. Hitherto the Gambia had been confounded with the Niger; it was thought that by ascending the former, the explorers might with comparative ease penetrate far into the interior, even to Timbuctoo. Stibbs declared that he had ascended the stream far enough to be able to judge of its size; he had seen no evidence of any great river; it issued from no lake, as the Niger was said to do; it was nowhere called by a name similar to Niger; the natives declared that at twelve days' journey above the falls it dwindled to a rivulet, which fowls might wade across. Despite the arguments which the English Company's factor on the Gambia drew from history, Stibbs persisted in the statement of facts of which he had personal experience. It came to be felt that the legends concerning the Niger were without foundation; and a degree of discouragement was experienced which for some time effectually put an end to the desire for exploring this portion of Africa. It does not seem to have suggested itself to them that the Niger might really exist, a little farther from England than the stream which they had assumed was the one that they sought.

While the English were exploring the Gambia, under the impression that it was the Niger, the French were making a similar mistake as to the Senegal. Shortly after the expedition commanded by Jobson, the French made a settlement near the mouth of the Senegal, which they named after the patron saint of their country and their king, Saint Louis. Accounts of this settlement were brought home, in 1637, by Jannequin, a young man of rank whose fancy sent him on a trip thither. For some time, however, the French seem to have made no great effort toward exploring the interior for any considerable distance.

The settlement had been made under the auspices of a company to which Louis XIV. had granted a patent, giving exclusive right of territory and privileges of settlement, trading, and exploration. This was the method employed by this king in furthering enterprises of the kind; and when one company became bankrupt, through extravagance or mismanagement, nothing was easier than to grant a patent for another. In this way four successive companies were formed having for their object the settlement and exploration of this part of Africa. It was not until 1697 that they were under the management of a man who seems to have been thoroughly enthusiastic over the purpose for which the company was organized. In that year, the Sieur Brue was appointed director-general of the company's affairs.

He at once began his preparations for penetrating into the interior, intending to visit the Siratik, or king of the Foulahs, whose territory lay four hundred miles up the river. He seems to have met with no difficulty in prosecuting his journey; but was well received, first by the envoys, and then by the king himself. Presents of great value in the eyes of the natives, but costing only about sixty or seventy pounds sterling, were tendered as an evidence of the friendly feeling of the white men, and graciously accepted. Having accomplished the immediate object of his journey, the Sieur returned to St. Louis.

He set out again the next year, having a more extended object in view. His first trip had been solely for the purpose of cultivating friendly feelings with the natives; in the second, he sought to ascend the Senegal as high as possible, and open up trade with the natives. He established the fort called St. Joseph, which was long the principal seat of French commerce on the upper Senegal; but failed to accomplish much beyond this; being compelled to return before the river fell so as to cut off his retreat. He obtained from the natives much information respecting the interior; unfortunately, their assertions were not always to be reconciled; especially was this the case in regard to the Niger, which seems for the first time to have been recognized as a stream distinct from the Gambia or the Senegal. According to the statement of some of the natives, the Niger flowed westward from the lake; according to others, it flowed eastward; the former account of it represented it as separating into the two channels of the Senegal and the Gambia; but the great French geographers of the time adopted the other opinion.

Brue wished to penetrate to the gold mines in the interior; but the tyranny of earliest Portuguese settlers had been such that the natives of that section were resolved not to permit the white men to enter their country again. Brue indeed secured the services of an intrepid advance, who, laden with presents, endeavored to persuade the natives to admit the party; but the project failed of accomplishment. Nor could Brue obtain from France the assistance which he required, if he made an effort to possess himself by force of the riches of the interior.

CHAPTER XI.

ROOSEVELT'S FIRST EXPERIENCE AS AN AFRICAN HUNTER.

He Kills a Gnu or Wild Beast—Despatches Three Lions in One Day—Kermit Makes an Expedition on His Own Hook—Smallpox Scare in the Camp—Other Thrilling Incidents.

ROOSEVELT'S first night under canvas in Africa was spent in the camp set up for the expedition in the vicinity of the railroad station at Kapoto Plains. Nothing disturbed the stillness of the tropical night except the monotonous concert of the beasts of prey, chief among whom was the lion, whose awe-inspiring roar, like the rumble of a distant thunder, when slowly dying away in repeated echoes among the mountains, sent an exerting thrill through the mighty hunter's heart.

The next morning he arose in splendid spirits and spent the day assorting his baggage and outfit, while his son Kermit, with some other members of the party, went out to try their luck with the rifles and succeeded in bringing down one antelope. "Bully, bully," exclaimed the ex-President with a face beaming from pleasure when the booty was laid at his feet.

He forbade the members of the expedition to give out any reports as to his movements and allowed only one representative of an English news agency and some American reporters to accompany him. This inspired the Nairobi newspapers to make a venomous attack on Roosevelt and the acting governor, and caused the British government to ask for an explanation from the local authorities.

A fine weather favored Roosevelt's first hunt, and he had many reasons to be "delighted," for he bagged two wildebeests and one gazelle the first day.

Next to the monkey, says an African traveler, I believe the gnu or wildebeest is the most inquisitive of all animals. A hunter often comes upon herds of twenty to fifty. As soon as they caught sight of us, he continues, they would begin curveting around the wagons, wheeling about in endless circles and cutting all sorts of curious capers.

While I was riding hard to obtain a shot at a herd in front of me, other herds charged down wind on my right and left, and, having described a number of circular movements, they took up position upon the very ground across which I had ridden only a few minutes before. Singly, and in small troops of four or five individuals, the old bull wildebeests may be seen stationed at intervals throughout the plains, standing motionless during a whole forenoon, coolly watching with a philosophic eye the movements of the other game, uttering a loud snorting noise, and also a short sharp cry which is peculiar to them. When the hunter approaches these old bulls, they commence whisking their long white tails in a most eccentric manner; then, springing into the air, begin prancing and capering, and pursue each other in circles at their utmost speed. Suddenly they all pull up together to overhaul the intruder, when the bulls will often commence fighting in the most violent manner, dropping on their knees at every shock; then, quickly wheeling about, they kick up their heels, whirl their tails with a fantastic flourish, and scour across the plain enveloped in a cloud of dust. In addition to their speed, wildebeest are remarkable for their extreme tenacity of life; and, owing to the vigorous use they make of their horns, are awkward creatures to hunt with dogs. Europeans find them good practice in rifle-shooting, as they will stand in herds at a distance which they think secure, say three hundred or four hundred yards, and watch the passer-by. Only occasionally can they be approached within easy range by fair stalking; although they may be killed by watching at their drinking-holes at night. During a thunderstorm of unusual intensity, I walked, hardly knowing where I was going, right into a herd of gnu. I did not see them until I was almost among them; but even had my gun not been hopelessly soaked, the fearful storm made self-preservation, and not destruction, one's chief thought. They were standing huddled in a mass, their heads together, and their sterns outwards, and they positively only just moved out of my way, much the same as a herd of cattle might have done.

The faculty of curiosity is largely developed in the gnu, which can never resist the temptation of inspecting any strange object, although at the risk of its life. When a gnu first catches sight of any unknown being, he sets off at full speed, as if desirous of getting to the furthest possible distance from the terrifying object. Soon, however, the feeling of curiosity vanquishes the passion of fear, and the animal halts to reconnoitre. He then gallops in a circle round the cause of his dread.

The native hunters are enabled to attract a herd of gnus, feeding out of shot, merely by getting up a clumsy imitation of an ostrich, by holding a head of that bird on a pole, and making at their back a peacock's tail of feathers. The inquisitive animals are so fascinated with the fluttering lure, that they actually approach so near as to be easily pierced with an arrow or an assegai.

The gnu, or wildebeest, inhabits Africa. At first sight it is difficult to say whether the horse, buffalo, or deer predominates in its form. It, however, belongs to neither of these animals, but is one of the bovine antelopes. The horns cover the top of the forehead, and then, sweeping downwards over the face, turn boldly upwards with a sharp curve. The neck is furnished with a mane like that of the horse, and the legs are formed like those of a stag.

His next victim was what is known as a Thompson gazelle. It was secured after several hours' hunt, from which the members of the party returned to the camp tired and exhausted.

The gazelle is regarded as the embodiment of grace and beauty, and is celebrated in song and story. It is usually of a sandy color and has a white streak on the side of the face from the base of the horn nearly to the nose, thus cutting off a dark triangular patch in the middle of the forehead, while the streak itself is bordered by a dark line. The horns, which are generally present in both sexes, are recurved and completely ringed throughout the greater part of their length. Most of the gazelles do not exceed thirty inches in height, although the mohr reaches thirty-six inches. There are about twenty-one living species.

The gazelle so famous in Oriental poetry inhabits Arabia and Syria. Its eyes are very large, dark and lustrous, so that the Oriental poets love to compare the eyes of a woman to those of a gazelle, just as Homer constantly applied the epithet ox-eyed to the more majestic goddesses, such as Juno and Minerva. It is easily tamed when young, and is frequently

seen domesticated in the court yards of houses in Syria. Its swiftness
is so great that even a greyhound cannot overtake it, and the hunters
are forced to make use of hawks, which are trained to strike at the head
of the gazelle, and thus confuse it and retard its speed, so as to permit
the dogs to come up. The color of this pretty little animal is a dark
yellowish brown, fading into white on the under parts.

A peculiar gazelle, known as the gerenuk, or Waller's gazelle, inhabits Eastern Africa, and is remarkable for the great length of its
neck, which has been likened to a miniature giraffe.

The gerenuk is found all over the Somali country in small families,
never in large herds, and generally in scattered bush, ravines and rocky
ground. I have never seen it in the cedar-forests, nor in the treeless
plains. Gerenuk are not necessarily found near water; in fact, generally in stony ground with a sprinkling of thorn-jungle. Its gait is
peculiar. When first seen, a buck gerenuk will generally be standing
motionless, head well up, looking at the intruder, and trusting to its
invisibility. Then the head dives under the bushes, and the animal goes
off at a long, crouching trot, stopping now and again behind some bush
to gaze. The trot is awkward-looking, and very like that of a camel;
the gerenuk seldom gallops, and its pace is never very fast. In the whole
shape of the head and neck, and in the slender lower jaw, there is a
marked resemblance between the gerenuk and the dibatag. It subsists
more by browsing than by grazing and it may not unfrequently be observed standing up on its hind-legs, with outstretched neck, and its forefeet resting against the trunk of a tree, in order to pluck the foliage.

A beautiful species of gazelle is the Dorcas, found in Egypt and Barbary, where it lives in large troops upon the borders of the cultivated
country, and also in the deserts. When pursued it flies to some distance, then stops to gaze a moment at the hunters, and again renews
its flight. The flock, when attacked collectively, disperse in all directions, but soon unite, and when brought to bay defend themselves
with courage and obstinacy, uniting in a close circle, with the females
and fawns in the center, and presenting their horns at all points to their
enemies; yet, notwithstanding their courage, they are the common prey
of the lion and panther and are hunted with great perseverance.

CHAPTER XII.

AFRICA'S GENERAL CHARACTERISTICS AND PARTITION AMONG EUROPEAN NATIONS.

Size of the Dark Continent—Natural Resources and Population—Climate and Geography—Rivers, Lakes and Mountains—Deserts and Vast Forests.

THE Continent Roosevelt selected as the battleground for his achievements as a hunter and a naturalist is one of the most interesting parts of the old world.

GIGANTIC STRIDES IN CIVILIZATION.

Has the average reader ever realized what the figures expressing the population of Africa mean? One hundred and seventy millions of people! Twenty-eight millions more than both North and South America together.

Little will be heard about "darkest Africa" in future generations. The advance of civilization to that continent has worked rapid changes in its people and in the country. As the great American desert has disappeared from modern maps of the United States, as well as from the minds of the people, so portions of the great Sahara Desert now bid fair to be reclaimed to usefulness. An enterprising American, after a survey by English and American engineers, has undertaken the irrigation of a large area of the Sahara Desert from the river Nile. It is claimed that it needs only water to transform it into a region of great fertility.

Africa, one of the three great divisions of the Old World, and the second in extent of the five principal continents of the globe, forms a vast peninsula joined to Asia by the Isthmus of Suez. It is of a compact form, with a few important projections or indentations, and having therefore a very small extent of coast-line (about 16,000 miles, or much less than that of Europe) in proportion to its area.

The continent extends from 37 degrees 20 minutes north latitude, to

34 degrees 50 minutes south latitude, and the extreme points, Cape Blanco and Cape Agulhas, are nearly 5,000 miles apart. From west to east, between Cape Verde, longitude 17 degrees 34 minutes west, and Cape Guardafui, longitude 51 degrees, 16 minutes east, the distance is about 4,600 miles. The area is estimated at 11,508,793 sq. miles, or more than three times that of Europe. The islands belonging to Africa are few; they include Madagascar, Madeira, the Canaries, Cape Verde Islands, Fernando Po, Prince's Island, St. Thomas, Ascension, St. Helena, Mauritius, Bourbon, the Comoros and Socotra.

THE PARTITION OF AFRICA.

The desperate struggle among the European powers for colonial possessions in Africa is of comparatively recent origin. While the earliest explorations began in 1553, when a body of British merchants sent out in search of trade a few vessels to Guinea, there was no thought of anything more than an effort to find a new market for English productions. It was more than forty years later, in 1595, that the Dutch followed the English merchants in the attempt to establish a trading station on the coast of Guinea. About the same time that the British traders began the exploration of the Guinea coast the French sent out on the same errand and located at what is now known as French Guinea. Thus at the beginning of the seventeenth century nearly all the portions of Africa that were held by the nations of Europe were the three divisions of the coast of Guinea that were known respectively as British, French and Dutch Guinea.

Even at the end of that century England and France were the principal rivals for African trade; but at the close of the French wars France had lost nearly all her possessions in Africa as well as elsewhere. In this war Great Britain acquired the ascendency in African affairs, which she stubbornly held for 200 years. Leaving the coast, they both pushed into the interior, which example was followed by other nations. Generally the partition of Africa went on slowly and peaceably, and it was not until the Brussels conference in 1878 that the unrestrained scramble began that has resulted in the division of the entire continent among the different nations of Europe. Thus in 1876, while

ZEBRA ATTACKED BY A LION.

Zebra are always found in herds but as soon as one is attacked or wounded it at once separates from the others, allowing its companions to get away safely while it fights for its life alone.

From Stereograph Copyright 1909, by Underwood & Underwood, N. Y.
CURING ANTELOPE FOR USE ON LONG FORCED MARCHES.
Contrary to popular ideas there are large sections of African Jungle and plain where Col. Roosevelt hunted, where food material of every sort is scarce and must be planned for beforehand. The native porters are here seen after the hunt curing strips of Antelope meat with which they sustain life while crossing the dreary wastes.

Great Britain, France, Spain and Portugal had located colonies on the coast of Africa, the interior was held by the wild tribes that occupied it against all foreign aggression. The Berlin conference in 1876 was the time at which the energetic division of the continent was inaugurated, and at the close of 1890 of the 11,508,793 square miles of territory composing the continent of Africa only some 1,500,000 remained open to seizure by the nations of Europe. There were even then some conflicting claims that had not been settled, as the conflicts between French, German and British interests on the Niger clearly testified. But these, together with the disputes between Portugal and England in the upper Zambesi, have been amicably settled, and it is mainly the claims that arise out of the British occupation of Egypt now that the British and Boers in South Africa have come to a settlement.

GENERAL CHARACTERISTICS.

The interior of Africa is as yet imperfectly known, but we know enough of the continent as a whole to be able to point to some general features and characterize it. One of these is that almost all round it at no great distance from the sea, and, roughly speaking, parallel with the coast-line, we find ranges of mountains or elevated lands forming the outer edges of interior plateaux.

The most striking feature of Northern Africa is the immense tract known as the Sahara or Great Desert, which is inclosed on the north by the Atlas Mountains (greatest height, 12,000 to 13,000 feet), the plateau of Barbary, and that of Barca, on the east by the mountains along the west coast of the Red Sea, on the west by the Atlantic Ocean, and on the south by the Sudan.

The Sahara is by no means the sea of sand it has sometimes been represented; it contains elevated plateaux and even mountains radiating in all directions, with habitable valleys between. A considerable nomadic population is scattered over the habitable parts, and in the more favored regions there are settled communities.

The Sudan, which lies to the south of the Sahara, and separates it from the more elevated plateau of Southern Africa, forms a belt of pastoral country across Africa, and includes the countries on the Niger, around Lake Tchad (or Chad), and eastwards to the elevated region of Abyssinia.

Southern Africa as a whole is much more fertile and better watered than northern Africa, though it also has a desert tract of considerable extent (the Kalahari Desert). This division of the continent consists of a table-land, or series of table-lands, of considerable elevation and great diversity of surface, exhibiting hollows filled with great lakes and terraces over which the rivers break in falls and rapids, as they find their way to the low-lying coast tracts.

The mountains which inclose Southern Africa are mostly much higher on the east than on the west, the most northernly of the former being those of Abyssinia, with heights of 10,000 to 14,000 or 16,000 feet, while the eastern edge of the Abyssinian plateau presents a steep un-broken line of 7,000 feet in height for many hundred miles. Farther south, and between the great lakes and the Indian ocean, we find Mounts Kenia and Kilimanjaro (19,500 feet), the loftiest in Africa, covered with perpetual snow.

Of the continuation of this mountain boundary we shall only men-tion the Drakenburg Mountains, which stretch to the southern extremity of the continent, reaching in Cathkin Peak, Natal, the height of over 10,000 feet. Of the mountains that form the western border the highest are the Cameroon Mountains, which rise to a height of 13,000 feet, at the inner angle of the Gulf of Guinea. The average elevation of the southern plateau is probably from 3,000 to 4,000 feet.

THE RIVER NILE.

The Nile is the only great river of Africa which flows to the Mediter-ranean. It receives its waters primarily from the great lake Victoria Nyanza, which lies under the equator, and its upper course is fed by tributary streams of great size, but for the last 1,200 miles of its course it has not a single affluent. It drains an area of more than 1,000,000 square miles.

The Indian Ocean receives numerous rivers; but the only great river of South Africa which enters that ocean is the Zambesi, the fourth in size of the continent, and having in its course the Victoria Falls, one of the greatest waterfalls in the world.

In Southern Africa also but flowing westward and entering the Atlantic is the Kongo, which takes origin from a series of lakes and marshes in the interior, is fed by great tributaries, and is the first in volume of all the African rivers, carrying to the ocean more water than the Mississippi. Unlike most of the African rivers, the mouth of the Kongo forms an estuary. Of the other Atlantic rivers, the Senegal, the Gambia, and the Niger are the largest, the last being third among African streams.

LAKES.

With the exception of Lake Tchad there are no great lakes in the northern division of Africa, whereas in the number and magnificence of its lakes the southern division almost rivals North America. Here are the Victoria and Albert Nyanza, Lakes Tanganyika, Nyassa, Shirwa, Bangweolo, Moero, and a few others.

Of these the Victoria and Albert belong to the basin of the Nile; Tanganyika, Bangweolo, and Moero to that of the Kongo; Nyassa, by its affluent the Shire, to the Zambesi, Lake Tchad on the borders of the Northern desert region, and Lake Ngami on the borders of the southern, have a remarkable resemblance in position, and in the fact that both are drained by streams that lose themselves in the sand.

CLIMATE.

The climate of Africa is mainly influenced by the fact that it lies almost entirely within the tropics. In the equatorial belt, both north and south, rain is abundant and vegetation very luxuriant, dense tropical forests prevailing for about 10 degrees on either side of the line. To the north and south of the equatorial belt the rainfall diminishes, and the forest region is succeeded by an open pastoral and agricultural country. This is followed by the rainless regions of the Sahara on the north and the Kalahari Desert on the south, extending beyond the tropics, and bordering on the agricultural and pastoral countries of the north and south coasts, which lie entirely in the temperate zone. The low coast regions of Africa are almost everywhere unhealthy, the Atlantic coast within the tropics being the most fatal region to Europeans.

Among mineral productions may be mentioned gold, which is found in the rivers of West Africa (hence the name Gold Coast), and in Southern Africa, but rarely in much abundance; diamonds have been found in large numbers in recent years in the south; iron, copper, lead, tin and coal are also found.

Among plants are the baobab, the date-palm (important as a food plant in the north), the doum-palm, the oil-palm, the wax-palm, the shea-butter tree, trees yielding caout-chouc, the papyrus, the castor-oil plant, indigo, the coffee-plant, heaths with beautiful flowers, aloes, etc.

Among cultivated plants are wheat, maize, millet, and other grains, cotton, coffee, cassava, ground-nut, yam, banana, tobacco, various fruit, etc.

Of African trade two features are the caravans that traverse great distances, and the trade in slaves that still widely prevails and is accompanied by an immense amount of bloodshed.

Among articles exported from Africa are palm-oil, diamonds, gold, ivory, ostrich feathers, wool, cotton, esparto, caoutchouc, etc.

The chief independent states in Africa are Morocco, Liberia, and Abyssinia. In 1891 Portugal annexed part of Loanda. To Great Britain belong the colonies of the Cape and Natal, with some large adjoining tracts, also British East Africa, Sierra Leone, the Gold Coast, the Niger territory, Zanzibar the Samali Coast, the islands of Sokotra, and Mauritius; to France belong Algeria and Tunis, Senegambia, and a considerable territory north of the Lower Congo; the western Sahara, Dahomey, a small territory on the Gulf of Aden, known as French Somali, and the Island of Madagascar and adjacent islands; the Portuguese possess a portion of the west coast of South Africa from about latitude 6 degrees south to 17 degrees south, and the east coast from about 10 degrees south to 27 degrees south, and a small tract on the west coast. Germany now has a portion of the southwest coast, and a large tract near Zanzibar, and the Kamerum and Togo on the Gulf of Guinea; to Turkey nominally belong Egypt, Barca and Tripoli; Spain has a part of the coast of Sahara. The Congo State is under the sovereignty of the King of Belgium.

CHAPTER XIII.

ROOSEVELT'S REMARKABLE SKILL AS A HUNTER.

Exciting Encounters with a Bull Rhinoceros—The First Elephant Falls for His Never Failing Bullet—Giraffes, Leopards and Other Beasts Bagged—Cubs Captured Alive.

ROOSEVELT'S success as a hunter in Africa during the first four months has already proved to be a record-breaking chain of surprising achievements. The first three months' hunting yielded 42 head of big game and among whom were seven lions, ten rhinoceros, 4 hippopotami, 4 giraffes, 3 wildebeests, 5 buffalos and one elephant.

During this brilliant career as a beast killer Roosevelt has time and again risked his life, and his success has been due to his undaunted courage, unerring aim and exceptional presence of mind.

All of these qualities of his combined brought death to a large bull rhinoceros near Machabos.

The long, low, uncouth-looking beast, of some five feet in height at the shoulder, and shaped much like an immense hog, came running full tilt at our nimrod.

The short, upright horn on the snout, the contour of the animal, and the loose folds of skin that covered his ribs, the maddened squeal that was heard above the snapping of the bush, proclaimed the arrival of the most dangerous of all wild animals, the African rhinoceros.

Roosevelt's resolution was taken in an instant. He must either kill the bull, or be killed himself almost inevitably. He was not ten feet from him when—

One flash! It was enough! Struck through the brain the old bull dropped instantaneously, and the ex-President was safe.

The rhinoceros is a favorite game in Africa. It has a ferocious disposition and is hard to kill. The easiest and least dangerous method is for the hunter to conceal himself and shoot it when it comes to drink at the pool. The true sportsman prefers to hunt it on horseback with dogs.

As the eyes of the rhinoceros are very small, it seldom turns its head and therefore sees nothing but what is before it. It is to this that it owes its death, and never escapes if there be so much plain as to enable the horses of the hunters to get before it. Its pride and fury then makes it lay aside all thoughts of escaping, except by victory over its enemy. For a moment it stands at bay; then at a start runs straight forward at the horse which is nearest. The rider easily avoids the attack by turn-ing short to one side. This is the fatal instant; a naked man who is

ONE FLASH ! AND THE OLD BULL LAY AT THE EX-PRESIDENT'S FEET.

mounted behind the principal horseman, drops off the horse, and, unseen by the rhinoceros, gives it, with a sword a stroke across the tendon of the heel, which renders it incapable either of flight or resistance.

Several travelers have mentioned that there are certain birds which constantly attend the rhinoceros, and give him warning of approaching danger. Their accounts were either received with silent contempt, or treated with open ridicule, as preposterous extensions of the traveler's privilege of romancing. I can bear witness to the truth of these reports, says a famous sportsman. Once while hunting the rhinoceros in Africa, I saw a huge female lying in the jungle asleep. My first thought was to photograph her and then attack her. I began to crawl toward her, but before I could reach the proper distance several rhinoceros-birds, by which she was attended, warned her of the impending danger, by sticking their bills into her ear, and uttering their harsh, grating cry. Thus aroused, she suddenly sprang to her feet, and crashed away through the jungle at a rapid trot, and I saw no more of her.

Next to the elephant in size, comes the rhinoceros, which with the hippopotamus, lays claim to bulk and ferocity unequalled by any other member of the animal kingdom. The rhinoceros is found in the rivers of Central Africa and Southern Asia. It can only live in tropical climates.

The length of the rhinoceros is usually about twelve feet, and this is also nearly the girth of its body. The skin, which is of a blackish color, is disposed, about the neck, into large plaits or folds. A fold of the same kind passes from the shoulders to the fore legs; another from the hind part of the back to the thighs. The skin is naked, rough, and covered with a kind of tubercles, or large callous granulations. Between the folds, and under the belly, it is soft, and of a light rose-color. The horns are composed of a closely-packed mass of horn fibers, growing from the skin, and having no connection with the bones of the skull, although there are prominences on the latter beneath each horn. All are mainly abroad at night, and while some resemble the tapirs in frequenting tall grass-jungles and swampy districts, others seem to prefer the open plains.

Some hunters have created the impression that the hide of the rhinoceros will turn a leaden bullet and sometimes an iron one. This is a popular error, for a common leaden ball will pierce the hide at a distance of thirty or forty paces, especially if a double charge of powder be used, which is the custom with all rhinoceros hunters. The most deadly aim is just behind the shoulder. The skull is too thick and the brain pan too small for a successful shot at the head.

The killing of the huge rhinoceros bull which was of unusual size and no doubt is one of the most valuable specimens in the Smithsonian collection called forth repeated cheers for Bwana Tambo from the sonorous throats of the natives.

The African elephant is a more dangerous animal than the Indian, and is more ready to charge. The first one killed by Roosevelt was a huge animal and the leader of a herd of about a dozen. At a distance of forty feet Roosevelt struck its heart and it went over dead. A baby elephant was captured an hour later and sent over to the New York Zoological Garden. The Arabs slay the elephant by hamstringing it with a long two-edged sword. They follow the animal until it faces its pursuers and prepares to charge. The hunter then puts his horse to a gallop, closely followed by the elephant. They follow at their best pace, and as soon as they come up with the fleeing animal, one leaps to the ground, and with one blow of his huge sword divides the tendon of the elephant's leg a short distance above the heel. The ponderous beast is at once brought to a standstill, and is at the mercy of his aggressors.

A leopard or African Panther was killed by our ex-President during the hunt and its cubs captured alive: The animal was dispatched at a distance of only six paces and already had mauled a beater and was charging Kermit when the fatal shot was fired.

Among the reptiles killed by Roosevelt was a python, measuring 23 feet. It was quietly making a meal of an antelope when the bullet struck it back of the head, cutting a vertebra. The naturalists of the party had collected two other pythons and four hundred birds and animals.

In Nairobi a splendid reception had been planned in his honor, but had to be abandoned owing to his expressed desire to spend the time writing. Half the distance Roosevelt rode with Major Mearns on the locomotive cowcatcher, for about 22 miles, and the scenery along the road delighted him, especially the Escarpment and the Rift Valley.

The highest point reached was the Kikuyu escarpment—7,830 feet—from where Roosevelt had a magnificent view down 2,000 feet into the great Rift Valley, where elephants, monkeys, etc., are plentiful, but fairly safe from the hunter owing to the thickness of the growth.

CHAPTER XIV.

ROOSEVELT VISITS CHRISTIAN MISSIONS IN AFRICA.

Religions of Africa—Fetichism—Devil Worship—Portuguese and Protestant Missions—London Missionary Society—Livingstone—Dutch Reformed Church—American Missions—Catholic Missions in Northern Africa—Persecutions—Martyrdoms—A Christian Ruler.

ROOSEVELT has always taken a deep interest in the efforts made by the missionaries to Christianize and civilize barbarian countries and during his stay in Africa had an excellent opportunity to study this work at close range.

The forms of religious beliefs professed by the inhabitants of Africa may be classed under three heads—Christian, Mohammedan, and pagan. The second form of faith was propagated in this continent at a very early period of Mohammedan history; and we find professors of it among many tribes which are not far removed from a state of savagery. These, however, are only nominally Mohammedans; in their gross superstitions, their ignorance, and their revolting practices, they are really pagans; and their profession of belief in the Prophet of Islam only serves to bring contempt upon his teachings, as too many who call themselves by a holier name bring contempt, by the manner of their lives, upon the religion which they profess.

It is difficult to speak in general terms of the faiths which are classed under the head of pagan. Some tribes appear to have a confused and gross belief in a future life; others declare that death ends all. Others again, believe in the transmigration of souls, and hold certain animals in reverence, as inhabited by the souls of dead friends. The negroes on the equatorial western coast of Africa believe that the souls of men frequently pass into gorillas, and that such animals are too cunning for the hunter. Some people have a well defined belief in a superior Being, who is good and beneficent; others, again, while they believe in spirits, cannot imagine one that is not malevolent; and are perpetually in terror of all supernatural agencies. But whatever rank these various religions may hold in point of purity or approach to reason, there is one thing in which they all agree: all teach a belief in magic, by whatever name it may be called; and the sorcerer is a person to be feared, the diviner to be honored.

AFRICAN SUPERSTITION—UNFAVORABLE PROPHECY.

One particular form of this belief in magic is Fetichism, or the belief in charms. A European explorer of recent years relates that on one occasion, when he had become unconscious from the effects of fever, he found, upon recovering his senses, that he was almost literally covered with charms which his faithful servitors had believed would restore him to health. But it was not even an opportunity for a faith cure; for he cast aside the antelope's horns, elephant's teeth and similar articles, and took a dose of quinine. The present writer is not prepared to say what are the peculiar virtues of the various fetiches, or whether the Africans are so ridiculous as to hang a horse-shoe over the stable-door for luck, or carry a horse-chestnut in the pocket (those of them who wear clothes) to ward off rheumatism.

From their universal belief in spirits, and that prevailing impression that spirits cannot be beneficent, arises what has been styled devil-worship. Much of that to which this name is applied is properly so called, since it is an effort to propitiate bad spirits; it may be that ignorance of their language and customs has caused some genuine worship of a Good Being to be so designated; since the stranger would suppose the god so worshipped to be, necessarily, a false one.

In 1481, the king of Portugal sent ten ships with five hundred soldiers and one hundred laborers, together with "a proper complement of priests," to Elmina. The mission thus founded lingered on for a period of 241 years, but does not seem to have made any impression upon the natives, except those who were immediately dependent upon the whites at the station. Finally, in 1723, the mission of the Capuchins at Sierra Leone was given up, and they disappeared altogether from West Africa. Whatever influence they may have had at the time has left no permanent traces.

An effort was made by the same authority to establish a mission station at the mouth of the Congo; but the natives proved too thoroughly wedded to their immoral practices to be really desirous of a purer mode of life. Somewhat of the story might be told, did our space admit; but the end is wrapped in darkness; vessels came from Portugal, and found that the missionaries had disappeared, and no one could or would tell them how.

The earliest Protestant efforts for the evangelization of Africa were made in 1736. In that year the Moravians determined to send out a missionary to the southern part of this great continent. The next year, George Schmidt arrived at the mouth of Sergeant's River. Though opposed and persecuted both by the government of the colony and by the native chiefs, he persevered, and at last succeeded in establishing a mission at Genadenthal, one hundred and twenty miles north of the Cape. The results of nine years' labor showed that forty-seven families had professed Christianity, and received baptism. He then returned to his native Holland, to seek for assistance; but not only did he find no others who would join him, but for some unexplained reason, he was not allowed to return. He passed the remainder of his days as a poor day-laborer in Germany, "with his heart in that southern land which he was never to see again."

On the west coast, the efforts of the Moravians were less successful. Beginning there at the same time that Schmidt went to South Africa, five different attempts were made to establish missionary stations; but they were made at the cost of eleven lives. Finally, in 1770, the effort was given up.

The Methodists were the next to seek to occupy the field. In the Minutes of the Conference for 1792, we find Africa, for the first time, set down as one of the missionary stations, Sierra Leone being the point selected. Four years later, the names of A. Murdoch and W. Patten are set down as missionaries to the Foulah country.

In 1798, the London Missionary Society sent out four missionaries, who arrived at the Cape the next year. Of these the most remarkable was Dr. Vanderkemp, who for years endured great hardships in his work of preaching the gospel to "his beloved Hottentots." But the most notable (with one great exception) of the missionaries sent out by this society was Robert Moffat.

He was a young man of but twenty-two when he offered himself for the work. Of his early training we have not space to say much; but volumes are told of the influences which had surrounded him at home, in the answer of his parents when he asked their consent to engage in this work: "We have thought of your proposal to become a missionary; we have prayed over it; and we cannot withhold you from so good a work." He never had any formal theological training; and seems, indeed, to have had but slight acquaintance with schools generally.

Great Namaqua-land was to be the scene of his earliest labors; a region where there had already been some effort at evangelization, so that the chief Africaner was thought to give evidence that would warrant a hope of his conversion. The missionary, of course, had landed at Cape Town; and the journey across Cape Colony was both toilsome and adventurous. It was late in January, 1818, when he arrived at Africaner's kraal, on the banks of the Orange River.

No sooner was he told that a white man had come, than Africaner appeared and demanded if Moffat were the missionary who had been promised. Receiving an answer in the affirmative, he turned to two women standing by, and commanded them to build a house for the missionary at once. They went to work with an alacrity that showed how pleasing the task was; and in an hour's time the "house" was finished. It is true that it was not a very substantial edifice; composed of native mats hung on poles, it was a shelter from neither rain nor sun, and frequently required extensive repairs after a storm. A dog could push aside the mats and enter at will; sometimes such an uninvited visitor would help himself to the missionary's stock of provisions for the next day. "Nor were these all the contingencies of such a dwelling; for as the cattle belonging to the village had no fold, I had been compelled to start up from a sound sleep, and try to defend myself and my dwelling from being crushed to pieces by the rage of two bulls which had met to fight a nocturnal duel."

But the hut, rude and unsubstantial as it was, was the best that they knew how to build; and Moffat felt himself more than repaid for such slight evils as bodily discomfort when the chief Africaner became an earnest Christian, and zealously seconded the efforts of the young missionary to teach his people not only the Gospel, but those lessons of industry and cleanliness which so powerfully assist the missionary in all countries to emphasize the blessings which his religion would teach the world.

Several efforts were made to find a place which would be more suitable for a missionary station than Africaner's kraal; it was desired to reach other peoples more directly; but these efforts were not successful. Finally, it was decided that Africaner's two brothers, who proved to be able and willing assistants, should conduct the services at the kraal when Moffat found it necessary to absent himself on missionary tours. These he made frequently. This missionary rode a borrowed horse, to the back of the saddle of which was tied a blanket, in which was wrapped his Bible and hymnbook. His guide rode an ox. They were not encumbered with useless baggage; they carried only a pipe, some tobacco, and a tinder-box—for it was before the days of matches. Their living they managed to get wherever they might be. After a day's ride through the hot sun, they would ask a drink of milk at the village to which they came; and then, assembling the people in a corner of the cattle-fold, the missionary would tell the glad tidings he had come so far to bring. His sermon done, and some talk held with the people individually, the

THE PROPHETESS AT WORK.

preacher would lie down on a mat in the corner of a hut for the night. After another address in the morning, the preacher and his companion would ride on toward another village, where the same thing would be repeated. Often their only breakfast was a drink of milk and sometimes, on arriving in the evening at a point where they had expected to find a village, they would discover that lack of grass and water had compelled the inhabitants to drive their flocks and herds, and remove their rude huts and few belongings to some other point.

Moffat spent forty years in this work; and lived to see the missionary stations 'pushed as far as the head-waters of the Limpopo, in twenty-four degrees south latitude; Kolobeng being then the farthest station in the interior. His daughter became the wife of the most famous African missionary—David Livingstone. It is useless here to follow his work in detail, since the country which he traversed has been explored by travelers who have noted more closely than he the characteristics of the country, because they were less concerned with the welfare of the people. Moffat was, above all else, a missionary; that work, in his eyes, far transcended anything else in importance; hence there is but little space for him in a volume on the history of African exploration.

In regard to the missionary labors of Livingstone, we shall here say nothing; but when he returned to England after his first great journey and long residence in Africa, his account of his experiences gave a greater impulse to the missionary effort for this part of the world than anything else had ever done. It is in place to sum up the results of ninety years' labor by the emissaries of the London Missionary Society in Africa. There are about twenty principal stations, with fifty-two branches, including the Tanganyika mission in Central Africa. One of the chief stations, Kuruman, seven hundred and fifty miles due north from the Cape, was founded by Moffat and Hamilton in 1817; it was here that Livingstone found a church-house, a well-stocked garden, and a printing-press—evidences of civilization that surprised the newly arrived missionary not a little. It was here, too, that he found Mary Moffat, who had not then (1840) dreamed that she would one day become Mary Livingstone.

Twenty-five English missionaries and something more than a hundred native preachers carry on the work so nobly begun, and the stations of the society now have forty-two schools, with more than two thousand pupils. The communicants number nearly twenty-five thousand.

The Dutch Reformed Church is naturally, from the number of Boers there resident, a strong one in South Africa; and from the settlements as a basis, missionaries have gone out among the surrounding tribes, until between four and five thousand of the aborigines have been brought into the church, while more than twenty thousand others are under instruction.

When Livingstone had aroused enthusiasm in England in regard to African mission work, the two great universities, Oxford and Cambridge, resolved to institute a mission at the mouth of the Zambesi. Bishop Mackenzie was selected to take charge of it; and accompanied

A SLAVE MARKET.

by six Englishmen, and five colored men from the Cape, he arrived at the scene of his intended labors in 1861. But he was not long to work here. He became entangled in the terrible slavery broils, and made frequent trips to a country far from healthful; he contracted a fever through these journeys, which was neglected because the press of his duties was so great. He sank rapidly, and died in the hut of a native, situated on the edge of a dark forest. His companion read the burial service over his body; but in a few days more, he too was cut down by the terrible fever, and was buried in that strange land. Another and another fell victims to the climate, and in 1862 the attempt was, for the time, given up. It has since been revived, however, and a mission instituted, with headquarters at Zanzibar, and twelve laborers in the field, with as many assistants.

Shortly after the death of Livingstone, the Free Church of Scotland resolved to establish a memorial mission. Livingstonia was adopted as the name, and the southern end of Lake Nyassa as the site. Ten thousand pounds was the sum subscribed, and the Free Church of Scotland, the Established Church of Scotland and the United Presbyterian Church united in the enterprise. The work received a severe blow when Dr. Black, a young man of great promise, died; his last words were: "Africa must not be given up, though it should cost thousands of lives." True to this watchword, the work in this section has been carried on with unextinguishable zeal; and a companion mission station called Blantyre established some two hundred miles from Livingstonia.

The American Board for Foreign Missions began its work on the west coast of Africa in 1834. by establishing a station at Cape Palmas.

The same point has been chosen as a station by the American Episcopalians, who have also stations at other places not far distant.

The efforts of the Baptists of this country have been most vigorous in Liberia and the Yarriba country, where churches and schools have been established, and much good has been accomplished among the natives of the vicinity.

Most of the American missions are on the west coast of Africa. The first established was that of the American Baptist Missionary Union, in Liberia, in 1821. After eleven years, this was followed by the establishment of another station in the same locality by the American Presbyterian Board of Missions. The same year (1832) the Methodist Episcopal Missionary Society sent a missionary to Liberia, who died shortly after reaching that country. The good work was carried on, however, and others followed him to the dangerous charge, but without suffering the same fatal results from the climate. The work is now carried on chiefly by native workers, who are less liable to the dreaded African Fever than strangers; and the work is under the charge of a colored bishop (Taylor).

The "American Board" of Missions began its African work in 1834 at Cape Palmas; and two years afterward, the Protestant Episcopal Church of the United States established a station at the same point. This church sent out three missionaries, who worked faithfully among the dense population of the surrounding country. Not a little of their success was due, speaking from a purely secular point of view, to the fact that one of these missionaries was a physician, and was enabled to win the confidence of the natives by attending to their physical ills. Native helpers have been trained, schools have been established and a newspaper is published in the interests of the mission.

In South Africa the Boers or descendants of Dutch colonists and French Huguenots have done much for the Christianizing of the inhabitants. Wherever the African farmer went he carried his old Dutch Bible with him and with it went the spirit of prayer and devotion which always has characterized the Dutch nationality. The Boers established municipal government and built churches and schoolhouses and while they originally were nothing but hunters and tradesmen, still they carried with them a spirit of thrift and piety, which has had a very wholesome effect on the native population. After long struggles with the savages and a wild nature, the Boers established two independent republics, which existed until the recent war with England, which resulted in their overthrow. They are now organized into a British Colony with their own parliament and colonial government. Christianity is gradually gaining in Africa and the time is not very far distant when the Dark Continent will have surrendered to Christ. In fact, our religion is making more rapid progress among the child-like, unsophisticated natives there than in Asia, where an old civilization and philosophical speculation of a mostly assertive nature has rather predisposed the inhabitants for a pantheistic view than for the stern monotheism of the Christian religion.

CHAPTER XV.

THE AFRO-AMERICAN NEGRO AND THE SLAVE TRADE.

How the Slave Trade Originated—Cruelty of the Slave Traders—Efforts to Suppress It—Liberia, the Afro-American Republic—Its People and Government—Sacrificing a Child—Roasting People Alive—Breaking the Bones of Victims—Adventures of the Cannibals—The Value of Female Slaves.

WHEN Roosevelt landed in Africa the iniquitous slave trade, which had flourished for centuries, had long ago been suppressed, and only a faint shadow of its horrors was still hovering over the eastern territories of the continent. The first traces of this nefarious trade can be noted as far back as 1619, when slaves were brought from the western coast of Africa to Virginia. It is said that the first load consisted to 14 blacks. The trade proved profitable and increased from year to year and at present the descendants of these African negroes amount to an eighth of our population.

This traffic was carried on to such an extent that during the eighteenth century more than two million slaves were imported into the English colonies and sold there. In one single year 192 slave-ships carried 47,146 slaves. This, however, excited a great agitation, and the following year, 1772, all slaves in the British dominions were set free.

The cruelties that characterized the slave-trade are too nerve-racking to be told. The following incident told by the famous African explorer, Captain Baker and relating to his visit to Fatino, once the headquarters of the Central African slave-trade, is quite interesting.

Baker reached this place before any knowledge of his coming had been received by the old slaver, who, therefore, was wholly unprepared for his visitor. Baker saw active preparations going on for secreting the slaves, but it was too late. The slaver, Abou Laood, greeted him in the most cordial manner professing great delight at his visit. Knowing what this hypocrisy meant Baker received the address with a similar manifestation of friendship. At the same time, however, he desired to show the slave hunter that he was at the head of a force sufficient to put a stop to the nefarious trade. Accordingly he let his regulars engage into a sham battle, and to heighten the effect the band played several military airs, which brought thousands of natives to the scene. The buglers, cymbals and bass-drums proved irresistable to the Africans, who are passionately fond of music; and the safest way to travel in those wild countries is to play the cornet, if possible without ceasing, which would secure a safe passage. An Italian organ grinder would

CAPTAIN SAMUEL BAKER.

march through Central Africa, followed by an admiring and enthusiastic crowd, who, if his tunes were lively, would form a dancing escort of most untiring material.

DANCING VENUSES.

As the troops returned to their quarters, with the band playing rather lively airs, women were observed running down from their villages, and gathering from all directions toward the common center. As they approached nearer, the charms of music were overpowering, and, halting for an instant, they assumed the most graceful attitudes, and then danced up to the band. In a short time the buglers could hardly blow their instruments for laughing at the extraordinary effects of the female dancers. A fantastic crowd surrounded them, and every minute added to their number. Even the babies were brought out to dance; and these infants strapped to their mothers' backs, and covered with pumpkin shells, like young tortoises, were jolted about by their infatuated mothers without the slightest consideration for the weakness of their necks. As usual among all tribes in Central Africa, the old women were even more determined dancers than the young girls. Several old Venuses made themselves extremely ridiculous, as they sometimes do in civilized countries when attempting the allurements of younger days.

When their king dies his body is slowly roasted on a gigantic gridiron over a fire until it resembles an overdone jack-rabbit. It is then wrapped in bark-cloths and lies in state until his successor is elected and ascends the throne after bloody fights with other pretenders that might last for years. An immense pit or trench is now dug, capable of containing several hundred people. This den is lined with bark-cloths. The late king's wives are seated at the bottom to receive upon their trembling knees the carcass of their departed lord. The previous night the king's body-guard surround the dwellings and seize the people indiscriminately as they issue from their doors and bring them to the pit's mouth. Their legs and arms are broken with warclubs, and they are pushed into the pit on the top of the king's body and his unfortunate wives. An immense din of drums, horns, flageolets and whistles, mingled with the yells of a frantic crowd, drown the shrieks of the sufferers, upon whom the earth is shoveled and stamped down by thousands of cruel fanatics, who dance and jump upon the loose mould so as to force it into a compact mass, through which the victims of their horrid sacrifice cannot grope their way. At length the mangled mass is buried and trodden down beneath a hummock of earth, and all is still.

A regular traffic was maintained between the traders of Uganda, in which young girls were made the object of barter. A plump, young girl was usually sold for a first-class elephant tusk or in some cases for a dozen needles and a new shirt. This was termed legitimate trade but some slavers took a less expensive way of securing female slaves, for they made war on the people, massacred the males and bore away the female prisoners as slaves. Slavery of girls was, moreover, encouraged by the shameful usuage of fathers selling their daughters to the highest bidder, who might use them either as slaves or wives. A large family of girls was, therefore, a source of revenue to the father, who disposed of them in exchange for trinkets or cows, of which latter usually twelve to fifteen are paid for a fine looking young girl.

Thanks to the efforts of the Christian missionaries and civilized governments of Europe and America these vicious practices had ceased long before Roosevelt put his foot on the soil where they once had been perpetrated. And had they not, we may rest assured that he would at once have put a stop to them.

Vile as the slave trade was it almost seems as if it had been a means in the hands of Divine Providence to help lift the Dark Continent out of the abyss of savagery and barbarism, for the descendants of the former slaves are returning to sow the seed of Christianity and organized government among their kindred. On the west coast of Africa is the little negro republic of Liberia with a coast line of about 300 miles and extending 250 miles into the interior, including about 75,000 square miles of territory.

The republic is at present inhabited by about 24,000 descendants of American negroes and 1,000,000 native Africans. The government is of course in the hands of the former, who speak the English language and try to uphold the banner of American civilization among the aborigines, who are divided in many tribes, speaking various dialects, and just emerging from the night of barbarism, under the dark shadow of which their ancestors not very long ago used to sacrifice children to propitiate their angry gods, roast people alive, break the bones of their victims, treat their women as slaves, and eat their enemies or captives. The torch of Christianity is now lighting up the darkness and spreading the gospel of Love and Wisdom in the former wilderness—thanks to the efforts of philanthropic Americans.

CHAPTER XVI.

LIVINGSTONE, THE MISSIONARY AND EXPLORER.

His Education and Early Ambitions—His Thirst for Knowledge—Studies Whole Morning in Factory—Intended to Go to China but Was Providentially Directed to Africa—His Exciting Experiences, Thrilling Adventures and Epoch-Making Discoveries in the Dark Continent.

AS Roosevelt sat on the deck of the magnificent steamer Hamburg, plying its way through the blue waves of the Mediterranean and leaving behind him Europe with its memories and ancient civilizations he might have been seen re-reading the fascinating life story of Livingstone, the great and famous explorer who first opened the Dark Continent to advancing civilization.

Livingstone's life excels in fascinating interest. It tells us about a youth who from his earliest years was inspired with an insatiable thirst for knowledge and actuated by high and noble motives. He tells us how at the age of ten he was put in a cotton factory to aid by his earnings in lessening his mother's anxiety. With part of his wages he bought books, attended an evening school and his mother often had to snatch the books out of his hands to prevent him from spending the whole night in studying. His working hours in the factory were from six in the morning till eight at night and his reading while at work was carried on by placing the book on a portion of the spinning jenny, so that he could catch sentence after sentence as he passed at his work. This enabled him to support himself while attending medical and Greek classes in Glasgow in winter and divinity lectures in summer. He never received a lift from anyone and no doubt should have accomplished his project to go to China as a medical missionary by his own efforts, had not friends advised him to join the London Missionary Society on account of its unsectarian character, which exactly agreed with his ideas, for in his own words it "sends neither Episcopacy, nor Presbyterianism, nor Independency, but the Gospel of Christ to the heathen."

This society sent him not to China, where the opium war then was raging, but to Africa, whose first successful apostle he was destined to become. He set sail for the Cape and from this point proceeded to Kuruman, the farthest inland station of the Society. Here he stayed six months to learn the language of the natives and then continued his journey partly on foot, because his oxen were sick, to the valley of Mobatsa, which he selected as the site of a missionary station. This village was much annoyed by lions and here occurred one of his most famous adventures. We let him tell it in his own words:

"It is well known that if one of a troop of lions is killed, the others take the hint and leave that part of the country. So, the next time the herds were attacked, I went with the people, in order to encourage them to rid themselves of this annoyance by destroying one of the marauders. We found the lions on a small hill about a quarter of a mile in length, and covered with trees. A circle of men was formed round it, and they gradually closed up, ascending pretty near to each other. Being down below on the plain with a native school-master, named Mebalwe, a most excellent man, I saw one of the lions sitting on a piece of rock within the now closed circle of men. Mebalwe fired at him before I could, and the ball struck the rock on which the animal was sitting. He bit at the spot struck, as a dog does at a stick or stone thrown at him; then leaping away, broke through the circle and escaped unhurt. The men were afraid to attack him, perhaps on account of their belief in witchcraft. When the circle was re-formed, we saw two other lions in it; but we were afraid to fire lest we should strike the men, and they allowed these beasts to break through also. If the Bakatla had acted according to the custom of the country, they would have speared the lions in the attempt to get out. Seeing we could not get them to kill one of the lions, we bent our footsteps toward the village; in going round the end of the hill, however, I saw one of the beasts sitting on a piece of rock as before, but this time he had a little bush in front. Being about thirty yards off, I took a good aim at his body through the bush, and fired both barrels into it. The men then called out: 'He is shot! He is shot!' Others cried: 'He has been shot by another man, too; let us go to him!' I did not see any one else shoot at him, but I saw the lion's tail erected in anger behind the bush, and turning to the people, said: 'Stop a little, till I load again.' When in the act of ramming down the bullets, I heard a shout. Starting and looking half round, I saw the lion just in the act of springing upon me. I was upon a little height; he caught my shoulder as he sprang, and we both came to the ground below together. Growling horribly close to my ear, he shook me as a terrier dog does a rat. The shock produced a stupor similar to that which seems to be felt by the mouse after the first shake of the cat. It caused a sort of dreaminess, in which there was no sense of pain nor feeling of terror, though quite conscious of all that was happening. It was like what patients partially under the influence of chloroform describe, who see all the operation, but feel not the knife. This singular condition was not the result of any mental process. The shake annihilated fear, and allowed no sense of horror in looking round at the beast. This peculiar state is probably produced in all animals killed by the carnivora; and if so, is a merciful provision by our benevolent Creator for lessening the pain of death. Turning round to relieve myself of his weight, as he had one paw on the back of my head, I saw his eyes directed to Mebalwe, who was trying to shoot him at a distance of ten or fifteen yards. His gun, a flint one, missed fire in both barrels; the lion immediately left me, and attacking Mebalwe, bit his thigh. Another man, whose life I had saved before, after he had been tossed by a buffalo, attempted to spear the lion while he was biting Mebalwe. He left Mebalwe and caught this man by the shoulder, but at that moment the bullets that he had received took effect, and he fell down dead. The whole was the work of a few moments, and must have been the paroxysms of his dying rage. * * * Besides crunching the bone into splinters, he left eleven teeth wounds in the upper part of my arm.''

Livingstone had attached himself to a tribe known as the Bakwains, whose chief was converted to Christianity. He thought that the missionary's methods were too slow and recommended whips of rhinoceros hide as more effective, which help in evangelizing of course was declined. The chief was a polygamist and a noted rain-doctor. But he finally consented to send away his many wives and instead of doctoring the skies dug an irrigation canal, which supplied the country with all the

ELEPHANT AND ITS YOUNG.

water it needed. After having staid there for some time, built school-houses and other buildings, and christianized the greater part of the tribe Livingstone continued his expedition northward until he discovered the shallow and muddy Lake Ngami.

They witnessed many sights peculiar to this part of the world. One occurrence that particularly excited their curiosity was the behavior of a herd of elephants when drinking at the river. These huge animals would play like so many children in the water, throwing great quantities of it over each other, and screaming with delight at the fun. On finishing their sport and endeavoring to leave the water at a point where the bank was quite steep, a comical sight ensued of their desperate struggles to get out. The elephants about Ngami, they observed, were much smaller than farther south, the variation in height being as much as three feet.

Several new kinds of animals were observed; and many different species of fish. The natives living along the Zouga are determined fishermen, for much of their food is drawn from the water. They use nets knotted like those of other countries; and also spear the fish with javelins having a handle so light that it readily floats on the surface. They show great dexterity in harpooning the hippopotamus; and the barbed blade of the spear being attached to a rope made of the young leaves of the palmyra, the animal cannot rid himself of the canoe, attached to him in whale fashion, except by smashing it, which he frequently does with his teeth or by a stroke of his hind foot.

Proceeding further to the north he discovered the majestic Zambesi River, one of the largest waterways of the world. The country being very unhealthy he now sent his wife and children back to England and turned his steps alone to the interior.

His journey was a slow one, delayed as it was by accidents and ravages of the Tsetse or fever fly. It was the last day of the year when he arrived at Kolobeng. By the middle of January they reached the Kalahari desert, but an unusual quantity of rain having fallen they did not suffer for water. Lions and ostriches are numerous in this country. Livingstone says of this bird:

"The ostrich is generally seen quietly feeding on some spot where no one can approach him without being detected by his wary eye. As the wagon moves far along to the windward he thinks it is intending to circumvent him, so he rushes up a mile or so from the leeward, and so near to the front oxen that one sometimes gets a shot at the silly bird. When he begins to run, all the game in sight follows his example. I have seen this folly taken advantage of when he was feeding quietly in a valley open at both ends. A number of men would commence running, as if to cut off his retreat from the end through which the wind came; and although he had the whole country hundreds of miles before him by going to the other end, on he madly rushed to get past the men, and so was speared. He never swerves from the course he once adopts, but only increases his speed.

OSTRICH HUNTING IN THE DESERT.

"When the ostrich feeds, his pace is from twenty to twenty-two inches; when walking, but not feeding, it is twenty-six inches; and when terrified, as in the case noticed, it is from eleven and a half to thirteen and even fourteen feet in length. Only in one case was I at all satisfied of being able to count the rate of speed by a stop-watch, and if I am not mistaken, there were thirty in ten seconds; generally one's eye can no more follow the legs than it can the spokes of a carriage-wheel in rapid motion. If we take the above number, and twelve feet stride as the average pace, we have a speed of twenty-six miles an hour. It cannot be very much above that, and is therefore slower than a railway locomotive. They are sometimes shot by a horseman making a cross cut to their unde-viating course, but few Englishmen ever succeed in killing them."

In May he arrived at Linganti, the capital of Makololo, where he was taken with the fever. Anxious to try the native cure for this disease he gave himself up to the treatment of one of the Makololo doctors. Of the result he says: "After being stewed in their vapor baths, smoked like a red herring over green twigs, and charmed secundum artem, I con-cluded that I could cure the fever much quicker than they." He offered to teach them to read but they declined alleging that it might make them content with one wife like other converts to Christianity.

After remaining at Linyanti for about a month, Livingstone set out to ascend the river, Sekeletu, who had volunteered to accompany him, being his companion, together with about one hundred and sixty of his tribe. They traveled on land for some distance, but finally took to the canoes, of which thirty-three were required for the transportation of their party.

The river was one which had never been explored by a white man thus far from the coast; and Livingstone could not sufficiently admire its grandeur. Along the banks were villages and fields which gave evi-dence of an industrious and prosperous people. They met with no particular difficulties in the ascent except at the cataract of Gouye, where the canoes had to be carried overland for more than a mile. The river was sufficiently high to make it possible to pass the rapids without portage.

Their journey, however, was not attended by any special adventure until they reached Njambi, a village of the Chiboque. They arrived here on Saturday, and the missionary expected to spend the ensuing Sunday in talking to the people. But his expectations were not fulfilled. The chief refused the gift of the hump and ribs of an ox which Living-stone had killed, and demanded that the traveler should present him with a man, an ox, or a gun. Oxen they had none to spare; of guns they had but five; and the missionary had no notion of leaving one of his faithful servants in slavery. The young Chiboque brandished their weapons threateningly, but Livingstone was firm. He declared that he and his people would not strike the first blow, but that if attacked they would defend themselves.

"It was rather trying for me, because I knew that the Chiboque would aim at the white man first; but I was careful not to appear flurried, and, having four barrels ready for instant action, looked quietly at the savage scene around. * * * The chiefs and counselors, seeing that they were in more danger than I, did not choose to follow our decision that they should begin by striking the first blow, and then see what we could do, and were perhaps influenced by seeing the air of cool preparation which some of my men displayed, and the prospect of a work of blood."

A compromise was finally effected, and the party passed on. But their experience here was only an earnest of what would await them in the country to the west.

In the meantime his Makololo attendants improved the time by becoming acquainted with the wonders of European architecture. They had been unable to comprehend how a house could be two stories high; since their huts are made by sticking the poles in the ground so as to form a cone, and covering that with skins or thatch, they could not understand how the poles for the second story were provided with a foundation, or what use the second floor would be, with the peak of the lower hut projecting above its floor. One of them, who had seen Livingstone's house at Kolobeng, described it as a mountain with several caves in it. Now, however, they all understood this much. The English vessels in port were another source of wonder; and they gravely pronounced these "towns;" designating them particularly as "towns that you climb into with a rope." The statement that these vessels, with their huge guns, were used to put down the slave-trade, afforded the poor creatures unalloyed gratification.

Some of the difficulties of traveling through an African forest are succinctly stated in the following lines:

"We pushed on through forests abounding in climbing plants, many of which are so extremely tough that a man is required to go in front with a hatchet; and when the burdens of the carriers are caught, they are obliged to cut the climbers with their teeth, for no amount of tugging will make them break. The paths in all these forests are so zig-zag that a person may imagine he has traveled a distance a thirty miles, which, when reckoned as the crow flies, may not be fifteen.''

During this journey Livingstone suffered from twenty-seven attacks of fever and, therefore, was glad to at last arrive at Libonta, where he and his party were particularly cordially received; for they were looked upon as men risen from the dead; the most skilful diviners having long before declared that they had perished. The missionary's means, acquired in Loanda, had all been spent, during a journey in which many delays had occurred, but this made no difference to the natives whose love had been won long before. They knew that Liv-

HIPPOPOTAMI.

ingstone had been engaged in an effort to open the country to trade, and to suppress the slave-trade, and that was enough for them. Even Livingstone's men said: ''Though we return as poor as we went, we have not gone in vain.''

One of the adventures of the party shortly after they left Libonta is worth recording, as a characteristic accident:

''I left Naliele on the 13th of August, and when proceeding along the shore at midday, a hippopotamus struck the canoe with her forehead, lifting one-half of it quite out of the water, so as nearly to overturn it. The force of the butt she gave tilted Mashauana out into the river; the rest of us sprang to the shore, which was only about ten yards off.

Glancing back, I saw her come to the surface a short way off, and look at the canoe, as if to see if she had done much mischief. It was a female, whose young one had been speared the day before. No damage was done except wetting person and goods. This is so unusual an occurrence, when the precaution is taken to coast along the shore, that my men exclaimed: 'Is the beast mad!' There were eight of us in the canoe at the time, and the shake it received shows the immense power of this animal in the water."

Long before this, Livingstone had heard that a party of Matabele had brought a number of parcels to the south bank of the Zambesi, and left them there in the care of the Makololo. The two tribes are sworn enemies, and the Makololo would not believe that Mr. Moffat had sent these goods to Dr. Livingstone, as the bearers told them. The Matabele answered:

"Here are the goods; we place them now before you, and if you leave them to perish the guilt will be yours."

After much divination, and with fear and trembling, the Makololo, who feared some attempt to bewitch them, built a hut over the parcels, and there Livingstone found them safe on his return in September, 1855, exactly a year after they reached that destination. Among other things, there was a copy of an address by Sir Roderick Murchison before the Royal Geographical Society, in which he stated his conviction that the interior of Africa was not a vast plateau, but a vast basin, flanked by mountains and highlands. This was the very same conclusion to which Livingstone had come, although with infinitely more difficulty:

"In his easy-chair he had forestalled me by three years, though I had been working hard through jungle, marsh, and fever, and since the light dawned upon my mind at Dilolo, had been cherishing the pleasing idea that I should be the first to suggest the idea that the interior of Africa was a watery plateau of less elevation than flanking hilly ranges."

From this point they went directly to Linyanti, where the men who had accompanied him were at last able to tell their own people of the wonderful things that they had seen. They had gone to the end of the world, and had only turned back when there was no more land.

Escorted by Sekeletu and his followers as far as the island of Kalai, two days' journey below the mouth of the Chobe, he determined to visit the great cataract of the Zambesi to which he has given an English name—Victoria Falls:

"Of these we had often heard since we came into the country; indeed, one of the questions asked by Sebituane was, 'Have you smoke that sounds in your country?' They did not go near enough to examine them, but viewing them with awe at a distance, said, in reference to the vapor and noise, *'Mosi oa tunya'* (smoke does sound there). It was previously called Shongwe, the meaning of which I could not ascertain. The word for a pot resembles this, and it may mean a seething caldron, but I am not certain of it. Being persuaded that Mr. Oswell and myself were the very first Europeans who ever visited the Zambesi in the center of the country, and that this is the connecting link between the known and the unknown portions of that river, I decided to use the same liberty as the Makololo did, and gave the only English name I have affixed to any part of the country. * * * * After twenty minutes' sail from Kalai we came in sight, for the first time, of the columns of vapor appropriately called 'smoke,' rising at a distance of five or six miles, exactly as when large tracts of grass are burned in Africa. Five columns now arose, and, bending in the direction of the wind, they seemed placed against a low ridge covered with trees; the tops of the columns at this distance appeared to mingle with the clouds. They were white below, and higher up became dark, so as to simulate smoke very closely. The whole scene was extremely beautiful; the banks and islands dotted over the river are adorned with sylvan vegetation of great variety of color and form. * * * * The falls are bounded on three sides by ridges 300 or 400 feet in height, which are covered with forest, the red soil appearing among the trees. * * * I did not comprehend it until, creeping with awe to the verge, I peered down into a large rent which had been made from bank to bank of the broad Zambesi, and saw that a stream of a thousand yards broad leaped down a hundred feet and then became suddenly compressed into a space, of fifteen or twenty yards. * * * On the left side of the island we had a good view of the mass of water which causes one of the columns of vapor to ascend, as it leaps quite clear of the rock, and forms a thick unbroken fleece all the way to the bottom. Its whiteness gave the idea of snow, a sight I have not seen for many a day. As it broke into (if I may use the term) pieces of water, all rushing on in the same direction, each gave off several rays of foam, exactly as bits of steel, when burned in oxygen gas, give off rays of sparks. The snow-white sheet seemed like myriads of small comets rushing on in one direction, each of which left behind its nucleus rays of foam. I never saw the appearance referred to noticed elsewhere. It seemed to be the effect of the mass of water leaping at once clear of the rock, and but slowly breaking up into spray."

It was nearly the end of November when Sekeletu parted from him and returned home; Livingstone then turned toward the north, and traveled for a few days over a beautiful but uninhabited district. There was a great abundance of game here, and on several occasions the lions approached unpleasantly close to their camp, but did no damage.

They had just passed Zumbo when the traveling procession was interrupted in a manner that is well worth description:

"Tsetse and the hills had destroyed two riding oxen, and when the little one that I now rode knocked up, I was forced to march on foot. The bush being very dense and high, we were going along among the trees, when three buffaloes, which we had unconsciously passed above the wind, thought that they were surrounded by men, and dashed through our line. My ox set off at a gallop; and when I could manage to glance back, I saw one of the men up in the air about five feet above a buffalo, which was tearing along with a stream of blood running down his flank. When I got back to the poor fellow, I found that he had lighted on his face, and though he had been carried about twenty yards on the horns of the buffalo before getting the final toss, his skin was not pierced nor was a bone broken. When the beasts appeared, he had thrown down his load and stabbed one in the side. It turned suddenly upon him, and before he could use a tree for defense, carried him off. We shampooed him well, and in about a week he was able to engage in the hunt again."

CHAPTER XVII.

LIVINGSTONE'S SECOND JOURNEY THROUGH AFRICA

The Expedition to the Zambesi River—Livingstone and his Makololo—The Elephant Marshes
—To the Great Lake—Hippopotamus Trap—The Great Unwashed—Lake Nyassa—Ascent
of Zambesi—Insolent Ferrymen—The Victoria Falls—"The White Man Must Be Saved"
—Freeing Slaves—Heart Rending Stories—Slave Hunters' Escape—A Desolated Country
—Robbed— Arrival of Slaves.

D URING the course of his first journey Livingstone had become
thoroughly well acquainted with the slave-trade as carried on
in the interior of Africa. He believed the great remedy for the
existing evil would be the opening up of the country to commerce; if
the tribes of the interior could trade directly with the white man, and
exchange their ivory and other articles of produce for the cloths and
manufactured goods which they covet, there would be no temptation
for them to capture slaves and trade them for these desired articles.
It was for this reason that, having failed to find a suitable place for the
establishment of a missionary station, he gave up that idea, and made
his way across the continent to Loanda, and then back again to the
mouth of the Zambesi. Returning to England, his narrative of the time
which he had spent in Africa aroused men to a longing to increase the
missionary aid sent to that continent.

But Livingstone had advanced beyond the position of a missionary;
his views had broadened so that he was no longer content to spend his
days in one place, teaching the people around him; he was eager and
anxious to put down the slave-trade, by showing the people who supplied
the market that a more lucrative business could be established in the
development of the agricultural and mineral resources of their country.
The government and the Royal Geographical Society lent him their
heartiest aid; and the expedition to the Zambesi was undertaken very
soon after his return to England.

Livingstone was made consul, which, of course, gave this undertaking a semi-national character, and enabled him to deal with other powers to much better advantage. The most liberal provision was made in the way of supplies, which even included a small steam-launch, named the "Ma-Robert." This was sent out from England in sections, and put together at the mouth of the Zambesi.

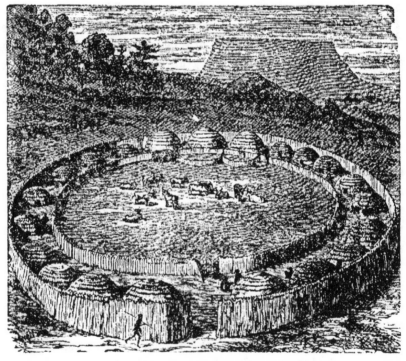

KAFFIR KRAAL.

Dr. Livingstone's brother, Rev. Charles Livingstone, who had been living for some years in the United States, was a member of the expedition; also Dr. Kirk, the celebrated botanist. They left England March 10, 1858, and reached the mouth of the Zambesi in May. Their instructions were to extend the knowledge already attained of the geography, and mineral and agricultural resources of Eastern and Central Africa; to improve their acquaintance with the inhabitants, and to endeavor to engage them to apply themselves to industrial pursuits and to the cultivation of their lands wih a view to the production of raw materials to be exported to England in return for British manufactures. Their first object was to explore the Zambesi, its mouths and tributaries, with a

SLAVES AND THEIR HARDSHIPS.

view to their being used as highways for commerce and Christianity to pass into the vast interior of Africa. They entered the River Luawe first, because its entrance is so smooth and deep that the vessel could easily go in without a boat sounding ahead. Here the Ma-Robert was screwed together, and launched as the proper vessel for these coast explorations.

They found the Luawe unnavigable at a short distance above its mouth, by reason of the vegetable matter in the channel; after ascending about seventy miles, it ended in a marsh, being only a tidal river after all. They now resolved to try the East Luabo, as the main stream of the Zambesi is called. This proved to be the river which they sought, although it was not then known that the Zambesi has four separate mouths.

The Pearl, the vessel in which they had come from England, accompanied the Ma-Robert as far as the Island of Simbo; when finding that the river was becoming too shallow for her draught (9 feet 7 inches) she steamed down the river, after having landed the goods belonging to the expedition on a small island; and the expedition to the Zambesi was fairly launched on its independent career.

The country around the mouth of the Zambesi had long been in the possession of the Portuguese; but their maps of it had been anything but reliable. It is charged that they had represented the Quillimane as the true mouth of the Zambesi, in order to promote and protect the slave trade; if the British vessels, and those of other nations, sent out to watch for slavers, could be persuaded to keep a close lookout on the Quillimane, as the outlet of the Zambesi, the slavers could readily sail down the true Zambesi and get safely out to sea before they should be discovered. Be this as it may, it is certain that one official Portuguese map had the mouth of the Mazaro, a narrow creek which in time of flood communicates with the Quillimane, as the point at which the Zambesi began to discharge its waters into the more northern river. As a fact, this creek is some six or eight feet above the level of the Zambesi, except, as mentioned, during periods of very high water.

Arrived at the mouth of this creek, the members of the expedition found that they had run into a veritable hornets' nest. A half-caste named Mariano or Matakenya had built a stockade near the mouth of the Shire, and carried on his trade as a slave-hunter. So long as he confined his depredations to the tribes of the interior, the indignation of the Portuguese settlers was not aroused; but he was allowed to send his kidnaped victims in chains to Quillimane, thence to be sent to the French Island of Bourbon. But as soon as Mariano began to practice violence on the people nearer at hand, under the very guns of the fort, the whites began to protest. Mariano paid no attention; and Dr. Livingstone was told, by a gentleman of the highest standing, that it was no uncommon occurrence for a slave to rush into the room where the informant's family was at dinner, pursued by one of Mariano's men with spear in hand to murder him.

War was declared against Mariano, and a force was sent to take him. He resisted for a time; but knowing that Portuguese governors have small salaries, and are amenable to bribery, he went down to Quil-

A ZULU DINNER PARTY.

limane to "arrange" with the governor. But that official was of a different stamp from most of his predecessors; and clapped the atrocious murderer into prison. When the English explorers came into the country, Mariano's brother, Bonga, was at the head of the rebel forces; and the contest was waging fiercely.

The fact that they were Englishmen proved to both parties at once what were their opinions regarding the slave trade; yet they were regarded as friends by Bonga's forces as well as by the Portuguese. On more than one occasion, they were almost in the midst of a fight; but happily escaped unharmed, and able to preserve their neutrality.

The right bank of the Zambesi is held by the Landeens or Zulus, to whom the Portuguese pay a pretty heavy annual tribute. Regularly every year the Zulus come to Senna and Shupanga to collect this tribute, which is really paid by the few wealthy merchants of Senna. They submit to pay two hundred pieces (sixteen yards each) of cloth, besides beads and brass wire, etc., to secure themselves from being plundered in war. The Zulu is like the Irish landlord of tradition; the more his tenants cultivate, the higher tribute he demands. On asking some of the Portuguese why they did not try to raise certain highly profitable products, the Englishmen received this characteristic reply:

"What's the use of our cultivating any more than we do? The Landeens would only come down on us for more tribute."

They arrived at Tette Sept. 8, and Dr. Livingstone at once went ashore. He was received by the Makololo with the most affecting joy; tempered with a ludicrous respect for his new clothes. Some were hastening to embrace him; when others cried out:

"Don't touch him; you will spoil his new clothes."

LIVINGSTONE AND HIS MAKOLOLOS.

Dr. Livingstone had heard, while he was in England, that his Makololos who had not returned to their own country were to receive from the Portuguese government a sufficient support; but he found now that no such rumor had ever reached Africa; they had been given hoes and land sufficient for gardens by a generous officer of that government, but it had been a gift paid for out his own pocket; and they had maintained themselves by means of these gardens, and by cutting and selling wood. These now readily attached themselves to the expedition; and the leader was only too glad to have assistants whose faithfulness had been tried.

Ascending the river, they carefully examined the Kebrabasa Rapids. After making their way seven or eight miles up through the swift current, they saw that this was not feasible until they knew what was to come next; and anchoring the little steamer below the rapids, proceeded to ascend the bank of the stream on foot. The stones upon the path were so hot that the soles of the Makololo's feet were blistered; but still they continued to advance. The Makololo told Dr. Livingstone that they had always thought that he had a heart, but that now they knew he had none; and appealed to Dr. Kirk to return, since the leader must have gone mad before he determined to go where no living foot could tread. Unfortunately for the Makololo, Dr. Kirk did not understand a word of their language; and Dr. Livingstone, knowing him to be as anxious as himself to explore the Kebrabasa, did not think it worth while to translate.

At last, however, they arrived at the cataract of Morumba, which is a sloping fall of about twenty feet in thirty yards. It is sufficient to stop all navigation except in the highest floods, when the river sometimes rises eighty feet above the level of the dry season.

They retraced their footsteps, then; although not exactly over the same path; they crossed Mount Morumba, which rises very near the fall, and camped on its side the first night of their return journey. As their guide had told them, the people were very ready to sell them provisions as long as they appeared to be leaving the country; in fact the ignorant people manifested the most unreasoning opposition to an expedition the objects of which were beyond their comprehension. The story is told that shortly after their departure from Tette, the river rose a foot and became turbid. A native Portuguese went to the governor with a grave face and complained that that Englishman was "doing *something* to the river."

Finding that it was impossible to take their steamer of only ten-horse-power through Kebrabasa, and convinced that, in order to force a passage when the river was in flood, much greater power was required, due information was forwarded to her majesty's government, and application made for a more suitable vessel. In the mean time, they turned their attention to the River Shire, a northern tributary of the Zambesi, which joins it about a hundred miles from the sea. The Portuguese could tell them nothing concerning this stream, except that it was covered with a mass of aquatic plants, which they pronounced impassable. They received a hint, however, that it was not the duckweed, but the hostility of the natives which had caused the one Portuguese expedition for the exploration of this river to return without making any considerable progress.

Their first trip to the Shire was in January, 1859. A considerable quantity of duckweed floated on the river for the first twenty-five miles, but not enough to obstruct navigation. They met with the first obstruction at the village of a chief named Tingane. This chief had always been the barrier to all intercourse between the Portuguese black traders and the natives farther inland; but on the explorers telling him that they had come neither to take slaves nor to fight, but only to open up a path by which their countrymen might come to purchase cotton or anything else that he had to sell (except slaves) he became at once quite friendly, and the men who had been dodging behind trees to take aim at the strangers with their poisoned arrows, came out and listened to the words of the missionary.

They ascended the Shire for a distance of about one hundred miles from its mouth; although the windings of the river are such that this distance represents about two hundred miles of actual travel. At this point, their further progress was stopped by the rapids, the first of which was named by them Murchison Falls. During the time that they were ascending the river, the natives kept a strong guard on the bank, night and day; apparently distrusting the strangers. The general opinion which the natives of this portion of Africa entertain in regard to white men does not speak well for the Portuguese, the first whites with whom they became acquainted.

THE ELEPHANT MARSHES.

A second trip up the Shire was begun about the middle of March. Thanks to their conciliating behavior on the previous journey, they found the natives extremely well disposed toward them. Leaving the banks of the river about ten miles below the falls, Drs. Livingstone and Kirk, with a number of Makololo, started on foot for Lake Shirwa. They traveled in a northerly direction over a mountainous country, among people who did not seem to be well-disposed, and with guides who were far from being trustworthy. This unreliability was partly due to their ignorance of the country and the language; they asked to be led to

"Nyanja Mukulu," or Great Lake, meaning thereby Lake Shirwa; but since the word Nyanja, or Nyanza, means a lake, river, marsh, or even a rivulet, the guides did not clearly understand them, and conducted them to the Great Elephant Marsh.

From this point, the party pressed on without guides, or with crazy ones. Regarding these, Dr. Livingstone says:

"They were often under great obligations to the madmen of the different villages; one of these honored them, as they slept in the open

IN THE GREAT ELEPHANT MARSH.

air, by dancing and singing at their feet the whole night. These poor fellows sympathized with the explorers, probably in the belief that they belonged to their own class; and uninfluenced by the general opinion of their countrymen, they really pitied, and took kindly to the strangers, and often guided them faithfully from place to place, when no sane man could be hired for love or money."

The perseverance of the party was finally crowned with success; for on April 18 they discovered Lake Shirwa, a body of bitter water, having no outlet, and containing leeches, fish, crocodiles and hippopotami. Their point of view was at the base of Mount Pirimiti or Mopeupeu, on its south-southwest side. Thence the prospect northward ended in a sea horizon with two small islands in the distance; a larger one, resembling a hill-top and covered with trees, rose more in the foreground. Ranges of hills appeared on the east, and on the west stood Mount Chikala. The shore, near which they spent two nights, was covered with reeds and papyrus.

From the people living near the lake, they gathered that there was a much larger one to the north, separated from Shirwa only by a tongue of land. But they considered that enough had been done for one expedition; it would be better to return from this point, and, having gained the confidence of the natives as far as this, make another trip for the exploration of countries beyond. They accordingly went back to their vessel on the Shire.

They reached Tette June 23, and from that point proceeded to the Kongone for the necessary repairs upon their vessel. They again ascended the Zambesi in August, and about the middle of that month reached the mouth of the Shire, which they proposed to ascend once more, and make, from the head of navigation, an overland trip to Lake Nyassa.

HIPPOPOTAMUS TRAPS.

They found the banks lined with hippopotamus traps; for the animals were evidently very plentiful, if the tracks on the bank were any guide. The hippopotamus feeds only on land, and crops the grass as short and even as a mowing machine. The trap consists of a beam five or six feet long, armed with a spear-head or hard-wood spike, covered with poison, and suspended from an overhanging branch by a cord, which, coming down to the path, is held by a catch, to be set free when the brute treads on it. Being wary beasts, they are very numerous, even where these traps are plentiful. One got frightened by the ship as she was steaming close to the bank. In its eager hurry to escape it rushed on shore, and ran directly under a trap, when down came the heavily weighted beam on its back, driving the poisoned spear-head a foot deep into its flesh. In its agony it plunged back into the river, to die in a few hours, and afterwards furnished a feast for the natives. The poison on the spear-head affects only that part of the flesh which is directly around the wound, and this is always thrown away. In some places the descending wood is weighted with heavy stones, but in others the hard, heavy wood needs no extra weight.

As they passed the neighborhood of the Great Elephant Marsh, they saw many elephants; but these sagacious animals soon learned that the

NATIVES HUNTING AN ELEPHANT.

puffing monster was a thing to be avoided, and fled in terror before the approach of the steamer. They succeeded, however, in catching a fine young elephant alive, as he was climbing up the bank to follow his dam; but after he was drawn on board, he was wounded by one of the men, and died in a few days.

They left ship August 28, 1859, for the discovery of Lake Nyassa. The party numbered four whites, thirty-six Makololo, and two guides.

The party was unnecessarily large, but it was thought that the strength of numbers would prevent attack from natives inclined to be hostile, and command respect from others. For the same reason, each one carried a musket, although many of the Makololo had never drawn a trigger. They were a week in crossing the highlands in a northerly direction; and having reached the Upper Shire valley, some 1200 feet above the sea-level, they were detained for some days by the sickness of one of the white men.

They found that the natives of this region were considerably advanced, in respect to their manufactures. They weave cotton cloth, by painfully slow processes; make pottery, and dig the iron ore out of the hills and make it into good axes, spears, needles, arrow-heads, bracelets, and anklets. Every village has its charcoal-burners, its smelting-house, and its blacksmiths. They weave neat baskets from split bamboos, and make fish-nets of a plant-fiber from their hills.

THE GREAT UNWASHED.

These people, judging from the old men and women who came to look on the white men, are generally long-lived; but they do not owe their longevity to cleanliness; an old man told them that he remembered to have washed once in his life, but it was so long ago that he had forgotten how it felt. They were much annoyed by one man, who persisted in preceding them from village to village and proclaiming that they had wandered; that they did not know where they were going. Persuasions and remonstrances were alike in vain; finally, he was informed that they were going to take him down to the river and wash him; he disappeared and was seen no more.

The language here was so unlike those dialects with which Dr. Livingstone was acquainted, that they were obliged to have recourse to an interpreter. This man, Masakasa, had an unbounded faith in anything that was said in a book; on one occasion, this faith served them well. The natives had persistently asserted that there was no such lake as that of which they were in search; but Masakasa knew that the lake was mentioned in a book, and grew indignant accordingly.

"There is a lake," said he to the natives, "for how could the white men know about it in a book if it did not exist?"

Then they admitted that there was a lake; and were probably not a little impressed by the white man's magical knowledge of things he had never seen. They pressed on, and discovered Lake Nyassa a little before noon of September 16, 1859. They could make out that there were hills on both sides of the lake, looking from their point of view at the southern end; but the haze from burning grass prevented their seeing very far. They learned afterward that they preceded a German explorer, Dr. Roscher, by about two months in the discovery of this lake. The only results of his discovery, however, were told in the depositions of his servants after they arrived at the Cape; for he was murdered by the natives shortly after reaching the lake.

THE SLAVE TRADE.

They were now among the Ajawa, who furnished a large number of slaves to the market, and are more debased in this traffic than most other tribes, since they sell each other. The chief with whom they remonstrated seemed ashamed of selling his own people, but apologized by saying that he sold only those who were bad. The party made but a short stay at Lake Nyassa, being, as usual, anxious to persuade the natives that they had no other object in view than to see the country. After a land-journey of forty days, they returned to the vessel October 6. It was necessary to send two of their number across the country from the Shire to Tette; and Dr. Kirk and Mr. Rae, the engineer, undertook the journey. But during their absence, the vessel began to leak so badly that they were obliged to go to the Kongone again for repairs. The steel plates were defective, and had been damaged by some chemical action shortly after the vessel was launched, so that they were full of minute holes. It leaked so badly that they were frequently compelled to mop up the cabin floor, and the engines proved so unsatisfactory that the Ma-Robert was re-christened the "Asthmatic." Returning from the sea, it was nearly the end of April, 1860, before they again reached Tette.

ASCENT OF ZAMBESI.

As they proceeded up the Zambesi toward the country of the Makololo, they found that many of the Makololo, who had descended the river
with Dr. Livingstone in 1856, deserted them; the reason of this was, that
these men had formed new ties in Tette, marrying slave-wives; they
could not take their wives or children with them, and gradually deserted
the party until all who had married in Tette had left.　Yet at setting

CRUELTY OF SLAVE TRADERS.

out, they had declared that they wished to return to their own country.

They of course left the Asthmatic below, as she could not ascend the
Kebrabasa; this was no matter of regret to the Makololo who had been
compelled to cut the wood for her fires on the former journeys.　One of
them laughingly exclaimed in broken English:

"Oh, Kebrabasa good, very good; no let shippee up to Sekeletu, too muchee work, cuttee woodyee, cuttee woodyee; Kebrabasa good."

They arrived at the Chicova plains, the level country above the Kebrabasa hills, June 7, and at Zumbo, on the left bank of the Loanwa, on the 26th. Here they had some difficulty in getting ferried across the river; the ferrymen were all tipsy, and did not come when they were expected. Having a waterproof cloak, which could be inflated into a small boat, they sent one of their attendants across in this improvised canoe. At the summons thus delivered, three men brought them the shaky canoes, lashed together. Five men were all that could be taken at a trip; and after four trips, the ferrymen began to clamor for drink. The travelers had none to give; and they became insolent, declaring that not another man should cross that day. One of the Makololo began to remonstrate with them, when a loaded musket was presented at him by one of the trio. In an instant the gun was out of the rascal's hands, a rattling shower of blows fell on his back, and he took an involuntary header into the river. He crawled up the bank a sad and sober man, and all three fell at once from the height of saucy swagger to a low depth of slavish abjectness. The musket was found to have an enormous charge, and might have blown the Makololo to pieces but for the promptitude with which his companions administered justice in a lawless band. They were all ferried safely across the river by eight o'clock in the evening.

On the 4th of August they reached Moachemba, the first of the Batoka villages which then owed allegiance to Sekeletu. From this point, they could see distinctly, with the naked eye, the columns of vapor rising from Victoria Falls, although the cataract was twenty miles away. Here they learned that many of the Makololo had been regarded as dead, not having been heard of since they accompanied Dr. Livingstone to the sea. They also learned that a recent effort to establish a missionary station at Linyanti had proved a failure and been abandoned. On the 9th, they set out to visit the falls, in the canoes of a native named Tuba Mokoro, who was said to possess the best "medicine" for ensuring safety in the rapids above the falls. This important personage forbade all talking while in the canoes, as it might impair the power of the medicine; and the white men, fearing to distract the steersman's attention when it might be critically necessary for him to attend to his business, obeyed unhesitatingly. They found that the hippopotami had trodden down the fruit trees which Dr. Livingstone had planted on his previous visit; and now erected a strong hedge for protection to newly sown seeds. There was not much hope, however, but what the same animals would break down the hedge.

LEPROSY.

Arriving at the town of Sekeletu, they found that, as they had been told, the chief was afflicted with the leprosy. He had been treated by several different doctors of his own tribe, and was now under the care of an aged negress who had come from some distance especially to take this case. Sekeletu, however, insisted upon placing himself at once under the care of the white doctor; and Drs. Livingstone and Kirk gave him the best remedies, internal and external, that their store of medicines afforded. He considered that his disease was the result of enchantment practiced by one of his enemies, and could not be persuaded otherwise. It was the opinion of his white physicians that the disease was rather due to the inordinate quantities of matokwane, or Indian hemp, which he smoked; and they could hardly induce him to give it up while he was under their treatment.

They found, indeed, that many of the natives are slaves of this pernicious habit, which makes the smokers feel strong in body, but weakens and finally destroys the mind. Both men and women indulge freely in its use; although the men do not like their wives to follow their own example, and sometimes forbid it entirely.

Dr. Livingstone determined now to go to Linyanti, in order to procure some medicines and other articles which he had left there in his wagon, eight years before. He found them all intact, and the wagon in fairly good condition, although the cover was, as might be expected, very rotten. The people inquired affectionately after "Ma-Robert" and her children, and asked why he had not brought them.

"Are we never more to know anything of them but their names?" asked the affectionate creatures, whose love had been won years before.

Returning to Shesheke by a trip which required three days, the party left that point September 17, 1860, taking with them a number of Makololo who were to return with additional medicines for Sekeletu. The path now pursued was a little nearer the river than that by which they had come, in order to see Kalunda and the Moamba Falls. They passed over a rugged country, with many hills and perennial streams, of which the Sindi was the finest for irrigation. They encamped on the Kolomo on the 1st of October; and on the 5th, after crossing some hills, rested at the village of Simariango.

LANDING OF THE EXPLORERS ON THE ZAMBESI.

A considerable part of their journey eastward was made by water; and in at least one instance, their attendants showed their faithfulness. Entering the narrow gorge called Karivua, the huge waves of the mid-current began at once to fill the canoes. With great presence of mind, and without the least hesitation, two men lightened each by jumping overboard; they then ordered a Batoka to do the same.

"I cannot swim," he replied.

"Jump out, then, and hold on to the canoe," they answered him; "for the white men must be saved."

Swimming alongside, they guided the swamping canoes down the swift current to the foot of the rapid, and then ran them ashore to bale them out. Thanks to the bravery of these poor fellows, nothing was lost, although everything was well soaked. A few hundred yards brought them to another rapid; but as this was worse than the first the canoes had to be unloaded, and the goods carried about a hundred yards.

They continued their voyage down the river, not leaving their canoes until they arrived at Kebrabasa; here their bearers complained much about having to carry the goods, and wished that they had tried the rapids. This difficulty over, they reached Tette early on the morning of the 23rd of November, having been absent a little over six months. The Zambesi being unusually low, they remained at Tette till it rose a little, and then left on the 3rd of December for the Kongone. Here their vessel was laid up for repairs; but the attempt was useless. New leaks broke out every day; the engine-pump gave way; the bridge broke down; three compartments filled at night. On the morning of the 21st the vessel grounded on a sandbank and filled; she could neither be emptied nor got off; the river rose during the night, and all that could be seen of her the next morning was about six feet of her two masts. Thus ended the Ma-Robert, otherwise the Asthmatic.

On the 31st of January, 1861, their new ship, the Pioneer, arrived from England, and anchored outside the bar of the Kongone; but the weather being stormy, she did not venture into the harbor until five days later. Two cruisers came at the same time, on board one of which were Bishop Mackenzie and his assistants, for the Universities' Missions.

The bishop desired them to take him and his colleagues up the Shire as far as Chibisa's, supposing that that would be a suitable place to establish the mission; but Dr. Livingstone, remembering the fate of the station at Linyanti, and fearful that, as there were no medical men on the bishop's staff, they might fall victims to the African fever, objected very strongly to this plan. In addition to this reason, was another: the Portuguese government refused to open the Zambesi to the ships of other nations, and it was therefore impolitic to expend so much labor at this point, when others that were equally important and more easily accessible were neglected. Finally, it was decided that the bishop should accompany the Zambesi expedition to the Rovuma, which their new instructions bade them explore, and ascertain whether the country

FISHING IN THE ZAMBESI RIVER.

around its headwaters was suitable for the establishment of a station. The other members of the mission were to proceed in one of the cruisers, to Johanna, and there await the orders of their superior.

Arriving at the mouth of the Rovuma toward the end of February, it was not until the 11th of March that they proceeded up the river, which had fallen four or five feet while they were delayed at the mouth, awaiting the arrival of the bishop; for he had chosen to go this far in the cruiser Lyra. But the river fell rapidly as they ascended, and as the March flood is the last of the season, they saw that the only thing to save the Pioneer from being hopelessly grounded was to get her back to salt water as quickly as possible. Had the expedition been absolutely unincumbered, they would have left the ship and pushed on in boats or on foot, and done what they could toward the exploration of the river and Lake Nyassa, from which it was supposed to flow; but they were anxious to advance the work of the mission; and therefore, decided to return to the Shire, see the mission party safely settled, and afterward explore Lake Nyassa and the Rovuma from the lake downward. Fever broke out on board the Pioneer at the mouth of the Rovuma, and the vessel was soon left, through the illness of the officers, to the management of Dr. Livingstone.

They arrived at the mouth of the Zambesi after a prosperous voyage, and steamed up to the mouth of the Shire without any special adventure. Their vessel, however, was not well adapted for their purpose in one particular: her draught was too great, being five feet, for the Shire. Much of their time was spent in getting her off sand-bars, and she could not venture down the river until a rise had increased its depth.

FREEING SLAVES.

Arrived at Chibisa's village, they left the river, July 15, and with a sufficiently strong party, went inland to show the bishop a suitable station for the mission. Halting at the village of Mbame, they were told that a slave party on its way to Tette would presently pass through. "Shall we interfere?" they asked of each other. The question was a difficult one to answer, for all of their valuable goods had been left at Tette, and if they were to interfere to free these slaves, the owners of them might retaliate by procuring the destruction of these stores. But the slave-hunters had taken advantage of the expedition's opening the country to white men, and had persistently dogged their footsteps in places where they had never dared to venture before. The Englishmen therefore resolved to run all risks and put a stop, if possible, to the slave-trade, which had followed on the footsteps of their discoveries. A few minutes after Mbame had spoken to them, the slave party, a long line of manacled men, women and children, came wending their way around the hill and into the valley, on the side of which the village stood. The black drivers, armed with muskets, and bedecked with various articles of finery, marched jauntily in the front, middle, and rear of the line; some of them blowing exultant notes out of a long tin horn. They seemed to feel that they were doing a very noble thing, and might proudly march with an air of triumph; but the instant the fellows caught a glimpse of the English, they darted off like mad into the forest—so fast, indeed, that they caught but a glimpse of their red caps and the soles of their feet. The chief of the party alone remained, and he, from being in front, had his hand tightly grasped by a Makololo. He proved to be a well-known slave of the late commandant at Tette, and for some time the Englishmen's attendant while there. On asking him how he obtained these captives, he answered that he had bought them; but on inquiry being made of the people themselves, all, save four, said they had been captured in war. While this inquiry was going on, he bolted, after his men.

The captives knelt down, and in their way of expressing thanks, clapped their hands with great energy. They were thus left entirely on the hands of the whites, and knives were soon at work, cutting the women and children loose. It was more difficult to cut the men adrift, as each had his neck in the fork of a stout stick, six or seven feet long, and kept in by an iron rod which was riveted at both ends across the throat. With a saw, luckily in the bishop's baggage, one by one the men were sawn out into freedom. The women, on being told to take the meal they were carrying and cook breakfast for themselves and the children, seemed to consider the news too good to be true; but after a little coaxing, went at it with alacrity, and made a capital fire by which to boil their pots with the slave sticks and bonds, their old acquaintances through many a sad night and weary day. Many were mere children of five years and under. One little boy, with the simplicity of childhood, said to one of the liberators:

"The others tied and starved us; you cut the ropes and tell us to eat; what sort of people are you? Where did you come from?"

HEART-RENDING STORIES.

The stories that the captives had to tell were heart-rending: two women had been shot the day before for attempting to untie the thongs; this, the rest were told, was to prevent them from attempting to escape. One woman had her baby's brains knocked out because she could not carry the load and it; and a man was dispatched with an

AFRICAN REVIEW OF TROOPS.

axe because he had broken down with fatigue. Eighty-four, chiefly women and children, were liberated; and on being told that they were now free, and might go wherever they wished, or remain with their liberators, they all chose to stay; and the bishop decided that they should be attached to the mission, to be educated as members of a great Christian family.

They proceeded next morning to Soche's with their liberated party, the men cheerfully carrying the bishop's goods. As they had begun, it was of no use to do the things by halves, so eight others were freed in a hamlet on their path; but a party of traders, with nearly a hundred slaves, fled from Soche's on hearing of these proceedings. Dr. Kirk and four Makololo followed them with great energy, but they got off clear to Tette. Six more captives were liberated at Mongazi's, and two slave-traders detained for the night, to prevent their carrying information to a still larger party in the front. Of their own accord they volunteered the information that the governor's servants had charge of the next party; but the Englishmen did not choose to be led by them, though they offered to act as guides to his excellency's own agents. Two of the bishop's black men from the Cape, having once been slaves, were now zealous emancipators, and volunteered to guard the prisoners during the night. So anxious were these heroes to keep them safe, that, instead of keeping watch and watch, both kept watch together till toward four o'clock in the morning, when sleep stole gently over them both, and the wakeful prisoners, seizing the opportunity, escaped. One of the guards, perceiving the loss, rushed out of the hut, shouting:

SLAVE HUNTERS ESCAPE.

"They are gone! The prisoners are off! And they have taken my rifle with them, and the women, too! Fire! Everybody fire!"

The rifle and the women, however, were safe enough, the slave-traders being glad to escape alone. Fifty more slaves were freed the next day in another village; and, the whole party being stark naked, cloth enough was left to clothe them, better probably than they had ever been clothed before. The head of this gang, whom the liberators recognized as the agent of one of the principal merchants of Tette, said that they had the license of the governor for all that they did. This was no news to the Englishmen, who were convinced that it was quite impossible for any enterprise to be undertaken there without the governor's knowledge and connivance.

They now approached the Manganja country, where they had seen such evidence, on the previous journey, of progress in manufactures. The country was now desolated by a war between the inhabitants and the Ajawas; the villages were all deserted; the stores of corn were poured out in cartloads, and scattered all over the plains, and all along the paths, neither conquerors nor conquered having been able to convey it away. About two o'clock they saw the smoke of burning villages, and heard triumphant shouts, mingled with the wail of Manganja women, lamenting over their slain. The bishop then engaged the company of Englishmen in fervent prayer; and on rising from their knees, they saw a long line of Ajawa warriors, with their captives, coming round the hill-side. The first of the returning conquerors were entering their own village below, and were welcomed back by the women with "lillilooings." The Ajawa head man left the path on seeing the whites, and stood on an ant hill to obtain a good view of their party. They called out that they had come to have an interview with his people, but some of the Manganja, who followed them, shouted:

"Our Chibisa is come!"

Chibisa being well known as a great conjurer and general. The Ajawa ran off, yelling and screaming:

"*Nkondo! Nkondo!*" (War! War!)

The whites heard the words of the Manganja, but did not think of them at the moment as neutralizing all their own expressions regarding peace. The captives threw down their loads on the path, and fled to the hills; and a large body of armed men came running up from the village, and in a few seconds were all around the whites, though mostly concealed by the projecting rocks and long grass. In vain the Englishmen protested that they had not come to fight, but to talk with them. They would not listen, having good reason in the cry of "Our Chibisa." Flushed with recent victory over three villages, and confident of an easy triumph over a mere handful of men, they began to shoot their poisoned arrows, sending them with great force upward of a hundred yards, and wounding one of the Makololo through the arm. The slow withdrawal of the English up the ascent from the village only made them more eager to prevent their escape; and in the belief that this retreat was the evidence of fear, they closed upon the little party with bloodthirsty fury. Some came within fifty yards, dancing hideously; others, having quite surrounded them, and availing themselves of the rocks, and long grasses hard by, were in-

KAFFIR WARRIORS SKIRMISHING.

tent on cutting them off, while others made off with their women and a large body of slaves. Four were armed with muskets; and the Englishmen were obliged in self-defense to return their fire and drive them off. When they saw the range of the rifles, they very soon desisted and ran away; but some of them shouted to the whites from the hill the consoling intimation that they would follow, and kill them where they slept. Only two of the captives escaped to the Englishmen, but probably most of those made prisoners that day fled elsewhere in the confusion. The whites returned to the village which they had left in the morning, after a hungry, fatiguing, and most unpleasant day.

Though the explorers could not blame themselves for the course which they had pursued, they felt sorry for what had happened. It was the first time they had ever been attacked by the natives or had come into collision with them; though they had always taken it for granted that they might be called upon to act in self-defense they were on this occasion less prepared than usual, no game having been expected here. The men had only a single round of cartridge each; their leader had no revolver, and the rifle he usually fired with was left at the ship, to save it from the damp of the season. Had they known better the effect of slavery and murder on the temper of these blood-thirsty marauders, they would have tried messages and presents before going near them.

The bishop, feeling as most Englishmen would at the prospect of the people now in his charge being swept off into slavery by hordes of men-stealers, proposed to go at once to the rescue of the captive Manganja, and drive the marauding Ajawa out of the country. All were warmly in favor of this save Dr. Livingstone, who opposed it on the ground that it would be better for the bishop to wait, and see the effect of the check the slave-hunters had just experienced. On the bishop inquiring if in the event of the Manganja asking aid against the Ajawa, it would be his duty to accede to the request:

"No," replied Dr. Livingstone, "you will be oppressed by their importunities, but do not interfere in native quarrels."

It would have been better if the bishop had followed this advice, which he mentions in his journal.

The members of the mission now having proceeded far enough to be able to form their own opinion of the country, the Zambesi expedition left them, and returned to the ship. A few days after their return, a party consisting of Dr. Livingstone, Dr. Kirk, and Charles Livingstone started for Lake Nyassa with a light four-oared gig, a white sailor, and a score of attendants. They hired people along the path to carry the boat past the forty miles of the Murchison Cataracts for a cubit of cotton cloth a day. This was such magnificent pay, that twice the required number of men eagerly offered their services; crowds followed them.; and it was only by taking down the names of the porters engaged in the morning that they could dispute claims made by those who had only helped during the last ten minutes of the evening.

After passing the cataracts, they launched their boat upon the broad and deep waters of the Upper Shire, and were virtually on the lake, for the gentle current shows but little difference of level. The natives regard the Upper Shire as a prolongation of Lake Nyassa; for where what the explorers called the river approaches Lake Shirwa, a little north of the mountains, they said that the hippopotami, "which are great night travelers," pass from one lake into the other. There the land is flat, and only a short land journey would be necessary.

The geographical features of the lake which they now entered have become comparatively well known since that day, so that it is unnecessary here to enlarge upon the subject; nor were they impressed, as other discoverers have been, with the grandeur of the scene before them when they first came in sight of it. At this second entrance into Lake Nyassa, as on the previous occasion, the air was full of smoke from burning grass, and their view was consequently extremely contracted.

By Chitanda, near one of the slave-crossing places, they were robbed for the first time in Africa, and learned by experience that these people, like more civilized nations, have expert thieves among them. It might have been only a coincidence, but they never suffered from imprudence, loss of property, or were endangered, unless among people familiar with slaving. They had such a general sense of security, that never, save when they suspected treachery, did they set a watch at night. Their native companions had, on this occasion, been carousing on beer, and had removed to a distance of some thirty yards; that their free and easy after-dinner remarks might not be heard by their employers. Two of the whites had a slight touch of fever. Between three and four o'clock in the morning some light-fingered gentry came, while the explorers slept ingloriously—rifles and revolvers all ready—and relieved them of most of their goods. The boat's sail, under which they slept, was open all around, so that the feat was easy. One of them felt his pillow moving, but in the delicious dreamy state in which he lay, thought it was one of the attendants adjusting his covering, and so, as he fancied, let well enough alone.

ROBBED.

Their consternation on awaking in the morning and finding their clothing, beads, and rice gone, may well be imagined. Their first question to each other was: "Is the cloth gone?" For the loss of that would have been equivalent to all their money. Fortunately, the parcel had been used as a pillow that night, and thus was safe. The rogues left on the beach a pair of boots and the aneroid barometer, also some dried plants and fishes; but they carried off many other specimens which had been collected, some of the notes of the journey, and nearly all of their clothing. They could not suspect the people of the village where they lay; they had probably been followed by the thieves for several days, watching their opportunity.

They found that the northern end of the lake was the scene of lawlessness and bloodshed. So threatening did the various parties of natives appear, that the attendants of the explorers, who were making the journey by land, while the white men kept to the boat, became afraid to go on, unless a white man should join their party; and indeed, the danger was not small. Dr. Livingstone accordingly left the boat, and having taken the first morning's journey along with them, and directing the boat to call for him at a bay in sight, both parties proceeded north. In an hour Dr. Livingstone and his party struck inland, on approaching the foot of the mountains which rise abruptly from the lake. Supposing that they had heard of a path behind the high range which there forms the shore, those in the boat held on their course; but it soon began to blow so fresh that they had to run ashore for safety. While delayed for a couple of hours, two men were sent up the hill to look for the land party, but they could see nothing of them, and the boat party sailed as soon as it was safe to put to sea, with the conviction that the missing ones would regain the lake in front.

The boat passed a couple of parties, evidently lake pirates, who · assured them that there was a path behind the hills. Pursued by another party of pirates, they put their boat to its utmost speed to escape; and after sailing twelve or fifteen miles north of the point where Dr. Livingstone had left them, a gale compelled them to seek shelter in a bay. A succession of gales prevented their advancing or going back to the point whence they had started.

In the meantime, Dr. Livingstone and his party had tried the path behind the hills, and found it so bad as to be almost impassable. They therefore turned back to the coast, expecting to find the boat; but only saw it disappearing away to the north. They pushed on as briskly as possible after it, but the mountain-flank which forms the coast proved excessively tedious and fatiguing; traveling all day, the distance made, in a straight line, was under five miles. As soon as day dawned the march was resumed; and after hearing at the first inhabited rock that their companions had passed it the day before, seven Mazitu suddenly appeared before them. These demanded presents, and became boisterous; but the quiet persistence of Dr. Livingstone made them retreat. Their presence showed that there was more or less danger to be encountered. The next night was spent, unconsciously, on the very brink of a precipice; the party having traveled during every moment of daylight, and fearing to kindle a fire lest it should attract the attention of the Mazitu. The next night was also spent without fire, except a little for cooking the flesh of a goat which they killed. The next day, Dr. Livingstone was delighted to see the boat coming back, having been separated from his companions for four days.

Their exploration of the lake extended from the 2nd of September to the 27th of October, 1861; and having expended or lost most of the goods they had brought, it was necessary to go back to the ship. They reached the vessel November 8, in a very weak condition, having suf- - fered more from hunger than on any previous trip. Bishop Mackenzie came down to the ship to visit them, and gave a glowing account of his success at the mission. It was hoped that it could soon be made self-sustaining to a considerable degree.

The river was rapidly and steadily falling; and they were obliged to wait until it should begin to rise, before the Pioneer could cross the bars. Not until January 7 did they leave their anchorage at Ruo, reaching the Zambesi on the 11th. Arrived at Tette, they expected to be called to account, in some way, for liberating the slaves; but beyond a mere mention of the fact by one of the owners of the liberated captives, nothing was said; all the others seemed to be ashamed to speak of it.

CANOES ON LAKE SHIRWA.

Descending the Zambesi, they anchored in the Great Luabo mouth; and here, January 30, the British vessel Gordon arrived, bringing Mrs. Livingstone and some ladies who were to join their relatives connected with the Universities' Mission. This vessel also brought out the sections of a new iron steamer intended for the navigation of Lake Nyassa, called the Lady of the Lake, or Lady Nyassa. Owing to the rivers being in flood, their progress up stream was extremely slow;

and they were finally obliged to put the hull of the Lady Nyassa together, and tow her up to Murchison Falls.

They were naturally anxious, as they progressed, to receive news of the mission; but it was some time before they were able to learn anything of it. At last, however, they learned that the bishop and Mr. Burrup had both died, from the consequences of exposure during a trip undertaken to rescue some of their "Mission family" of liberated slaves, who had been recaptured. The bishop's sisters and Mr. Burrup's wife had arrived on the Gordon, and just reached the Shire in time to learn the sad news of the two deaths.

Shortly after this, the surviving members of the mission decided to remove to the lower Shire valley—a course which had the fatal consequences that Dr. Livingstone foresaw.

DEATH OF MRS. LIVINGSTONE.

Many members of the Zambesi expedition were prostrated by the fever, which seems to have raged with unusual virulence this year; and they noticed that an extraordinary number of natives wore the stripes of palm-leaf which are their sign for sickness and mourning. In April, Mrs. Livingstone was taken down; and after a few days' illness, died April 27, 1862. She had come out again to Africa, thinking to assist her husband in his work as she had done before; but was taken before she could reach those who affectionately remembered "Ma-Robert." She was buried at Shupanga, under the shade of a wide-spreading baobab tree.

After many delays, the Lady Nyassa was launched on the 23rd of June. In accordance with their customs, the natives hotly discussed the question of what would be the result of putting so much iron in the water; some affirming that it would go to the bottom at once, others asserting that the white men had powerful medicine that would enable them to keep even iron from sinking. Dr. Livingstone frequently notes the warm discussions which the negroes of this part of Africa hold over any question upon which they chance to differ; these discussions often ending in laying wagers as to the event of a given course.

15

When the discussion cannot be settled this way, one party will challenge the other to a foot-race, and the winner is held to have been in the right.

The Portuguese officials threw so many obstacles in the way of ascending the Zambesi, that they at last concluded to explore the Rovuma, at least until the water of the Zambesi should be at a stage which would not assist these officers in their efforts to detain them. They accordingly sailed for the mouth of the Rovuma. The first people with whom they met were inclined to be hostile; but as they ascended the river, they found them more friendly. At last, after traveling about a hundred and forty miles by the river's course from the sea, or nearly two degrees of longitude in a straight line from the coast, they were obliged to stop. The river was narrow and full of rocks, with a rapid divided into such narrow passages that only a native canoe could pass through them. The natives reported a worse place above their turning-point, the passage being still narrower. They now saw that their easiest path to Nyassa was by way of the Shire, even with the Portuguese officials in the way; and they decided to return and try that path again. They reached the Pioneer October 9, and put to sea nine days later.

Their destination as the Zambesi, but their fuel failed, and they were obliged to put into Quillimane. The delay thus occasioned brought them to the Zambesi so late in the season, that that river was very low, and their progress was correspondingly impeded. While waiting the March rise, they unscrewed the Lady Nyassa at a point about five hundred yards below the first cataract, and began to make a road over the thirty-five or forty miles of land portage by which to carry her up piecemeal.

The valley of the Shire had been well populated when they saw it on their former expeditions; but now, the results of the slave-trade, combined with those of a famine induced by drought, had turned the once smiling country into a wilderness. Everywhere that they turned, they saw desolation; and the living were not enough to bury the dead. Decaying corpses poisoned the atmosphere, or floated down the river in too great numbers for the over-gorged crocodiles to consume. The effect upon the spirits of the explorers may be imagined; and when to this feeling was added sickness, it was judged best that the two who suffered most severely physically, should return home. These were

CARRYING THE SILLL BOAT AND CUTTING A PATH THROUGH THE FOREST.

Dr. Kirk and Charles Livingstone. The parting took place May 19; and with them went all the whites that could be spared.

On the 2nd of July, a dispatch was received from Earl Russell, containing instructions for the withdrawal of the expedition. The attempt to open up this portion of Africa to trade was regarded as practically hopeless, while the Portuguese government maintained such an attitude—counteracting the effect of its open instructions to its

officials by actual private instructions, or by allowing abuses of authority which practically nullified the laws made in Lisbon. In the
then condition of the river, however, it was useless to attempt a return
to the sea.

They accordingly decided to make an exploratory journey on foot
to the northward. Crossing the country to the southern shores of
Lake Nyassa, they skirted the western coast of that body of water almost half-way to the northern end; then, by a three days' journey to
the westward, reached a village on the banks of a tributary of the
Loangwa. It was now the latter part of September; and if they were
to take advantage of the winter floods, they could not afford to go
farther. From this point, their path was, with slight variations, that
by which they had come. Reaching the ship, they took advantage of
a rise about the middle of January to sail down the Shire, and, after
some delays, occasioned by waiting to take on board some members of
the helpless "Mission family" of Bishop Mackenzie, the mission having now been abandoned, they reached Zanzibar April 16, 1864; and
after two weeks spent there, directed the course of the Lady Nyassa
to Bombay. Early in June, after sailing more than twenty-five hundred
miles, they sighted Bombay; the expedition to the Zambesi had come
to an end.

CHAPTER XVIII.

LIVINGSTONE'S LAST EXPEDITION.

THE Zambesi expedition, described in the previous chapter, was
substantially a failure; and no one felt this more keenly than
its illustrious leader. Not only had he spent thousands of pounds
of the Government's money and of his own, without attaining any ap-
preciable result, or at least any such result as had been expected, but
his failure had brought the whole subject of African exploration into
disfavor with his countrymen. He returned to England, a disappointed
man. But although the popular feeling was now as much against the
exploration of Africa as at the close of the first journey it had been in
favor of it, there were some whose interest was not lightly to be
changed. The president of the Royal Geographical Society still held
the work as of the same importance; and it was Sir Roderick Murchison who, almost as soon as he had returned, proposed that the explorer should undertake a third journey, for the purpose of fixing the
true water-shed of Inner Southern Africa. After much difficulty, Sir
Roderick persuaded that Government to advance five hundred pounds
for this purpose; the Council of the Royal Geographical Society subscribed as much more; and "a valued private friend" of Dr. Livingstone's placed a further thousand pounds at his disposal.

The expedition was organized at Bombay, and proceeded thence
to Zanzibar. From this point, Livingstone sailed down the coast to
Mikindany Bay, near the mouth of the Rovuma River; thence they
were to proceed overland to Lake Nyassa.

ATTENDANTS AND ANIMALS.

His attendants numbered thirty-six. Of these, three had been with him on the previous trip, employed, not at the beginning, but after the arrival of the Pioneer; of these we shall have occasion hereafter to single out Susi by name. Two of his attendants were among the slaves liberated by the party when Bishop Mackenzie was with it; of these, Chuma is the one whose name has been perpetuated by what he did for his master.

TRAVELERS AND THE MIRAGE.

Six camels, two buffaloes and a calf, two mules, and four donkeys, were the animals attached to the expedition. It should be noted that while the bite of the tsetse is fatal to the horse and to cattle, it does not affect the donkey or the mule any more than it injures the wild beasts or man. This fact will explain the reason for selecting these animals.

They reached Rovuma Bay March 22, 1866; and landed April 6, at the point chosen. Then the march began, nearly due west, as they followed the course of the river. The journey to the lake is marked only by misfortunes. The camels proved as vulnerable to the tsetse as cattle, and all died from the bites. The mules and three donkeys succumbed to the ill-usuage of their drivers. The thirteen Sepoys mutinied, and then proved so worthless that Dr. Livingstone was obliged to dismiss them; the ten Johanna men deserted in a body; one of the nine Nassick boys died, and another met some of his friends and concluded to remain with them. Thus the expedition of thirty-seven which had left Zanzibar had dwindled down to a little group of twelve persons.

The first hundred pages of his journal of this expedition are melancholy reading; containing, as they do, little beyond the record of events which would have discouraged a less determined explorer to the point of retracing his footsteps and giving up the effort: and of devices for easing the pangs of hunger; for which the folly and laziness of the attendants themselves were largely responsible. But Livingstone's was too great a mind to be shaken by such adverse winds as these; and he pressed steadily forward.

THE OPEN SORE OF THE WORLD.

There is yet another element of sadness in these early pages of his journal. Even in the first stages of his journey, there was again laid bare to his eyes "the great open sore of the world," as the slave-trade has fitly been styled. In a little more than two months after leaving the coast, the first indications that they were on the track of the slave-traders appeared. First, they passed by a woman tied by the neck to a tree, and dead; the people of the surrounding country explained that she had been unable to keep up with the other slaves in a gang, and her master had determined that she should not become the property of any one else if she recovered after resting a time. They saw others tied up in a similar manner, and others lying in the path shot or stabbed, a pool of their own blood surrounding them. The explanation which the traveler invariably received was that the Arab who owned these victims was enraged at losing his money by the slaves be-coming unable to march, and vented his spleen by murdering them. Dr. Livingstone remarks that the traders are quite well aware that such an example as this spurs the others to renewed endeavors to keep up with the march, even when their strength is rapidly failing them. In other cases, they found slaves who were dying of starvation, having been abandoned because they could not go on, or because the trader found his stock of provisions insufficient for those under his charge.

On the 8th of August, he again reached the shores of Lake Nyassa, this time at the mouth of the Masinje River. "It was as if I had come back to an old home I never expected again to see," he writes; "and pleasant to bathe in the delicious waters again, hear the roar of the sea, and dash in the rollers." He remained at this point for several days, taking observations, and writing up his journal fully. Then he skirted the southern shore of the lake, reaching the western borders September 25.

It had been his intention to strike directly north-west from Nyassa for the exploration of Lake Tanganyika; but the intervening country was filled with hostile Mazitu, and it was not safe for his little party to attempt to cross it. He therefore resolved to journey directly west until he reached the Zalyanyama Mountains, and then to proceed nearly due north until the lake was reached.

AN AFRICAN SPONGE.

Most of the country crossed in this westward journey was lowland, of the kind known in Africa as "sponges." Wherever a plain sloping toward a narrow opening in hills or higher ground exists, we have the conditions requisite for the forming of an African sponge. The vege-tation, not being of a peat-forming kind, falls down, rots, and then forms a rich black loam. In many cases, a mass of this loam, two or three feet thick, rests on a bed of pure river sand, which is revealed by crabs and other aquatic animals bringing it to the surface. In the dry season, the black loam is cracked in all directions, and the cracks are often as much as three inches wide, and very deep. The whole surface falls down and rests on the sand; but when the rains come, the first supply is nearly all absorbed in the sand. The black loam forms soft slush, and floats on the sand. The narrow opening prevents it from moving off in a landslip, but an oozing spring rises at that spot. All the pools in the lower portion of this spring-course are filled by the first rains, which happen south of the equator when the sun goes vertically over any spot. The second, or greater rains, happen in his course north again, when all the bogs and river-courses being wet, the supply runs off, and forms the inundation. This was cer-

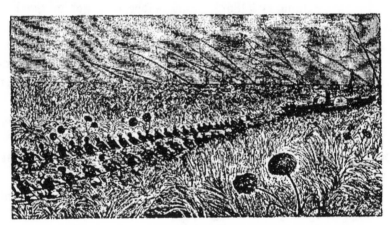

HAULING OF STEAMER THROUGH THE VEGETATION.

tainly the case which Livingstone had observed on the Zambesi and the Shire; and taking the different times for the sun's passage north of the equator, he considered that it explained the inundation of the Nile.

It may be inferred that traveling over ground of this nature was not the easiest thing in the world; but so long as the little party was not thrown among hostile tribes, it did not matter so much. The people through whose territory they were passing were Manganja, a very industrious race, combining agriculture and hunting with nets with various handicrafts, such as weaving and working in iron.

The Manganja are very ceremonious in their demeanor toward

each other; and were very friendly to the strangers. In return for the food and native sweet beer with which the chiefs generally provided them at each stopping-place, Livingstone usually gave a "cloth," (two yards of unbleached muslin), and so little clothing is worn in this country that this was considered quite a munificent payment. Owing, however, to the raids and forays of the Mazitu, food was very scarce in some localities, and more than once the caravan was almost on the verge of starvation.

They crossed the Loangwa, the great northern tributary of the Zambesi, the middle of December; and reached the Chambeze late in the following January (1867). But before they got to the banks of this latter river, they had met with a loss which affected the whole after history of the expedition; and the editor of Livingstone's Last Journals has advanced the statement that this loss materially hastened his death, by leaving him without the means of counteracting fever, and thus allowing his constitution to be undermined.

The desertion of so large a number of his men in the very outstart of the expedition had made him dependent upon the people of the country through which he passed for porters and for guides; the Johanna men had been intended chiefly for the latter purpose.

They were traveling through the forest near the Lobo, having just set out from Lisunga. Their guides were two Waiyau who had joined them some time before, and who were considered perfectly trustworthy because of their uniform good conduct ever since they had joined the caravan. A boy named Baraka, who was very careful, had charge of the medicine box, which was packed with a parcel containing five large cloths and all Baraka's clothing and beads. The Waiyau offered to exchange burdens for a while with Baraka, his own being the lighter (his real reason was that his own contained no cloth). Baraka consented. The fugitives watched their chance, and suddenly disappeared in the dense forest. Besides Baraka's package, they took all the dishes, a large box of powder, some flour, for which a high price had been paid, the tools, two guns, and a cartridge-pouch. The loss of these things was bad enough, but the great loss was the medicine. Livingstone says: "I felt as if I had now received the sentence of death, like poor Bishop Mackenzie," whose medicines had been wetted and rendered worthless by the upsetting of a boat.

The caravan returned to Lisunga, and men were at once sent out to scour the surrounding country for a trace of the fugitives. Livingstone was aware that they could attach no value whatever to the medicine-chest but would throw it and its precious contents away as soon as they had got the clothing and beads out of the parcel.

They remained for two days at Lisunga, and then, having bought all the provisions which the chief had to sell, were obliged to push forward in spite of the rain. For the next few days, they had much difficulty in obtaining food; but looked forward to great plenty when they should have reached the village of the powerful Chitapangwa.

This was called Molemba; and they came to it about noon of the last day of January. It was surrounded by a triple stockade, the inner being defended also by a deep, broad ditch, and a hedge of a thorny shrub, resembling the tomato or nightshade family. Chitapangwa sent to inquire if they desired an audience; and the messenger informed them that they must take something in their hands the first time they went to see so great a man. Dr. Livingstone was tired from marching, and sent word that he would not come until evening. About five o'clock he sent notice of his coming. They passed through the inner stockade, and then to an enormous hut, where sat Chitapangwa, with three drummers and ten or more men, with two rattles in their hands. The drummers beat furiously, and the rattlers kept time to the drums, two of them advancing and receding in a stooping posture, with rattles near the ground, as if doing the chief obeisance; but still keeping time with the others. The traveler declined to sit on the ground, and so an enormous tusk was brought for him. The chief saluted courteously. He had a fat, jolly face, and legs loaded with brass and copper leglets. Dr. Livingstone mentioned his losses by the desertion of the Waiyau, but as power is merely nominal, Chitapangwa could do nothing. After talking a while, he conducted his guest to a group of cows, and pointed out one.

"That is yours," he said politely.

The tusk on which the explorer had sat was also sent after him to his quarters, as being his. Before they separated, Chitapangwa put on the cloth which Livingstone had given him, as a token of acceptance; and further showed his gratitude by sending two large baskets of sorghum to the stranger's hut after dark. The gift of the cow, however, proved a delusion and a snare; for when the traveler would have it killed the next day, a man interfered, and pointed out a much

THE COURT OF A BLACK KING.

smaller one; an appeal to the chief ended in his having to pay Chitapangwa about four times the value of the animal in cloth, and then the savage was not satisfied.

Sending a number of letters from this point by means of a small party of Arab slavers, who were on their road to Zanzibar, Dr. Livingstone remained at this village about three weeks. This stay was partly on account of illness, as he was taken down with the fever, which he had no means of curing. But much of the time was spent in negotiating for food with Chitapangwa.

About the middle of March, they met with an enemy who had not before been encountered. Dr. Livingstone says:

"A shower of rain set the driver-ants on the move, and about two hours after we had turned in we were overwhelmed by them. They are called kalandu, or nkalanda. To describe this attack is utterly impossible. I wakened covered with them; my hair was full of them. One by one they cut into the flesh, and the more they are disturbed, the more vicious are their bites; they become quite insolent. I went outside the hut, but there they swarmed everywhere; they covered the legs, biting furiously; it is only when they are tired that they leave off."

They reached Lake Tanganyika the 1st of April, viewing it from the summit of the ridge two thousand feet above its level, which forms the southern boundary of its cup-like bed. The village at this point, Pambete, is surrounded with palm-oil-trees, tall and graceful as those found upon the west coast.

But the leader of the expedition was too weak and ill to make journeys about the lake. At one time, he was unconscious for several hours from the effects of fever; and finally his faithful servants hung a blanket before the entrance to his hut, that the curious natives might not be witnesses of his weakness. Nor could he learn anything by inquiry of the people. Either they were wholly ignorant, or they mistrusted him so much that they would give no information.

They remained at this village a month, before the leader was able to travel; and then he was far from being well. Toward the end of May, they arrived at Chisaka, Chitimba's village, and here they were detained for more than three months, owing to trouble between a party of Arab traders and a native chief, Nsama. Dr. Livingstone frankly says he heard but one side of the story, that of the Arabs, and hence cannot pretend to state the case truly; but the fact that the native chiefs generally condemned Nsama seemed to indicate that he was in the wrong. About the middle of September, however, the Arabs having lost about fifty men and Nsama probably twice as many, negotiations for a peace were entered upon; and as was often the case among civilized nations in other days, this peace was to be cemented with a marriage, Nsama promising to give one of his daughters to Hamees, one of the Arabs, as a wife. She came riding pick-aback on a man's

THE KING ADDRESSING HIS SUBJECTS.

shoulders into the village where her future lord was for the time, "a nice, modest, good-looking young woman, her hair rubbed all over with nkola; a red pigment made from the cam-wood, and much used as an ornament. She was accompanied by about a dozen young and old female attendants, each carrying a small basket with some provisions, as cassava, ground-nuts, etc. The Arabs were all dressed in their finery, and the slaves, in fantastic dresses, flourished swords, fired guns, and yelled. When she was brought to Hamees' hut she descended, and with her maids went into the hut. She and her attendants all had small, neat features. I had been sitting with Hamees, and now rose up and went away. As I passed him, he spoke thus to himself: 'Hamees Wadim Tagh! see to what you have brought yourself!' "

Nsama had been a great conqueror in his time, and with bows and arrows as the arms of his enemies, he was invincible; but the Arabs had of course been provided with fire-arms, and it was to the supremacy of weapons, not of generalship, that he had been obliged to yield so far as to consent to a peace. Dr. Livingstone visited his village, Itawa, and found the people particularly handsome. Nsama was very gracious, and promised guides and porters; but showed so much distrust that the traveler finally decided to go on without the proffered assistance.

Keeping to the north of Nsama's country after this brief visit, the party moved westward until it reached the north end of Moero. This was Nov. 8; it was the rainy season again, and the explorer was obliged to be very careful where he traveled, lest he again fall a victim to that fever against which he was now defenseless.

Their next visit of note was to a chief of Lunda, called the Casembe. This word, which means simply a general, has been applied as a proper name both to the chief and to the village where he lives. The Portuguese had used it in the latter sense; and their various observations as to the location of the village Casembe did not agree very closely, for the simple reason that each Casembe, as he came into office, removed the village from its previous site to one which pleased him better. The town at the time of Livingstone's visit was situated on the east bank of the lakelet Mofwe, and one mile from its northern end. The plain extending from the Lunde to the town of Casembe is level, and studded pretty thickly with red-ant hills, from fifteen to twenty feet high. Casembe had made a broad path from his town to the Lunde, a distance of about a mile and a half. The town consisted of a space a mile square, dotted over with cassava plantations, in the midst of which were the huts. The court or compound of Casembe was surrounded by a hedge of high reeds, ornamented with about sixty human skulls. Before the gigantic hut within this enclosure, which was Casembe's abode, the chief sat on a square seat placed on lion and leopard skins; he was dressed in a coarse blue and white print edged with red baize, arranged in large folds "so as to look like a crinoline put on wrong side foremost." His arms, legs, and head were covered with sleeves, leggings, and cap made of various colored beads arranged in patterns; a crown of yellow feathers surmounted his cap, and he considered himself a model of royal magnificence.

While at this village, Dr. Livingstone was provided with food on a liberal scale; and his presents seemed to be fully appreciated. His first gift to the chief consisted of eight yards of orange-colored serge, a large striped table-cloth, another large cloth, and a large richly gilded comb for the hair, such as ladies wore about 1820. As Lunda fashions in coiffure are various, this could not fail of being a welcome gift.

Casembe showed himself very friendly, although the traveler, remembering the skulls, and noting that many of his attendants had their ears cropped or their hands lopped off in token of their master's displeasure, could not trust him entirely. Although the Portuguese had visited this country, it is to be noted that Casembe thought there were only two sovereigns in the world, Queen Victoria and the sultan of Zanzibar.

As they came down the watershed toward Tanganyika, they entered an area of the earth's surface still disturbed by internal igneous action. A hot fountain in the country of Nsama, they found, was often used to boil cassava and maize. Earthquakes are no rarity in this section of the country, and one was experienced which shook their hut, and set the fowls to cackling, in the middle of the night. The most remarkable effect of this earthquake was, that it changed the rates of the chronometers, and stopped one entirely.

Dr. Livingstone was so affected by the climate that he was unable to leave Casembe's town until late in June, 1868, although he had arrived there in the previous autumn. His desire was to explore Lake Bangweolo, but the shores of it were so marshy, and the intervening country so overflowed during the wet season that it was highly imprudent for him to attempt it.

THE CONGO KING.

DISCOVERY OF LAKE BANGWEOLO.

It was on the 18th of July, 1868, that Dr. Livingstone discovered this lake, one of the largest in central Africa. It is extraordinary to note the total absence of all pride and enthusiasm as, almost parenthetically, he records the fact in these few brief words:

16

"Reached the chief village of Mapuni, near the north bank of Bang-weolo. On the 18th I walked a little way out, and saw the shores of the lake for the first time, thankful that I had come safely hither."

His intention to explore the lake was not carried out for a week, a strong and unfavorable wind detaining him on shore. But his return was much delayed by the condition of the country. We have already referred to that contest between Nsama and the Arab traders, which was apparently settled by the marriage of Hamees to Nsama's daughter. But this alliance did not accomplish this result; for the lady, hearing what seemed to her an indication that her father was to be attacked by her husband's people, departed quietly from her new home, and was seen no more. The other native chiefs, beginning to be alarmed at the encroachments of the Arabs, joined forces and attempted to storm the stockade of one of their leaders. They suffered a severe defeat in this attempt; and the whole country was thrown into turmoil and confusion. For several months travel or exploration was impossible; and several times the life of the stranger was in imminent danger. During this period, he occupied his time in writing out an exceedingly valuable treatise on the subject of the periodical floods which drain the enormous cistern-lakes of Central Africa. It would manifestly be out of place to transfer that treatise to these pages; and the reader who would study the subject is referred to the work of which the present chapter is substantially an abridgment—"The Last Journals" of David Livingstone in Central Africa.

At last, a cruel outrage perpetrated by one of the Arabs on the natives of Kizinga so exasperated the latter that they declared war; and although badly defeated in the first instance soon compelled the slave-traders to leave the country. With a party of these, led by Mohammed Bagharib, Livingstone started to Ujiji on December 11. The march to the nearest point on Lake Tanganyika occupied just two months, but was entirely uneventful, except that just before reaching the lake, Livingstone had an attack of pneumonia, accompanied by spitting of blood and distressing weakness. He had to be carried for sixteen days, during part of which time he was insensible, and lost count of the days of the week and the month. And this was the man who at the start, had been able to outstrip all his companions in walking, and was often obliged to loiter on the way because the caravan could not keep up with his swift, steady pace.

He had arranged for a quantity of goods to be sent from Zanzibar to Ujiji by one of the caravans trading along this route; and fully expected to find at this point, not only cloth and beads for propitiating the natives along his way, but a supply of the sorely needed medicines. Unfortunately, the goods had been intrusted to a scoundrel, who had helped himself most liberally to them. Sixty-two out of the eighty pieces of cloth had been stolen, and most of his best beads. Medicines, wine, and cheese had been left at Unyanyembe, thirteen days' journey east of Ujiji. Nor was the distance the only difficulty; the way was blocked by a Mazitu war, so that he must wait at Ujiji until the governor of Unyanyembe should have an opportunity of forwarding the goods in safety.

At Ujiji, however, he found a supply of flannel, which was very beneficial worn next to the skin, in his present condition. He also received a present of Assam tea from Calcutta, and his own supply of coffee and a little sugar had not been stolen.

The next month was occupied in writing letters home; and on the 27th of April he records that he had finished forty-two. He had great difficulty in persuading any one to undertake to deliver these at Zanzibar; the probability is, that even those who were not directly implicated in the theft of his goods were afraid that they would be accused of it; at last, however, he found messengers who promised to take them; and to their charge the documents were confided. That is the end of the history of the letters then written; for they never reached their destination.

EXPLORING THE RIVER LUALABA.

July 12, he set out to explore the Manyuema country, hitherto a country wholly unknown. Securing canoes, he skirted the edge of the lake for a short distance, then crossed it, and struck along the coast on foot. They passed through Uguha, or the country of the Waguha, and came to the territory occupied by the Manyuema.

Late in October, 1869, being thoroughly rested, he determined to cross the country to the Lualaba, and buy a canoe for its exploration. It is scarcely necessary to say that at the period of which we write, the course of this river was shrouded in mystery. Their route was west and south-west, through a country of beauty so great that he seems never tired of praising it. But they found the people far from friendly.

COOKING THE LOCUSTS.

A slave-trader had been through there, and had treated the people with great severity; in spite of the difference of color, they persisted in looking upon Dr. Livingstone as akin to the Arab. Owing to this state of feeling, they found it impossible to buy a canoe in which to cross the Luamo, the banks of which they reached November 17. Finally the party returned to Bambarre.

A second trip was begun the day after Christmas, the route being slightly altered, so that they struck the Luamo at a higher point than before. Their course from Bambarre for a number of days was nearly due north. They found the people civil, as a rule, but like noisy children, all talking and gazing when they entered a village. But weakness and sickness delayed them, and it was a month and more before they reached the Lualaba.

The incidents of the next few months need not be recorded in detail. He made but little progress, and even after reaching the banks of the Lualaba he turned aside, to visit Arab traders who had come for ivory, and with whom he was good friends. Under the date of June 26, we have this entry:

"Now my people failed me; so, with only three attendants, Susi, Chuma and Gardner, I started off to the north-west for the Lualaba."

SUFFERS FROM SORE FEET.

But this was another false start. For the first time in his life his feet failed him; and learning that the Lualaba took a great bend to the west-south-west, he gave up the quest, and limped back to Bambarre with his three faithful servants. Fairly baffled by the difficulties in his way, and sorely troubled by the demoralized state of his men, who had been seduced by the Arabs to a more lucrative employment, the explorer turned back from this point. He was laid up for some time with the sores on his feet, which became irritable eating ulcers, so painful that sometimes he could not sleep.

While he was thus rendered helpless, the few men that had not deserted him occupied much of their time in hunting. The chief game about this point was the soko, a species of the chimpanzee which has sometimes been identified with the gorilla; but no white scientist has ever seen the soko, and those Africans who came to England after the death of Dr. Livingstone failed to recognize the gorilla, stuffed, which is in the British Museum, as a soko. Nor do the descriptions of soko-hunts lead us to believe that they are the same as that powerful and ferocious animal of Western Equatorial Africa, which Du Chaillu has described. The soko is represented by some to be extremely knowing, successfully stalking men and women while at their work, kidnapping children and running up trees with them; he seems to be amused by the sight of the young natives in his arms, but comes down when tempted by a bunch of bananas, and as he lifts that, drops the child. One man was cutting honey from a tree, when a soko suddenly appeared and caught him, and then let him go. Another man was hunting, and missed in his aim when he attempted to stab a soko; it seized the spear and broke it, then grappled with the man, who called for help to his companions; it bit off the ends of his fingers and escaped unharmed. Another still was caught by a soko while hoeing; he roared out, but the soko giggled and grinned, and left him as if it had attacked him in play. A child caught up by a soko is often abused by being pinched and scratched and let fall.

His friend Mohammed, the chief of the ivory traders, offered to go with him to see the Lualaba; the explorer explained that it would not be sufficient for him to see it, he must descend the stream and see whither it flowed. Mohammed then offered to provide him with men; and this offer was accepted, the equivalent of two hundred and seventy pounds sterling being paid as amends for the injury to his ivory trade which the loss of these men would occasion.

Eighty days had passed since Dr. Livingstone first knew that his feet had failed him, before he was able to use them again. He was, by the journey which he was now beginning, entering upon the solution of a vexed geographical problem. It was a vexed problem, because the assumption of a point as true had caused errors which could not be corrected as long as this error obtained. This mistake was in identifying the Chambeze with the Zambesi. The map of Africa which Dr. Livingstone carried with him upon this expedition contained this error; the map-maker showing the river as running up-stream, and between three and four thousand feet up-hill, in order to reach the Zambesi which was known through Livingstone's former expedition, as well as by the settlements of the Portuguese.

Upon this trip, the explorer departed from the course which he had previously marked out for himself, to give no European name to any natural feature; this rule had been broken but once before, when he gave to the great cataract of the Zambesi the name of Victoria Falls; he now gave English names to the lakes which are the head-waters of the Congo—Palmerston Fountain, Frere Fountain, and Lake Lincoln, thus perpetuating, in the interior of Africa, the names of three men who had been, in his own day, most prominent in their efforts to suppress slavery.

But his effort to descend the Lualaba was not without hindrance. Under date of December 10, 1870, he says:

"I am sorely let and hindered in this Manyeema. Rain every day, and often at night. * * * This is the sorest delay I ever had."

BROKEN HEARTS.

While detained thus at Bambarre, Dr. Livingstone became acquainted with a curious disease—the strangest disease which he had seen in that country, he declared. Freemen who were taken as slaves died without any assignable cause, the only pain which they suffered being in the region of the heart. He regarded their death as due to that much scoffed-at trouble, a broken heart.

Late in December, the traveler's goat, on which he depended for milk, was killed by a leopard. A gun set for the animal went off at ten o'clock at night. The next morning, some of the attendants of the explorer set off on a hunt, and tracked him to his lair. The ball had broken both hind-legs and one fore-leg; yet he sprang viciously upon the foremost of the hunters, and bit him badly. Speared by the comrades of the man attacked, he proved to be a splendid specimen of his kind, being six feet eight inches from tip of nose to end of tail.

They left Bambarre February 16, but progressed very slowly. Their way lay across a great bend of the Lualaba, and they traveled on foot. After a journey lasting about six weeks, they came once more to the bank of the Lualaba, a mighty stream, at least three thousand yards broad, and so deep that the people living near by declared it could never, at any time of the year, be forded. The current, he found to be about two miles an hour.

But having reached the banks of this mighty river, the traveler found that he could go no farther, for the present at least; the suspicions of the natives prevented him from obtaining canoes either for descending or for crossing it. Here he remained from March 31 until

July 20, hoping day by day to be able to obtain canoes; getting bits of uncertain information now and then from the people about the rivers of the surrounding country, and striving to teach those with whom he came in contact. Finally, there was a terrible fight at this point, which was a market-place for the whole surrounding country. A quarrel between the natives and a slave of the ivory-traders who had come hither was taken up by all interested, and between three and four hundred persons killed. Livingstone, powerless to prevent the slaugh-

GREAT HONEY GUIDE.

ter, could only look on at the affrighted people struggling in the river into which they had plunged for safety, and, when the fight was over, intercede for those who had fled to him for safety. So far had the people been carried by their anger, that after it was all over, no one could give a connected account of the reasons for the fight. They had seen their friends fighting, and had joined in.

On July 20, he started back to Ujiji, but the journey back was different from anything that this old traveler had yet experienced. The ivory-traders had passed through this country, and maltreated the natives to such an extent that the whole country was aroused; and Dr. Livingstone being constantly taken for an Arab, was in perpetual danger of his life. Three times in one day (August 8) was he delivered from impending death.

A DANGEROUS PATH.

In passing along the narrow path, with a dense wall of vegetation touching either hand, the party came to a point where an ambush had been placed, and trees cut down to obstruct their passage while the assailants speared them; but for some reason it had been abandoned. Nothing could be detected; but by stooping down toward the earth and looking up toward the sun, a dark shade could sometimes be seen; this was an infuriated savage, and a slight rustle in the dense vegetation meant a spear. A large spear from Livingstone's right lunged past, and, almost grazing his back, stuck firmly in the soil. The two men from whom it came appeared in an opening in the forest only ten yards off, and bolted, one looking back over his shoulder as he ran. As they are expert with the spear, the traveler could only account for its missing by supposing that the man had been too sure of his aim, and by attributing his safety to the protecting care of his Father.

Shortly after this, another spear was hurled at him, missing him by about a foot in front. Guns were fired into the thick forest, but with no effect, for nothing could be seen; but they heard the savages jeering and denouncing them close by. Two of Livingstone's men were killed by them.

The third danger was not from concealed spearmen. Coming to a part of the forest cleared for cultivation, the explorer noticed a giant tree, made to appear still taller by growing out of an ant-hill twenty feet high; it had fire applied near its roots.

Dr. Livingstone heard a crack, which told that the fire had done its work in felling the tree; but he felt no alarm until he saw the mass of wood sway and then descend directly toward him. He ran a few paces back, and down it came to the ground within a yard of where he paused; breaking into several lengths, it covered him with a cloud of dust. Had the branches not been rotted off previously, he could scarcely have escaped.

His attendants, who had been scattered in all directions, regarded this as a good omen, taken in connection with his other escapes that day, and came running toward him, crying out:

"Peace! Peace! You will finish all your work in spite of these people, and in spite of everything!"

Reaching Ujiji October 23, he found that all his goods had been sold by an Arab, Shereef, to his friends, at nominal prices. In spite of the protests of other traders, more than three thousand yards of calico and seven hundred pounds of beads had been thus sacrificed. Shereef had the assurance, however, even after this was fully made known to Dr. Livingstone, to come to shake hands with him; and when the long-suffering traveler rebelled against such behavior at last, and refused to do so, the Arab assumed an air of displeasure, as if he had been badly treated. He afterward came twice a day with his salutation of "*Balghere* (good luck)!" until Livingstone told him, that if he were an Arab, his (Shereef's) hand and both ears would be cut off for thieving; and the traveler wanted no salutations from him.

DESTITUTE.

He was now utterly destitute, and with no prospect of further supplies for months to come; for letters must be dispatched to the coast before such would be sent to him; and how to pay the bearers of such letters, except in promises, he could not tell. He had made up his mind, if he could not get people at Ujiji, to wait until men should come from the coast; but to wait in beggary, was what he had never contemplated; and he "now felt miserable."

The few simple words are significant enough, if we consider the patience of the man. Livingstone's journals are unlike those of every other African traveler in the brevity and lack of enthusiasm with which the events are chronicled; the cold and undemonstrative nature of the Scotchman shows itself most plainly in this way; and especially in respect to his own sufferings. But in this case, we must remember that it is something more than natural reluctance to enlarge upon his feel-

ings; it is even more than the manly reticence regarding personal physical pain, which is shown by the great majority of the explorers; it is
the patience of the Christian, who sees in all the suffering and trouble
which come upon him, the trial which is to fit him for his Master's purpose.

Just as his spirits had reached their lowest ebb, the dawn began to
break; an Arab merchant, who said that he himself had no goods, offered to sell some ivory, and give the goods so obtained to the stranger.
This was encouraging; but Livingstone felt that he was not yet at the
point of accepting such an offer.

"Not yet, but by and by," he said to the Arab.

He had still a very few goods for barter remaining, goods which had
been left in the care of another Arab than the one who had stolen his
new stock, which he had deposited before going to Manyuema, in case
of returning in extreme need. These he was now resolved to use, to
get to the coast a letter, if possible. He had been full two years without
any tidings from Europe whatever; he had sent dispatches during that
time, but as we have seen, they had not reached the coast.

Such were the circumstances surrounding this great explorer when
his servants brought him word that an Englishman was approaching
the town. Susi came running to his master at the top of his speed, and
in great excitement. He breathlessly gasped out:

"An Englishman! I see him!"

In an instant he was off. Dr. Livingstone followed him to the door,
and saw the caravan approaching the town. Bales of goods, a tin bath,
huge kettles, cooking-pots, tents, and all the paraphernalia of a well-
equipped traveler through a country where few or no conveniences were
to be expected, struck him with a sense of the difference between himself and the approaching stranger.

"This must be a luxurious traveler," he told himself, "and not one
at his wit's end like me."

THE STARS AND STRIPES.

The first glance at the caravan had showed him that Susi had been
mistaken in one particular—this was not an Englishman, for at the

head of the caravan floated the flag of England's eldest daughter, the United States. The stranger was Henry M. Stanley.

Of the meeting, we need not here give details. Overwhelmed as Livingstone was by surprise at the coming of this man, sent by a

MEETING BETWEEN STANLEY AND LIVINGSTONE.

stranger through the heart of Africa especially to find him if alive, and to bring back his bones if he were dead, we could hardly expect that his narrative of the meeting would be clear and succinct; he was too bewildered, probably, in spite of his Scotch coolness of head, to remember just what took place. Little by little the whole wonderful story came home to him, and he realized that he was once again in communication with the outer world. And with this realization, came renewed vigor; he was no longer the broken-down old man, spiritless, bitterly disappointed at the failure to reach the points which he had endeavored to attain, heart-sick at the duplicity which had left him well-nigh without resources in the heart of this great continent; a new life seemed to fill his veins, and emotions that had lain dormant in Manyuema revived at the tidings that he had to tell. But while struggling to express the flood of feeling which so nearly overwhelmed him, these are the words he uses:

"I really do feel extremely grateful, and at the same time I am a little ashamed at not being more worthy of the generosity."

Mr. Stanley brought news that Sir Roderick Murchison most earnestly desired that Lake Tanganyika should be fully explored, and accordingly, after a little more than two weeks spent at Ujiji, the whole party set out for the north of the lake. The start was made November 16, but a cruise to the head of the lake failed to reveal any passage into the Nyanza, or any stream flowing out of Tanganyika; the natives appeared to know nothing of any large lake to the north, and they returned to Ujiji a month after they had left it.

Directly after their return, they made ready for a journey towards the east to secure Dr. Livingstone's goods, the English government having granted one thousand pounds for supplies for the explorer, in addition to the assistance which Mr. Bennett had commissioned Stanley to bring. Owing to the illness of the younger traveler, however, they did not leave Ujiji until two days after Christmas. The same cause which had detained them at Ujiji delayed their journey somewhat after they had started; and during one stage, Mr. Stanley had to be carried on a cot. After a march of fifty-four days, they reached Unyanyembe, over three hundred miles away.

Mr. Stanley was extremely anxious to have Dr. Livingstone return to England with him, to recruit his strength; but the old explorer was by no means ready to do so. His own judgment told him:

"All your friends will wish you to make a complete work of the exploration of the sources of the Nile before you retire."

His daughter Agnes had written:

"Much as I wish you to come home, I would rather that you finished your work to your own satisfaction than return merely to gratify me."

In spite of the persuasions of his newly found friend, then, he resolved to remain until this work should be accomplished. Probably, in the enthusiasm which had been re-awakened in his breast, and the return of a measure of good health, he did not realize what inroads upon his constitution had been made by the fever from which he had suffered so much after the theft of his medicines. Feeling so much better, he fancied himself a strong man again.

They remained at Unyanymebe until the 14th of March, Dr. Livingstone preparing dispatches and letters for the outer world to which his companion was so shortly to return. On the date mentioned, they separated; communication between them was kept-up for some time; and it was arranged that Mr. Stanley was to procure men for Dr. Livingstone in Zanzibar, and send them forward to Unyanyembe, where he was to await them. The time thus spent in waiting was utilized by completing many calculations which lack of time had caused him to leave unfinished, and by planning his work for the future. Briefly stated, it was his intention to allow the remainder of the year 1872 (at that time, five months,) for the journey to his new field of exploration; devote the whole of 1873 to his work, and return in 1874 to home and a well-earned repose.

It was the middle of August before the caravan of porters arrived at Unyanyembe. They numbered fifty-seven. Besides these new men, of whom John and Jacob Wainwright are to be remembered, Dr. Livingstone had five old servants with him—Susi, Chuma and Amoda, who had been employed by him during the Zambesi expedition, and Mabruki and Gardner, two of the Nassick boys who had left Zanzibar with his caravan at the beginning of the present journey.

Leaving a sufficient quantity of goods with Sultan bin Ali to secure their return journey from Unyanyembe to the coast, the caravan set out August 23. A week later, the two Nassicks had, "from sheer laziness," allowed all the cows to stray; they were found a long way off, but one was missing, and was never recovered. One cow, their best milker, had been lost three days after starting. Two of the pagazi, engaged at a village on their road, deserted, taking with them a quantity of calico belonging to the men. Thus the story goes on.

The latter half of September, they were much delayed by sickness, both of the leader and of his followers. They came in sight of Tanganyika October 8, and slowly approached the lake from which so short a distance seemed to divide them. Their course was nearly due south to Fipa, as that was the town to which their steps were now directed; they had been many times assured in Unyanyembe that the route to this point was much shorter and less difficult than that to Ujiji.

From this point they skirted the shores of the lake; and early in November came within sight of the Luazi. For some time past, Livingstone had been tormented by doubts about the Lualaba; he was in search of the ultimate sources of the Nile, not considering that the discovery of the two Nyanzas had settled this vexed question; what if, after all, the Lualaba should prove to be a tributary of the Congo? The question occurs more than once in his journal, even before the meeting with Stanley, showing that the idea was gaining hold upon his mind. Still, he pressed on, resolved to find out for himself what was the destination of this great river.

The journey now turned toward the southwest, for he wished to visit Lake Bangweolo again, and ascertain what connection it might have with a great river-system. The journey was without special incident; there was the same old story of natives angered by the outrageous treatment of Arab traders, and consequently jealous of all strangers; of efforts to get food, sometimes unavailing because of this jealousy; of sickness of the men; and finally, here and there we find the simple word "ill" among the entries in his journal, coupled sometimes with a statement of the length of time during which his illness had continued. Occasionally, the feeble writing testifies more plainly than words that his strength was failing.

February 13, they arrived within sight of Lake Bangweolo; the plain surrounding the lake was under water, and it was necessary to obtain canoes to make their way along the shore of the enlarged lake. Halting at the village of a chief named Matipa, they entered into negotiations for these vessels. Matipa showed himself at first very friendly, but on one pretext or another, put off the arrival of the canoes in a sufficient number to serve their purpose. At last, they found that he was deliberately acting treacherously; Dr. Livingstone then took possession of Matipa's own hut, fired his pistol through the roof, and left ten men to guard the village. Matipa fled to another village, while his people sent off and brought a number of canoes, so that Livingstone's men were enabled to embark at once. Later intercourse showed that Matipa was thoroughly frightened by the warlike demonstration, and became once more very friendly.

HARDSHIPS.

An entry under date of March 24 will give some idea of the hardships endured at this time, when the end was so rapidly approaching:

"We punted six hours to a little islet without a tree, and no sooner did we land than a pitiless, pelting rain came on. We turned up a canoe to get shelter. We shall reach the Chambeze to-morrow. The wind tore the tent out of our hands, and damaged it, too; the loads are all soaked, and with the cold, it is bitterly uncomfortable. A man put my bed into the bilge, and never said 'Bale out,' so I was safe for a wet night, but it turned out better than I expected. No grass, but we made a bed of the loads, and a blanket fortunately put into a bag."

It is interesting, in this portion of his journal, to note what care Susi and Chuma took of their master. He does not seem to realize it himself, yet from his own record we see that, day by day, their watchfulness over him was increasing, as they saw his strength diminishing. It was on this journey that, for the first time, he was unable to wade the streams which they crossed on foot; and all the way to Bangweolo, wherever they came to a sponge or a river, Chuma carried his master on his strong and willing shoulders, even though the main stream came up to Susi's mouth as they waded along.

The voyage over this overflowed land was far from easy sailing. On the seventh of April, he records that they were lost for five hours on the grassy prairies, which were covered with from three to five feet of water. The next morning they obtained guides from a village within bearing, who caused them to take their large canoe along a course where the water was sometimes but fifteen inches deep; and although the men put all their strength to her, she stopped at every haul with a jerk, as if in a bank of adhesive plaster.

But exertion and exposure.had further weakened him; and a few days later we find the entry that he was so weak he could hardly walk, but tottered along nearly two hours, and then lay down quite done over. At this resting-place, he made coffee—the last of his stock—and tried to go on again; but in an hour's time was compelled to give it up. Even then, he was very unwilling to be carried, but, "on being pressed," allowed the men to help him on by relays to Chinama, a highly cultivated region.

From this point forward we carry the story forward by means of the narration of his two faithful servants. April 21, he tried to ride the donkey, but was so weak that he fell to the ground utterly exhausted and faint. Chuma carried him back to the village which they had just left, and placed him in his hut. The next day, they contrived a sort of litter, known to the natives at a kitanda, a framework covered with grass, and having a blanket laid upon it. On this he was placed, while Chuma walked by his side, to steady the sick man when the bearers stopped; for he was so weak that he could not otherwise have kept from falling off.

HIS LAST SICKNESS AND DEATH.

They arrived at the village of Kalunganjova, on the banks of the Molilamo, April 27. From this point, they sent out to buy food. The effort was unsuccessful, for the Mazitu had made raids through that country, and taken everything. The chief, nevertheless, made them a substantial present of a kid and three baskets of ground-nuts; and those who had food were quite willing to sell it for beads. The chief visited Dr. Livingstone on the morning of the 29th, and assured him that he would personally accompany the caravan to the crossing-place of the river, in order to be sure that canoes were furnished as he wished them to be.

But when they were ready to set out, Dr. Livingstone was too weak

17

to walk from his bed in the hut to the kitanda at the door. It was therefore necessary, because the door was so narrow, to break down one of
the frail walls of the hut; through the breach thus made, the bearers
brought the litter close to the sick man's bed, and he was carefully
lifted upon it.

LIVINGSTONE'S LAST JOURNEY.

With almost incredible gentleness, when we remember that only
love had taught them how to deal with the sick, these men, who had until the last few years been rude and untaught savages, lifted him from
the kitanda into the canoe, and again into the litter when they had
crossed the river; for the canoe was not wide enough to admit the
kitanda with the sick man upon it. Susi hurried on ahead of the caravan, that a hut might be built at Chitambo's village, which was their
present destination, by the time that his master arrived.

The natives stood in silent wonder as he was helped from his litter
into the hut, for his praises had reached them long ago. This was the
"good man," as he was emphatically called by the tribes that knew

him best; and they watched him till he was lost to their view inside the hut.

The next day, the chief paid a visit of ceremony to his guest; but Dr. Livingstone was obliged, after an effort to talk to him, to send him away, telling him to come again the next day, when he hoped to have more strength. The day wore on, and night came; some of the men took to their huts; it was the duty of others to keep watch. The boy who was appointed to sleep just within his master's hut, summoned Susi about eleven o'clock; Livingstone asked a few questions, first about noises that he heard outside, and then about distances, the latter showing that his mind was wandering. An hour later, the man was again summoned, and attended to his master's wants, getting the medicine which was required.

"All right; you can go out now," said the white man.

The hours passed on; it was not yet dawn when the boy came to Susi again, this time in fright:

"Come to Bwana; I am afraid; I don't know if he is alive."

Susi called his immediate companions, and six men went to the doctor's hut. A candle, stuck by its own wax to a box, was burning at the head of the rude bed; the light showed their master's form, kneeling by the side of the bed, his head buried in his hands upon the pillow. He gave no sign of hearing them; one of them gently touched his cheek; it was quite cold; at some time between midnight and dawn, of the 1st of May, 1873, David Livingstone had knelt in prayer, and died upon his knees.

Livingstone's remains were taken back to England and interred in Westminster Abbey.

Just one year before the day that he died he had finished a letter to the New York Herald, trying to enlist American zeal to stop the east-coast slave-trade. His concluding words were: "All I can add, in very loneliness, is, may Heaven's rich blessing come down on every one, American, English or Turk, who will help to heal the open sore of the world." Nothing could better represent the man, and these words consequently were inscribed on the tablet at his grave in Westminster.

THE PROMISED LAND—END OF THE GREAT CONGO FOREST.

CHAPTER XIX.

STANLEY'S SEARCH FOR LIVINGSTONE.

Birth and Youth of Stanley—To America—In the Confederate Army—In the U. S. Navy—
Adventures in Turkey—In Abyssinia—In Spain—Find Livingstone—Off to Zanzibar—
Shooting Hippopotami—News of Livingstone—An Insolent Fellow—Attempt to Assassin-
ate Stanley—Fever—War—Mirambo and His Misdeeds.

WHILE Livingstone for years was lost in the wilds of Africa several unsuccessful attempts were made to locate him. Only one man succeeded in accomplishing what so many had attempted, viz., Henry M. Stanley, and the story of his adventurous journey sounds like a tale from the Arabian Nights.

In the year 1840, there was born, near the town of Denbigh, in Wales, a boy, who was named after his father and grandfather, John Rolland, or Rowlands, as the name is sometimes anglicized. His father died when he was but two years old; his mother married again, not many years afterward. He was for several years a pupil at the poor-house of St. Asaph, where he procured the best education that that institution of learning could afford. Leaving this, he was employed for a year as a teacher at Mold, in Flintshire; but finding this quiet life very little to his taste, he made his way to Liverpool, and there shipped as cabin-boy in a vessel bound for New Orleans. There, while looking for employment, he came into contact with a wealthy, childless merchant named Stanley. This gentleman liked the boy so well that he employed him about various parts of his extensive business, promoting him rapidly; and finally adopted him as his own son, promising to provide liberally for him.

But the youth had a restless spirit, and could not be prevailed upon to settle down and enjoy the good things of this life unless a great deal of the spice of variety could be added to them. He wandered away into the wildest parts of Arkansas; thence he made his way overland to

California, making friends with many of the Indians on the way, and sitting gravely by their council fires when it so pleased him to do. At last, he returned to New Orleans. His adopted father had given him up as dead, and welcomed him as one who had come back from beyond the grave.

The trial of thus losing his adopted son, as he thought that he had, had been a severe one to Mr. Stanley; but he was not destined to suffer again from the young man's roving disposition. Shortly after his return, the elder Stanley (for of course his adopted son had assumed his name) died suddenly; investigation showed that he had left no will; and the angry relatives whom young Rollant-Stanley was to have supplanted as the heir, inherited all his fortune. The young man was turned adrift, receiving from the affectionate adopted father nothing but the name of Henry Moreland Stanley.

IN THE CONFEDERATE ARMY.

Very shortly afterward, the war between the States broke out; and young Stanley, being in New Orleans, and surrounded by Confederate influences, enlisted in the Southern army. After various adventures and some hair-breadth escapes, he was captured by the enemy, and held as a prisoner of war. The case was a hopeless one; there was no chance of regaining his late comrades; and the soldier promptly took the oath of allegiance to the United States and enlisted in the United States navy. It would seem that he had none of the qualities which would recommend him for promotion on board of a man-of-war where the discipline was peculiarly rigid, as it was on the iron-clad Ticonderoga; but in a few months' time we find him acting ensign.

After the war was over, his ship was sent to the Mediterranean. Here he obtained leave, and, with two of his comrades, started on a pedestrian tour of a part of Syria. They were attacked by Turkish brigands, and only with great difficulty were they able to make their way back to Constantinople, there to appeal to the American minister for assistance and redress. But for the excellent generalship of Stanley, they would never have reached the Turkish capital.

It is a little doubtful whether this adventure occurred before or after he had left the United States service; although the probabilities are that it was previous to doffing his uniform. Whatever the truth may be in the case, he left the navy about this time, and before he revisited his native place, a very few months after his Turkish adventure.

WITH THE NEW YORK HERALD.

Returning to America, he was employed as special correspondent of the New York *Herald*, and given a roving commission. His duties first took him to Abyssinia, where the British were then waging war

THE ALOETOGU.

against King Theodore. It is (or was) an article of firm belief in England that the government receives the earliest news from the seat of war, and gives out the information to the newspapers; and that newspaper correspondents are-simply to fill up the outlines thus kindly furnished by the authorities. Mr. Stanley somewhat astonished the people of the War Department by providing the London newspapers with information which had not then reached the office of the Minister. It was one evidence of the energy which was derived in part from

Mother Nature, and in part learned from the people of his adopted country.

The war over, he returned to the United States, and was attached, still in the capacity of special correspondent of the *Herald*, to the Indian Commission of 1867. In 1868-9, we find him in Spain, following the fortunes of the royal forces and those of the republicans, as the latter strove to dethrone Isabella II. While he was portraying the situation for the benefit of the readers of the *Herald*, he received, October 16, 1869, a dispatch from Paris. It ran thus:

"Come to Paris on important business," and was signed by James Gordon Bennett, Jr., the manager of the New York *Herald*. The telegram reached him at ten A. M.; he at once proceeded to make ready; his pictures and books were packed in a hurry; his laundress was not given time to finish drying his clothes; by noon he was ready, having only to say good-bye to his friends.

At three in the afternoon, that being the hour at which the first express left Madrid after the receipt of the telegram, he was on his way, arriving in Paris the following night. He went straight to the Grand Hotel, and knocked at the door of Mr. Bennett's room.

A voice bade him enter; he found Mr. Bennett in bed.

"Who are you?" was the first question.

"My name is Stanley," was the reply.

"Ah, yes, sit down; I have important business for you."

Throwing over his shoulders his robe de chambre, Mr. Bennett asked:

"Where do you think Livingstone is?"

"I really do not know, sir," rejoined the subordinate, rather taken aback (if Stanley ever was taken aback) at the suddenness of the question.

"Do you think he is alive?"

"He may be, and he may not be."

"Well, I think he is alive, and that he can be found, and I am going to send you to find him.".

"What!" ejaculated Stanley; "do you really think that I can find Dr. Livingstone? Do you mean me to go to Central Africa?"

"Yes, I mean that you shall go and find him wherever you may hear that he is, and to get what news you can of him and perhaps"—delivering himself thoughtfully and deliberately—"the old man may be in want; take enough with you to help him, should he require it. Of course you will act according to your own plans, and do what you think best —but

FIND LIVINGSTONE."

The subordinate wondered at the cool order of sending one to Central Africa to search for a man whom most men believed to be dead; and asked:

"Have you considered seriously the great expense you are likely to incur on account of this little journey?"

"What will it cost?" asked the chief, abruptly.

"Burton and Speke's journey to Central Africa cost between three thousand and five thousand pounds, and I fear it cannot be done under two thousand five hundred pounds."

"Well, I will tell you what you will do. Draw a thousand pounds now; and when you have gone through that, draw another thousand, and when that is spent, draw another thousand; and when you have finished that, draw another thousand, and so on; but, FIND LIVING-STONE."

He was not to go directly to Africa; or at least not to the part where he might expect to find Livingstone. He was to go first to the inauguration of the Suez Canal; then proceed up the Nile, find out what he could about Baker's expedition under the authority of the Khedive (the celebrated Englishman was then just starting for Upper Egypt), write up a practical guide for Lower Egypt, go on to Jerusalem, visit Constantinople, the Crimea and its battle-grounds, cross the Caucasus to the Caspian Sea, write up Persepolis and Bagdad, get to India by a journey across Persia, and thence start to Zanzibar, if news of Livingstone had not been received in the meantime. Having mapped out this little program, Mr. Bennett told him that this was all, and bade him goodnight.

He followed out his instructions to the letter, arriving in India in

August, 1870; on October 12, he sailed from Bombay to Mauritius, the journey occupying thirty-seven days; and at last arrived at Zanzibar, January 6, 1871. Here he was well received by the United States consul, Captain Webb; and had the good fortune, as he then esteemed it, to meet with Dr. Kirk, the coadjutor of Dr. Livingstone during the Zambesi expedition.

Many questions now occurred to the traveler, which he had no means of answering. They were such as these: How much money is required? How many pagazis, or carriers? How many soldiers, free black men, natives of Zanzibar, or freed slaves from the interior? How much cloth? How many beads? How much wire? What kinds of cloth are required for the different tribes? He studied the volumes of African travels at his command, chiefly Burton, Speke, and Baker; but information such as he sought was not to be found in them. Even the hints in Baker's "Ismailia" were not available, for the materials for that volume had not yet been collected; and Baker does not answer there such questions as these.

PREPARATIONS FOR THE JOURNEY.

An insuperable obstacle to rapid transit in Africa is the want of carriers; and as speed was the main object of the expedition under his command, his duty was to lessen this difficulty as much as possible. His carriers could only be engaged after arriving at Bagamoyo, on the main land. He had over twenty good donkeys ready, and he thought a cart adapted for the goat-paths of Africa might prove an advantage. Accordingly, he had one constructed, eighteen inches wide and five feet long, supplied with two fore-wheels of a light American wagon, more for the purpose of conveying the narrow ammunition-boxes. He estimated that if a donkey could carry to Unyanyembe a load of four frasilahs, or one hundred and forty pounds, he ought to be able to draw eight frasilahs on such a cart, which would be equal to the carrying capacities of four stout pagazis.

When his purchases were completed, and he beheld them piled up, tier after tier, and row upon row, he was rather abashed at his own temerity. Here were nearly six tons of material; and as a man's maximum load does not exceed seventy pounds, his eleven thousand pounds would require about one hundred and sixty men.

Shortly before their departure from Zanzibar, Mr. Stanley was presented to the sultan, who gave him letters to his officers at Bagamoyo and Kaole, and a general introductory letter to all Arab merchants whom he might meet on the road; and concluded his remarks to the traveler with the expressed hope that, on whatever mission he was bound, he would be perfectly successful.

THE LESSER CIVET.

OFF FOR CENTRAL AFRICA.

By the fourth of February, all his preparations were completed; and on the fifth, the New York *Herald* expedition sailed from Zanzibar to the mainland. This space has been devoted to the fitting out of the expedition, because only a fairly detailed account can give any idea of the difficulties which an experienced traveler, of more than ordinary intelligence and energy (to put it mildly) encounters in organizing an expedition to Central Africa, even with unlimited means at his command.

On the 25th of March, exactly seventy-three days after his arrival at Zanzibar, Stanley's fifth caravan, led by himself, left the town of Bagamoyo for the first journey westward. The other caravans had preceded him, some by as much as a month. They left Bagamoyo, the attraction of all the curious, with much eclat; and defiled up a narrow lane shaded almost to twilight by the dense umbrage of two parallel rows of mimosas. They were all in the highest spirits. The first camp, Shamba Gonera, they arrived at in one hour and thirty minutes, equal to three and one-fourth miles. The first or "little journey," was performed very well, "considering," as the Irishman says. The boy Selim upset the cart not more than three times; Zaidi, the soldier, only once let his donkey, which carried his master's box of ammunition and one bag of his clothes, lie in a puddle of black water. The clothes had to be re-washed; the ammunition-box, thanks to its owner's prevision, was water-proof. Kamma perhaps knew the art of donkey-driving, but had sung himself into oblivion of the difficulties with which an animal of the pure asinine breed has to contend, such as not knowing the road, and inability to resist the temptation of straying into a manioc-field; and the donkey, misunderstanding the direction in which he was required to go, ran off at full speed along an opposite road, until his pack got unbalanced, and he was fain to come to the earth. But these incidents were trivial, of no importance, and natural to the first "little journey" in Africa.

The road was a mere foot-path, and led over a soil which, though sandy, was of surprising fertility, producing grain and vegetables a hundred fold, the sowing and planting of which was done in the most unskilful manner. In their fields, at heedless labor, were men and women in the scantiest costumes, compared with which Adam and Eve, in their fig-leaf apparel, must have been modesty indeed.

JUNGLES AND OTHER OBSTACLES.

They were detained for three days at this first stopping-place; but shortly after leaving it reached the turbid Kingani, famous for its hippopotami. They began to thread the jungle along its right bank until they were halted point-blank by a narrow sluice having an immeasurable depth of black mud. The difficulty presented by this was very grave, although its breadth was barely eight feet; the donkeys, and least of all the horses, could not be made to traverse two poles like the biped carriers, neither could they be driven into the sluice, where they would quickly founder. The only available way of crossing it in safety was by means of a bridge, to endure in this conservative land for generations as the handiwork of the Wasungu. So they set to work, there being no help for it, with American axes, to build a bridge. It was compassed of six stout trees thrown across; over these were laid crosswise fifteen pack saddles, these covered again with a thick layer of grass. All the animals crossed it safely; and then for the third time that morning the process of wading was performed.

A half-mile to the north, and they reached the ferry; while the work of unloading the donkeys was going forward, Stanley sat down on a condemned canoe to amuse himself with the hippopotami by peppering their thick skulls with his No. 12 smooth-bore. One old fellow, with the look of a sage, was tapped close to the right ear by one of his smaller bullets; instead of submerging himself as others had done, he coolly turned round his head as if to ask:

"Why this waste of valuable cartridges on us?"

The response to this mute inquiry of his sageship was an ounce and a quarter bullet from the smoothbore, which made him bellow with pain, and in a few moments he rose again tumbling in his death agonies. As his groans were so piteous, the sportman refrained from a useless sacrifice of life, and left the amphibious horde in peace.

Mr. Stanley was anxious to try what a good watch-dog might do to protect him from the unmannerly Wagogo, of whom he had heard much from the Arabs; and had accordingly brought one with him. He found it of very great use, in keeping out of his tent these ruffians of the wilderness. Shortly after crossing the above-named river, the fifth caravan became the fourth, by reason of delays which sickness imposed upon that which had started the earlier.

AN OLD HIPPOPOTAMUS WITH THE LOOK OF A SAGE.

THE RAINY SEASON.

They pushed on toward Kingaru, the rainy season having now begun, and made travel very difficult. The natives poured into camp from the villages in the woods with their vendibles. Foremost among these, as in duty bound, came the chief, bearing three measures of matama and a half-measure of rice, of which he begged, with paternal smiles, the traveler's acceptance. But under the smiling mask, bleared eyes, and wrinkled front of him was visible the soul of trickery, which was of the cunningest kind. Responding under the same mask adopted by this knavish elder, Stanley said:

"The chief of Kingaru has called me a rich sultan. If I am a rich sultan why comes not the chief with a rich present to me that he might get a rich return?"

Said he, with another leer of his wrinkled visage:

"Kingaru is poor, there is no matama in the village."

To this appeal, Mr. Stanley replied that since there was no matama in the village, he would pay the chief half a shukka, or a yard of cloth, which would be exactly equivalent to his present; that if the chief preferred to call his small basketful a present, the white man would be content to call his yard of cloth a present. With this logic the chief had to be satisfied.

One of the two horses brought from Zanzibar died the next day, and by the orders of the leader, was buried, in order that the decaying flesh might not affect the health of the people of Kingaru. This consideration, however, was but poorly repaid; for the chief demanded that the white man should pay a fine of two doti of Merikani for his presumption in burying the horse within his domain. To this Stanley replied by demanding how many soldiers he had. The question was repeated before the answer was given that he had none, only a few young men. To this the white man retorted:

"Oh, I thought you might have a thousand men with you, by your going to fine a strong white man, who has plenty of guns and soldiers, two doti for burying a dead horse."

The chief was staggered but not convinced; whereupon Stanley,

after explaining the sanitary reasons for burying the animal, generously offered to repair his error at once:

"This minute my soldiers shall dig him out again, and cover up
the soil as it was before; and the horse shall be left where he died.
Ho! Bombay, take soldiers with jembes to dig my horse out of the
ground, drag him to where he died, and make everything ready for
a march to-morrow morning."

AZARA'S AGOUTI.

Kingaru, his voice considerably higher, and his head moving to
and fro with emotion, cries out:

"No, no, master! Let not the white man get angry. The horse is
dead, and now lies buried; let him remain so, since he is already there,
and let us be friends again."

The second horse died that night. Other misfortunes came. Out
of a force of twenty-five men, one deserted, and ten were on the sick-

list. They left Kingaru April 6; and the long stay there had completely demoralized soldiers and pagazis. Only a few of them had strength to reach Imbiki before night; the others, attending the laden donkeys, put in an appearance next morning, in a lamentable state of mind and body.

At Muhalleh, which they reached a little after the middle of April, they met Selim bin Bashid, bound eastward, with a huge caravan carrying three hundred ivory tusks. This good Arab, besides. welcoming the newcomer with a present of rice, gave him news of Livingstone. He had met the old traveler at Ujiji, had lived in the next hut to him for three weeks, described him as looking old, with long gray mustaches and beard, just recovered from severe illness, looking very wan; when fully recovered Livingstone intended to visit a country called Manyuema by way of Marungu.

AN INSOLENT FELLOW.

But illness was not the only danger with which he had to contend. Of the two white men hired at Zanzibar, Farquhar had shown himself to be inexcusably extravagant in the expenditure of the stores committed to his care. He was continually crying out like a sick baby for half a dozen people to wait upon him, and if they did not happen to understand the English language in which he addressed them, he poured out a volley of the most profane abuse that ever offended the ears of a Christian gentleman. The soldiers were in such dread of his insane violence that they feared to go near him. He was ill with a disease of which Stanley could secure no definite description of the symptoms; and by his weight and see-sawing method of riding killed every donkey that he rode.

But Shaw was even worse to deal with than Farquhar; and since he had been with the caravan which Stanley led in person, the leader's patience, so far as he was concerned, was about exhausted, when on May 15th, the crisis came. It was at breakfast time; the meal had just been served, and Stanley had asked Shaw to carve.

"What dog's meat is this!" he asked, in the most insolent way imaginable.
18

"What do you mean?" asked Stanley.

Then ensued a volley of abuse, tempered with profanity; to which the indignant chief replied by a recapitulation of what they had brought upon him; closing with an expostulation at being sworn at at his own table, and reminding Shaw that he was his (Stanley's) servant. An oath was the rejoinder; but before Mr. Shaw could say more, he had measured his length on the ground.

He thereupon demanded his discharge; to which Stanley most willingly agreed; giving orders at once that Shaw's tent should be struck, and that he and his baggage should be escorted two hundred yards outside the camp. After breakfast was over, Stanley explained to Farquhar how necessary it was for him to be able to proceed; that as Farquhar was sick, and would probably be unable to march for a time, it would be better that he should be left in some quiet place, under the care of a good chief, who would, for a consideration, look after him until he got well. To this Farquhar had agreed.

Stanley had barely finished speaking before Bombay came to the door and informed him that Mr. Shaw would like to speak to him. He went out to the gate of the camp, and there met Shaw, looking extremely penitent and ashamed. He commenced to ask pardon, and began imploring Stanley to take him back again; promising that he should never find fault with him again. Stanley held out his hand to him, saying:

"Don't mention it, my dear fellow. Quarrels occur in the best of families. Since you apologize, there is an end of it."

That night as Stanley was falling asleep, he heard a shot, and a bullet tore through his tent, a few inches above his body. He snatched his revolvers and rushed out of his tent, and asked the men about the watchfires, "Who shot?" They had all jumped up, rather started at the sudden report.

"Who fired that gun?"

"Bana Mdogo," said one, (the little master, i. e., Shaw).

Stanley lit a candle, and walked with it to Shaw's tent.

"Shaw did you fire?"

There was no answer. He seemed to be asleep, he was breathing so hard.

"Shaw! Shaw! did you fire that shot?"

"Eh—eh?" said he, suddenly awaking—"me?—me fire? I have been asleep."

Stanley's eye caught sight of his gun lying near him. He seized it, felt it, put his little finger down the barrel. The gun was warm, his finger was black from the burnt gunpowder.

"What is this?" he asked, holding his finger up; "the gun is warm. The men tell me you fired."

"Ah, yes," replied Shaw; "I remember it. I dreamed I saw a thief pass my door, and I fired. Ah—yes—I forgot. I did fire. Why, what is the matter?"

"Oh, nothing," said Stanley. "But I would advise you in future, in order to avoid all suspicion, not to fire into my tent, or at least so near me. I might get hurt, you know, in which case ugly reports would get about, and this perhaps would be disagreeable, as you are probably aware. Good night."

But what a clumsy way to murder! Surely, had he done so, Stanley's own men would have punished him as the crime deserved. A thousand better opportunities than this would be presented in a month's march. Stanley could only account for it by supposing he was momentarily insane.

The next thing which must be done was to provide a home for Farquhar until he should be able to return to the coast. Leucole, the chief of the village, with whom Stanley made arrangements for Farquhar's protection and comfort, suggested that he should appoint some man in his employ to wait on him, and interpret his wishes to Leucole's people. Making inquiry, Stanley was assured by Bombay that any soldier whom he might appoint for this purpose would obey him until he was gone, and then run away. Despite Bombay's assertion, the leader inquired of each man personally whether he would be willing to stay behind, and wait on the sick Musungu (white man). From each man he received an answer in the negative; they were afraid of him, he damned them so; and Ulimengo mimicked him so faithfully, yet so ludicrously, that it was almost impossible to abstain from laughing. As, however, the sick man absolutely needed some one to attend him, Stanley was compelled to use his authority; and Jako, who could speak English, was, despite his protestations and prayers, appointed. Six months provisions of white beads, besides a present for Leucole, a carbine, ammunition and tea were set aside for Farquhar's wants.

This took place in the neighborhood of the Mpwapwa range of mountains, a country memorable to the traveler by reason of its plentiful and excellent milk, and its equally plentiful earwigs, for which he did not feel quite so grateful as for the milk. Second to the earwigs in importance and numbers he found the white ants, whose powers of destructiveness were simply awful. Mats, cloth, portmanteaus, clothes, in short, every article he possessed, seemed to be on the verge of destruction; and as he witnessed their voracity, he felt anxious lest his tent should be devoured while he slept.

MIRAMBO AND HIS MISDEEDS.

The road to Ujiji was closed by Mirambo, chief of Uyoweh; what was to be done? Stanley found himself in the midst of preparations for war on the part of the Arabs of Unyanyembe.

This Mirambo of Uyoweh, it seems, for the past few years had been in a state of chronic discontent with the policies of the neighboring chiefs. Formerly a pagazi for an Arab, he had now assumed regal power, with the usual knack of unconscionable rascals who care not by what means they step into power. When the chief of Uyoweh died, Mirambo, who was head of a gang of robbers infesting the forests of Wilyankuru, suddenly entered Uyoweh, and constituted himself lord paramount by force. Some feats of enterprise, which he performed to the enrichment of all those who recognized his authority, established him firmly in his position. This was but a beginning; he carried war through Ugara to Ukonongo, through Usagozi to the borders of Uvinza, and after destroying the population over three degrees of latitude, he conceived a grievance against Mkasiwa, and against the Arabs, because they would not sustain him in his ambitious projects against their ally and friend with whom they were living in peace.

The first outrage which this audacious man committed against the Arabs was the halting of an Ujiji-bound caravan, and the demand for five kegs of gunpowder, five guns, and five bales of cloth. This extraordinary demand, after expending more than a day in fierce contro-

THE GEMSBOK.

versy, was paid; but the Arabs, if they were surprised at the exorbitant blackmail demanded of them, were more than ever surprised when told to return the way that they came; and that no Arab caravan should pass to Ujiji except over his dead body.

THE ZEBRA.

One road to Ujiji had been tried, and had been found impassable. The southern route was not well known to those about him; and they vaguely hinted of want of water and robber Wazavira as obstacles in the way.

But before he could venture on this new route, he had to employ a new set of men, as those whom he took to Mfuto considered their engagement at an end, and the fact of five of their number being killed rather damped their ardor for traveling. It was useless to hope that Wanyamwezi could be engaged, because it was against their custom to go with caravans, as carriers, during war-times. His position was most serious; but although he had a good excuse for returning to the coast, he felt that he must die sooner than return.

While Stanley was still uncertain what to do, or how to procure a sufficient number of pagazis, firing was heard from the direction of Tabora, where the Arabs were still encamped. Some of the men who were sent out to ascertain the cause came running back with the information that Mirambo had attacked Tabora with over two thousand men, and that a force of over one thousand Matuta, who had allied themselves with him for the sake of plunder, had come suddenly upon Tabora, attacking from opposite directions. Later in the day, or about noon, the way was crowded with fugitives from Tabora, who were rushing to Kwihara for protection. From these people, Stanley received the sad information that the noble Khamis bin Abdullah, with many of his adherents, had been slain. Perceiving that his people were ready to stand by him, Stanley made preparations for defense by boring loop-holes for muskets into the stout clay walls of his tembe. They were made so quickly, and seemed so admirably adapted for the efficient defense of the tembe that his men got quite brave; and Wangwana refugees with guns in their hands, driven out of Tabora, asked to be admitted to this tembe to assist in its defense. Livingstone's men were also collected, and invited to help defend their master's goods against Mirambo's supposed attack. By night, Stanley had one hundred and fifty armed men in his courtyard, stationed at every possible point where an attack was to be expected. The next day, Mirambo had threatened, he would come to Kwihara; Stanley hoped that he would come, and was resolved that if he came within range of an American rifle, it should be seen what virtue lies in American lead.

The tembe was fortified so strongly that Stanley expressed it as his firm conviction that ten thousand Africans could not take it; four or five hundred Europeans without cannon, or fifty with its aid, he adds, might take it. But having expended all this care, and waited so anxiously to give Mirambo a taste of American lead, that gentleman chose to avoid the place where such a reception had been prepared for him, and turned his attention to Mfuto.

KALULU, STANLEY'S FAVORITE SERVANT.

While he was anxiously gathering up a sufficient number of men to transport his necessary baggage to Ujiji, Stanley received a present. This was nothing less than a little boy slave, named Ndugu M'hali. The name did not suit his fancy, and he called the chiefs of his caravan together and asked them to choose a better one. Various names were suggested, but Ulimengo, after looking at his quick eyes, and noting his celerity of movement, pronounced the name "Ka-lu-lu" best for him, "Because," said he, "just look at his eyes! So bright! Look at his form! So slim! Watch his movements! So quick!"

"Yes, bana," said the others, "let it be Kalulu."

Kalulu is a Kisawahili term for the young of the blue-buck antelope.

·"Well, then," said Stanley, water being brought in a huge tin pan, Selim, who was willing to stand god-father, holding him over the water, "let his name henceforth be Kalulu, and let no man take it from him."

MIRAMBO'S ATTACKS.

The next day (Sept. 8) word was received that Mirambo had attacked Mfuto; the result of the engagement was not told until the next day; when the welcome news was received that Mirambo had been repulsed with severe loss. From this point forward, Mirambo had but little terror for the people at Kwihara, and Stanley was able to carry on his work of getting ready for the journey to Ujiji, unhindered by any circumstance except the sickness of Shaw and Selim.

A farewell banquet was given on the 17th; two bullocks were barbecued; three sheep, two goats, and fifteen chickens, one hundred and twenty pounds of rice, twenty large loaves made of Indian corn flour, one hundred eggs, ten pounds of butter, and five gallons of sweet milk were the contents of which the banquet was formed.

The march was without other incidents for several days. It was Oct. 2 that they caught sight of a herd of giraffes, whose long necks were seen towering above a bush they had been nibbling at. This sight was greeted with a shout, for they knew that they had entered the game country, and that near the Gombe, where they intended to halt, they would find plenty of these animals.

Three hours brought them to Manyara. Arriving before the village-gate, they were forbidden to enter, as the country was throughout in a state of war, and the villagers did not wish to be compromised. The travelers were directed to ruined huts outside the town, near a pool of clear water. After they had built their camp, the guide was sent to buy food; he was informed that the chief had forbidden his people to sell any grain whatever. Two royal cloths were selected, and sent by Bombay to propitiate the chief; but proved useless; and all the caravan went supperless to bed.

The bale of choice cloths was opened again the next morning and four royal cloths were this time selected, and two dotis of Merikani, and Bombay was again dispatched, burdened with compliments and polite words. It was necessary to be very politic with a man who was so surly, and too powerful to make an enemy of. What if he made up his mind to imitate the redoubtable Mirambo, king of Uyoweh! The effect of Stanley's munificent liberality was soon seen in the abundance of provender which came into the camp. Before an hour went by, there came boxes full of choroko, beans, rice, matama or dourra, and Indian corn, carried on the heads of a dozen villagers; and shortly

THE PICHICIAGO.

afterward the Mtemi himself came, followed by about thirty musketeers and twenty spearmen, to visit the first white man ever seen on this road. Behind these warriors came a liberal gift fully equal in value to that sent to him, of several large gourds of honey, fowls, goats, and enough vetches and beans to supply the caravan with four days' food.

STANLEY MEETS MIRAMBO.

Stanley met the chief at the gate of his camp, and bowing profoundly, invited him to his tent, which he had arranged as well as his circumstances would permit, for this reception. His Persian carpet and bear skin were spread out, and a broad piece of bran-new crimson cloth covered his kitanda, or bedstead.

The chief, a tall, robust man, and his chieftains were invited to seat themselves. They cast a look of such gratified surprise at their host, his face, his clothes, and guns, as it is impossible to describe. They looked at him intently for a few seconds, and then at each other, which ended in an uncontrollable burst of laughter, and repeated snappings of the fingers. After a short period expended in exchanging compliments, the chief desired Stanley to show him his guns. The Winchester rifle elicited a thousand flattering observations from the excited man; and the tiny deadly revolvers, whose beauty and workmanship they thought superhuman, evoked such gratified eloquence that the American was glad to try something else. The double-barreled guns fired with heavy charges of powder caused them to jump up in affected alarm, and then to subside to their seats convulsed with laughter. As the enthusiasm of the guests increased, they seized each other's index fingers, screwed them and pulled at them until the host feared they would end in their dislocation. After having explained to them the difference between white men and Arabs, Stanley pulled out his medicine chest, which evoked another burst of rapturous sighs at the cunning neatness of the array of vials. He asked what they meant.

"*Dowa,*" replied Stanley, sententiously; a word which may be interpreted, medicine.

"Oh-h, oh-h," they murmured, admiringly. The white man succeeded, ere long, in winning unqualified admiration; and his superiority, compared with the best of the Arabs they had seen, was but too evident. "*Dowa, dowa,*" they added.

"Here," said Stanley, uncorking a vial of medicinal brandy, "is the Kisungu pombe (white man's beer); take a spoonful and try it," at the same time handing it.

"*Hacht, hacht,* oh, *hacht!* What! Eh! What strong beer the white men have! Oh, how my throat burns!"

"Ah, but it is good," said Stanley; "a little of it makes men feel strong and good; but too much of it makes men bad, and they die."

"Let me have some," said one of the chiefs; and the request was echoed until all had asked.

The exhibitor next produced a bottle of concentrated ammonia, which he explained was for snake-bites, and headaches; the sultan immediately complained he had a headache, and must have a little. Telling him to close his eyes, Stanley suddenly uncorked the bottle, and presented it to his majesty's nose. The effect was magical, for he fell back as if shot, and such contortions as his features underwent are indescribable. His chiefs roared with laughter, and clapped their hands, pinched each other, snapped their fingers, and did many other ludicrous things. Finally the sultan recovered himself, great tears rolling down his cheeks, and his features quivering with laughter; then he suddenly uttered the word "*Kali,*" strong, quick, or ardent medicine. He required no more; but the other chiefs pushed forward to get one wee sniff, which they no sooner had than all went into paroxysms of uncontrollable laughter. The entire morning was passed in this state visit, to the satisfaction of all concerned.

"Oh," said the sultan at parting, "these white men know everything! The Arabs are dirt compared to them."

October 4, they left their camp here, and traveled toward Gombe, which is four hours and a quarter from Manyara. Here, at last, was the hunter's paradise. Hunters were now directed to proceed east and north to procure meat, because in each caravan it generally happens that there are fundi, whose special trade is to hunt for meat for the camp. Some of these are experts in stalking, but often find themselves in dangerous positions, owing to the near approach necessary before they can fire their most inaccurate weapons with any degree of certainty.

CHAPTER XX.

HOW STANLEY FOUND LIVINGSTONE.

A Mutiny—Stanley's Life Again Attempted—Attack of a Leopard—Lions near the Camp—
"A White Man at Ujiji"—Silencing a Woman — Tanganyika — "Dr. Livingstone, I Pre-
sume?"—Under the Palms of Ujiji—A Lion in the Grass—Parting from Livingstone—
"Drop That Box, and I'll Shoot You"—Going Home.

We have not space here to detail Stanley's prowess in hunting,
since it brought nothing of special adventure; we must pass on to a
more dangerous incident.

The caravan remained two days at this camping-place, the hunters
procuring plenty of meat, which the others cut and sliced so that it
might be dried for future use; and even then the meat-loving, lazy
Wangwana did not wish to go. They delegated Bombay early in the
morning of the 7th to speak to Stanley, and entreat him to stop one
day longer. Bombay was well scolded for bearing any such request
after two days' rest; and Bombay was by no means in the best of
humors; flesh-pots full of meat were more to his taste than a constant
tramping, and its consequent fatigues. Stanley saw his face settle
into sulky ugliness, and his great nether lip hanging down limp, which
means, as if expressed in so many words:

"Well, get them to move yourself, you wicked, hard man! I shall
not help you."

An ominous silence followed Stanley's order to the kirangozi to
sound the horn, and the usual singing and chanting were not heard.
The men turned sullenly to their bales, and Asmani, the gigantic guide,
was heard to say grumblingly that he was sorry he had engaged to guide
the Musungu to the Tanganyika. However, they started, though re-
luctantly. Stanley stayed behind with the gun-bearers, to drive the
stragglers on. In about half an hour he sighted the caravan at a
dead stop, with the bales thrown on the ground, and the men standing
in groups talking angrily and excitedly.

Taking his double-barreled gun from Selim's shoulder, he selected a dozen charges of buckshot, and slipping two of them into the barrels, and adjusting his revolvers in order for handy work, he walked on toward them. He noticed that the men seized their guns as he advanced. When within thirty yards of the groups, he discovered the heads of two men appear above an ant-hill on his lift, with the barrels of their guns carelessly pointed toward the road.

He halted, threw the barrel of his gun into the hollow of the left hand, and then, taking a deliberate aim at them, threatened to blow their heads off if they did not come forward to talk to him. These two men were gigantic Asmani, and his sworn companion Mabruki, the guides of Sheikh bin Nasib. As it was dangerous not to comply with such an order, they presently came; but keeping his eye on Asmani, Stanley saw him move his fingers to the trigger of his gun, and bring his gun to a "ready." Again the white man lifted his gun, and threatened him with instant death, if he did not drop his musket.

Asmani came on in a sidelong way, with a smirking smile on his face, but in his eyes shone the lurid light of murder as plainly as it ever shone in a villain's eyes. Mabruki sneaked to Stanley's rear, deliberately putting powder in the pan of his musket; but sweeping the gun sharply around, the Musungu planted the muzzle of it about two feet from his wicked-looking face, and ordered him to drop his gun instantly. He let it fall from his hand quickly; and, giving him a vigorous poke in the stomach with the double-barrel, which sent him reeling a few feet, Stanley turned to Asmani, and ordered him to put his gun down; accompanying the order with a nervous movement of his own weapon, pressing gently on the trigger at the same time. Never was a man nearer his death than was Asmani during those few moments. The white man was reluctant to shed his blood, and he was willing to try all possible means to avoid doing so; but if he did not succeed in cowing this ruffian, authority was at an end. The truth was, they feared to proceed farther on the road, and the only possible way of inducing them to move was by an overpowering force and exercise of his power and will in this instance, even though he might pay the penalty of his disobedience with death. As Stanley was beginning to feel that Asmani had passed his last moment on earth, as he was lifting his gun to his shoulder, a form came up behind him, and Mabruki Speke cried in horror-struck accents:

"Man, how dare you point your gun at the master?"

Mabruki then threw himself at Stanley's feet, and endeavored to kiss them, and entreated him not to punish him:

"It is all over now," he said, "there will be no more quarreling; we will go to the Tanganyika, without any more noise; and *Inshallah!* we shall find the old Musungu at Ujiji! Speak, men, freedmen, shall we not? Shall we not go to the Tanganyika without any more trouble? Tell the master with one voice."

"*Ay Wallah! Ay Wallah! Bana yango! Hamuna manneno mgini!*" which, being literally translated, means:

"Yes, by God! Yes, by God! my master! There are no other words."

"Ask the master's pardon, man, or go thy way," said Mabruki, peremptorily, to Asmani; which Asmani did, to the gratification of them all. It only remained for Stanley to extend a general pardon to all, except to Bombay and Ambari, the instigators of the mutiny, which was now happily quelled. For Bombay could by a word, as the captain, have nipped all manifestation of bad temper at the outset, had he been so disposed. But no, Bombay was more adverse to marching than the cowardliest of his fellows, not because he was cowardly, but because he loved indolence, and made a god of his belly. So, snatching up a spear, Stanley laid its staff vigorously on Bombay's shoulders, and then sprang upon Ambari, whose mocking face soon underwent a remarkable transformation; and then clapped them both in chains, with a threat that they would be kept chained until they knew how to ask their master's pardon. Asmani and Mabruki were told to be cautious not to exhibit their ugly tempers any more, lest they might taste the death they had so fortunately escaped.

Again the word was given to march, and each man, with astonishing alacrity, seized his load, and filed off quickly out of sight; Bombay and Ambari in the rear in chains, with Kingaru and Asmani, the deserters, weighted with the heaviest loads. They had barely traveled an hour from the Gombe before Bombay and Ambari in trembling accents implored their master's pardon; he permitted the n to continue for half an hour longer, when he finally relented, releasing them both from their chains, and restoring Bombay to his full honors as captain.

THE WILD BOAR.

They traveled fourteen days in a southwesterly direction and Stanley intended to have gone still further south; but rumors of war on the path before them induced him to change this plan. After consulting with Asmani, the guide, he decided to strike across toward the Tanganyika, on a west-by-north course through the forest, traveling, when it was advantageous, along elephant tracks and local paths.

All were firm friends now; all squabbling had long ceased. Bombay and his master had forgotten their quarrel; the *kirangozi* and Stanley were ready to embrace. Confidence returned to all hearts; for now, as Mabruki Unyanyembe said: "They could smell the fish of the Tanganyika."

They were now in a country where the most dangerous animals were to be found; Stanley had already seen the first herd of elephants in their native wilds; and their camp on the Mtambu proved to be near the lairs of leopards and of lions. As some of the men were taking the two donkeys to water from this camp, a leopard sprang upon one of the animals, and fastened its claws in his throat. The frightened donkey began to bray so loudly, and was so warmly assisted by its companions, that the leopard bounded away through the brake, as if in sheer dismay at the noisy cries which the attack had provoked. The donkey's neck exhibited some frightful wounds, but the animal was not dangerously hurt.

MEETS A WILD BOAR.

Stanley, thinking that possibly he might meet with an adventure with a lion or leopard in that dark belt of tall trees, took a stroll along that awesome place with the gun-bearer, Kalulu, carrying an extra supply of ammunition and an additional gun. But after an hour's search for adventure he had encountered nothing, and strolled further in search of something to shoot. Presently he saw a huge wild boar feeding quietly at some distance from him. He got two shots at this animal, but his bullets were not heavy enough to penetrate his thick hide and do any material damage, so that the boar escaped. As it was now getting late, and the camp was three miles away, they were obliged to return without the meat. On their way to camp they were accompanied by a large animal which persistently followed them on their left. It was too dark to see plainly, but a large form was visible, if not very clearly defined. It must have been a lion.

About eleven that night, they were startled by the roar of a lion very near the camp; soon it was joined by another and another, and the novelty of the thing kept the white man awake. He endeavored to sight a rifle; but the cartridges might as well have been filled with sawdust for all the benefit which he derived from them. Disgusted with the miser-able ammunition, he left the lions alone, and turned in, with their roar as a lullaby.

November 3, being then in Uvinza, they saw a caravan which came from the direction of Ujiji, consisting of about eighty Waguhha. They asked the news, and were told that a white man had just arrived at Ujiji from Manyuema. This news startled them all.

"A white man?" Stanley asked.

"Yes, a white man," was the reply.

"How is he dressed?"

"Like the master," they said, referring to Stanley.

"Is he young or old?"

"He is old. He has white hair on his face, and he is sick."

"Where has he come from?"

"From a very far country away beyond Uguhha, called Manyuema."

"Indeed! And is he stopping at Ujiji now?"

"Yes, we saw him about eight days ago."

"Do you think he will stop there until we see him?"

"*Sigue*" (don't know).

"Was he ever at Ujiji before?"

"Yes, he went away a long time ago."

It must be Livingstone. It can be no other; but still—he may be some one else—some one from the west coast—or perhaps he is Baker. No, Baker has no white hairs on his face. But they must now march quickly, lest he hears that they are coming, and runs away. Stanley addressed his men, and asked them if they were willing to march to Ujiji without a single halt: and then promised them, if they acceded to his wishes, two doti for each man. All answered in the affirmative, almost as much rejoiced as he was himself. But he was madly re-joiced, intensely eager to solve the burning question: "Is it Dr. Liv-ingstone?" He did wish there was a railroad, or at least horses in this country; with a horse he could reach Ujiji in about twelve hours.

DELAYS AND DANGER.

But the time necessary was much longer than this. They must pass through Uhha, and there they were subject to many delays. The messenger of the king demanded *hongo*, or tribute, to an enormous extent. After considerable haggling, this was paid; a few miles further on, the king himself demanded *honga*, and denied all knowledge of his supposed agent. This, too, had to be paid. Yet farther, the king's brother required *honga*, for he was almost as powerful as the king.

Upon consultation with his chief men, Stanley decided that the only way to escape absolute penury as the result of a journey through Uhha,

THE ALPINE MARMOT.

was to keep away from the villages and roads, and, trusting only to the compass, plunge boldly into the forests and make their way, by a hitherto untrodden path, out of the country. Provisions sufficient to last six days were purchased, the guides were given an extra *douceur*, orders for the strictest silence throughout the march were issued, and the caravan marched.

They stole out of their camp near a village at 3 A. M.; and by 8 had reached the Rusugi, where they camped in a clump of jungle near its banks. An hour after they had rested, some natives, carrying salt from the Malagarazi, were seen coming up the right bank of the river. When abreast of the hiding-place they detected the strangers, and dropping their salt-bags, they ran to give the alarm to the neighboring villages, four miles away. The men were immediately ordered to take up their loads, and in a few minutes they had crossed the Rusugi, and were making direct for a bamboo jungle which appeared in their front. Almost as soon as they entered, a weak-brained woman raised a series of piercing yells. The men were appalled at this noisy demonstration, which would call down upon their heads the vengeance of the Wahha for evading the tribute to which they thought themselves entitled. In half an hour they would have hundreds of howling savages about them in the jungle, and probably a general massacre would ensue. The woman screamed fearfully, again and again, for no cause whatever. Some of the men with the instinct of self-preservation, at once dropped their bales and their loads, and vanished into the jungle. The guide came rushing back to Stanley, imploring him to stop her noise. The woman's husband, livid with rage and fear, drew his sword, and asked his master's permission to cut off her head at once. Had Stanley given the least signal, the woman had paid for her folly with her life. He attempted to hush her cries by putting his hand over her mouth, but she violently wrestled with him, and continued her cries worse than ever. There remained nothing else for him to do but to try the virtues of his whip over her shoulders. He asked her to desist after the first blow. No! She continued her insane cries with increased force and volume. Again his whip descended upon her shoulders. "No, no, no!" Another blow. "Will you hush?" "No, no, no!" Louder and faster she cried, and faster and faster he showered the blows for the taming of this shrew. However, seeing he was as determined to flog as she was to cry, she desisted before the tenth blow, and was silent. A cloth was folded over her mouth, and her arms were tied behind her; and in a few moments, the runaways having returned to their duties, the expedition moved forward again with redoubled pace.

Still keeping silence, they at last passed through Guhha, and were out of danger of extortion. They arrived at a point whence the Tanganyika could be seen, November 10. It was the fifty-first day after leaving Unyanyembe, and the two hundred and thirty-sixth after leaving Bagamoyo. They now pushed on rapidly, lest the news of their coming might reach the people of Bunder Ujiji before they came in sight and were ready for them. They halt at a little brook, then ascend the long slope of a naked ridge, the very last of the myriads they have crossed. They arrive at the summit, travel across and arrive at its western rim, and the port of Ujiji is below them, embowered in the palms, only five hundred yards from them. Their hearts and feelings are

THE WATER DEERLET, OR CHEVROTAIN.

with their eyes, as they peer into the palms and try to make out in which hut or house lives the white man with the gray beard they heard about on the Malagarazi.

"Unfurl the flags, and load your guns!"

"*Ay Wallah, Ay Wallah, bana!*" respond the men eagerly.

"One—two—three—fire!"

A volley from nearly fifty guns roars like a salute from a battery of artillery; we shall note its effect presently on the peaceful-looking village below.

"Now, *kirangozi*, hold the white man's flag up high, and let the Zanzibar flag bring up the rear. And you men keep close together and keep firing until we halt in the market-place, or before the white man's house. You have said to me often that you could smell the fish of the Tanganyika—I can smell the fish of the Tanganyika now. There are fish, and beer, and a long rest waiting for you. MARCH!"

FORWARD!   MARCH!

Before they had gone a hundred yards their repeated volleys had had the effect desired. They had awakened Ujiji to the knowledge that a caravan was coming, and the people were witnessed rushing up in hundreds to meet them. The mere sight of the flags informed every one at once that they were a caravan, but the American flag borne aloft by gigantic Asmani, whose face was one vast smile on this day, rather staggered them at first. However, many of the people who now approached them remembered the flag. They had seen it float over the American consulate and from the mast of many a ship in the harbor of Zanzibar; and they were soon welcoming the beautiful flag with cries of *Bindera Kisuggu!*—a white man's flag! *Bindera Merikani* —the American flag!"

Then the newcomers were surrounded by them; by Wajiji, Wanyamwezi, Wangwana, Warundi, Waguhha, Wamanyuema and Arabs, and were almost deafened with shouts of "*Yambo, yambo, bana! Yambo, bana! Yambo bana!*" To all and each of Stanley's men the welcome was given.

They were now about three hundred yards from the village of Ujiji, and the crowds were dense about them. Suddenly Stanley heard a voice on his right say: ·

"Good morning, sir."

Startled at hearing this greeting in the midst of such a crowd of black people, he turns sharply around in search of the man, and sees him at his side, with the blackest of faces, but animated and joyous—

a man dressed in a long white shirt, with a turban of American sheeting around his woolly head; and he asks:

"Who the mischief are you?"

"I am Susi, the servant of Dr. Livingstone," said he, smiling and showing a gleaming row of teeth.

"What! Is Dr. Livingstone here?"

"Yes, sir."

ANT BEAR.

"In this village?"

"Yes, sir."

"Are you sure?"

"Sure, sure, sir. Why, I leave him just now."

"Good morning, sir," said another voice.

"Hallo," said Stanley. "Is this another one?"

"Yes, sir."

"Well, what is your name?"

"My name is Chuma, sir."

"What, are you Chuma, the friend of Wekotami?"

"Yes, sir."

"And is the doctor well?"

"Not very well, sir."

"Where has he been so long?"

"In Manyuema."

"Now you, Susi, run and tell the doctor I am coming." ·

"Yes, sir;" and off he darted like a madman.

But by this time they were within two hundred yards of the village, and the multitude was getting denser, and almost preventing their march. Flags and streamers were out; Arabs and Wangwana were pushing their way through the natives in order to greet the new-comers; for according to their account, the strangers belonged to them. But the great wonder of all was:

"How did you come from Unyanyembe?"

Soon Susi came running back, and asked Stanley his name; he had told the doctor that a white man was coming, but the doctor was too surprised to believe him; and when asked the white man's name, Susi was rather staggered. But during Susi's absence, the news had been conveyed to the doctor that it was surely a white man that was coming, whose guns were firing and whose flag could be seen; and the great Arab magnates of Ujiji had gathered together before the doctor's house, and the doctor had come out from his veranda to discuss the matter and await his arrival.

In the meantime, the head of the expedition had halted, and the kirangozi was out of the ranks, holding his flag aloft; and Selim said to his master:

LIVINGSTONE FOUND.

"I see the doctor, sir. Oh, what an old man! He has got a white beard."

And Stanley—what would he not have given for a bit of friendly wilderness, where he might vent his joy in some mad freak, such as idiotically biting his hand, turning a somersault, or slashing at trees, in order to allay those exciting feelings that were well nigh incontroll-able. His heart beat fast, but he must not let his face betray his emo-tions, lest it shall detract from the dignity of a white man appearing under such extraordinary circumstances.

So he did that which he thought was most dignified. He pushed back the crowds, and passing from the rear, walked down a living ave-nue of people, until he came in front of the semi-circle of Arabs, in the front of which stood the white man with the gray beard. As he advanced slowly toward him, he noticed that the great explorer was pale, looked wearied, had a gray beard, wore a bluish cap with a faded gold band round it, had on a red-sleeved waistcoat, and a pair of gray tweed trousers. Stanley would have run to him, only he says, "I was a coward in the presence of such a mob—would have embraced him, only, he being an Englishman, I did not know how he would receive me; so I did what cowardice and false pride suggested was the best thing —walked deliberately to him, took off my hat, and said:

" 'Dr. Livingstone, I presume?' "

"Yes," said he, with a kind smile, lifting his cap slightly.

Stanley replaced his hat on his head, and Livingstone put on his cap; and they both grasped hands; and Stanley then said aloud:

"I thank God, Doctor, that I have been permitted to see you."

"I feel thankful," replied Livingstone, "that I am here to welcome you."

Stanley turned to the Arabs, took off his hat to them in response to the saluting chorus of *"Yambos"* he received, and the doctor in-troduced them to him by name. Then oblivious of the crowds, obliv-ious of the men who had shared dangers with him, Livingstone and Stan-ley turned their faces toward the elder man's tembe. They are seated with their backs to the wall. The Arabs take seats on their left. More than a thousand natives are in front of them, filling the whole square densely, indulging their curiosity, and discussing the fact of two white men meeting at Ujiji—one just come from Manyuema, in the west, and one from Unyanyembe in the east.

Conversation began; questions innumerable, yet of the simplest kind; then Livingstone began to tell the story of his travels, while Stanley listened entranced. The Arabs rose with a delicacy of which the white men approved, as if they intuitively knew that they ought to be left to themselves. Stanley sent Bombay with them, to give them the news they also wanted so much to know about the affairs at Unyanyembe; they all had friends there, and it was but natural that they should be anxious to hear of what concerned them.

"No, doctor," was the reply, "read your letters first, which I am sure you must be impatient to read."

"Ah," said he, "I have waited years for letters, and I have been taught patience. I can surely afford to wait a few hours longer. No, tell me the general news: how is the world getting along?"

"You probably know much already. Do you know that the Suez canal is a fact—is opened, and a regular trade carried on between Europe and India through it?"

"I did not hear about the opening of it. Well, that is grand news! What else?"

Shortly, Stanley found himself acting the part of an annual periodical to him. There was no need of any exaggeration—of any penny-a-line news, or of any sensationalism. The world had witnessed and experienced much during the past few years. The Pacific railroad had been completed; Grant had been elected President of the United States; Egypt had been flooded with savans; the Cretan Rebellion had been terminated; a Spanish Revolution had driven Isabella from the throne of Spain, and a regent had been appointed; General Prim was assassinated; a Castelar had electrified Europe with his advanced ideas upon the liberty of worship; Prussia had humbled Denmark, and annexed Schleswig-Holstein, and her armies were now around Paris; the "Man of Destiny" was a prisoner at Wilhelmshohe; the Queen of Fashion and the Empress of the French was a fugitive; and the child born in the purple had lost forever the imperial crown intended for his head; the Napoleon dynasty was extinguished by the Prussians, Bismarck and Von Moltke; and France, the proud empire, was humbled to the dust. What could a man have exaggerated of these facts? What a budget of news it was to one who had emerged from the depths of the primeval forests of Manyuema!

CHAPTER XXI.

STANLEY'S TRIUMPHANT MARCH ACROSS THE DARK CONTINENT.

Stanley Explores Same Ground as Roosevelt—Preparations for the Journey—Departure—Interviewed by Lions—A Three Days' Fight—Crocodiles and Hippopotami—Sickness and Death in the Camp—A Murderous Outbreak—A Fight and a Fine——Uganda and Its People—Panic in the Camp—The Terror of Africa—In Dwarf Land—Cataracts and Cannibals—The Congo—Struggling On—Victoria and Albert Nyanza.

WHEN Stanley set out to find the outlet of Lake Tanganyika and the sources of the Nile and to explore the then unknown western half of the African continent hardly anyone realized the wonderful resources of that rich and undeveloped country.

His equipment included guns, ammunition, ropes, saddles, medical stores, provisions, gifts for native chiefs, scientific instruments, stationery, etc., pontoons and boats. He was accompanied by three young stalwart English boatmen, two magnificent mastiffs, a retriever, a bulldog and a bull-terrier. When they left Zanzibar (in November, 1874) the party were 356 in number, including 36 women and 10 boys, the line being nearly half a mile in length. Their first march through Ugogo was a progress in a country of starvation, for the improvident savage natives had no provisions and on one occasion they were reduced to two cupfuls of oatmeal mush for each person.

SICKNESS AND HUNGER.

They were much troubled by sickness among the caravan; and Edward Pocock was dangerously ill. But the discontent of the people at the difficulty of obtaining food was such that Stanley judged it best to keep moving, if only two or three miles a day. Accordingly, those who were in the worst condition were carried in hammocks, and they proceeded by easy stages. They reached Chiwyu January 18, and had just begun to erect grass huts, when the sick European died from typhus fever. Here they buried him at the foot of a hoary acacia with wide-spreading branches, and the lessened group of Europeans, with their army of black attendants, took up their journey westward

HENRY M. STANLEY.

the next day. This was by no means the first death in the expedition, although it was the first white man. Since leaving Bagamoyo, twenty had died, and no less than eighty-nine had deserted.

Hitherto, in the case of all explorers, the story has rather been one of difficulties resulting from the nature of the country than from the hostility of the natives. Mungo Park alone, of the great African explorers, met with his death at the hands of Africans. But the story of Stanley's journey across the continent is, throughout, a story of battle. He had learned forbearance, he tells us, from Livingstone, but this is a virtue which savage adversaries seldom appreciate, mistaking it for weakness and cowardice.

While encamped at Vinyata, they received a visit from a great magic doctor, who brought them the welcome present of a fine fat ox. Repaid about four-fold for it, he came again the next day, bringing some milk, and again received a present.

WAR ABOUT A GLASS OF MILK AND AN ASS.

Many were the difficulties they encountered often for very trivial reasons. One day some of his native helpers had stolen some milk from the savage tribe, through whose territory they were journeying, and this being considered a sufficient cause for war they suddenly found themselves surrounded by a howling mob of bloodthirsty warriors. A brisk encounter was sustained for an hour, and then, having driven the savages away they returned to camp. But the next day the hostile natives gathered again in their front larger than before in numbers and still fiercer for fight; the whole neighboring country seemed to have been aroused. Stanley and his men were in no mood for fighting. They were hungry, exhausted and wretched, and the danger of starvation or extinction seemed the only end in view. Time and again the savages attacked and were driven back but only to return in larger number. Stanley himself gives this graphic description of the perilous situation of his command:

"Our position, as strangers in a hostile country, is such that we cannot exist as a corporate expedition, unless we resist with all our might and skill, in order to terminate hostilities and secure access to the western country. We therefore wait until they advance upon our camp, and drive them back from its vicinity as we did the day before. In half an hour our people are back, and organized into four detachments of ten men each under their respective chiefs, two more detachments of ten men each held in reserve, and one other, of ten also, detailed for the defense of the camp. They are instructed to proceed in skirmishing order in different directions through the hostile country, and to drive the inhabitants out wherever they find them lodged, to a distance of five miles east and north, certain rocky hills, the rendezvous of the foe, being pointed out as the place where they must converge. Messengers are sent with each detachment to bring back information.

"The left detachment, was thrown into disorder, and were killed to a man, except the messenger who brought us the news, imploring for the reserve as the enemy were now concentrated on the second detachment. Manwa Sera was dispatched with fifteen men, and arrived at the scene only in time to save eight out of the second detachment. The third plunged boldly on, but lost six of its number; the fourth behaved prudently and well, and as fast as each inclosed village was taken set it on fire. But ten other men dispatched to the scene retrieved what the third had lost, and strengthened Safeni.

"Our losses in this day's proceedings were twenty-one soldiers and one messenger killed, and three wounded.

"On the morning of the 25th we waited until 9 A. M., again hoping that the Wanyaturu would see the impolicy of renewing the fight; but we were disappointed, for they appeared again, and apparently as numerous as ever. After some severe volleys we drove them off again on the third day, but upon the return of the Wangwana, instead of dividing them into detachments, I instructed them to proceed in a compact body. Some of the porters volunteered to take the place of the soldiers who perished the previous day, and we were therefore able to show still a formidable front. All the villages in our neighborhood being first consumed, they continued their march, and finally attacked the rocky hill, which the Wanyaturu had adopted as a stronghold, and drove them flying precipitately into the neighboring country, where they did not follow them.

"We knew now that we should not be disturbed. * * * Our losses in Ituru were twenty-four killed and four wounded, and as we had twenty-five men on the sick-list, it may be imagined that to replace these fifty-three men great sacrifices were necessary, and much in-

FIGHT AND BURNING OF VILLAGES.

genuity had to be exercised. Twelve loads were accordingly placed on the asses, and ten chiefs were detailed to carry baggage until we should arrive in Usukuma. Much miscellaneous property was burned, and on the morning of the 26th, just before day-break, we resumed our interrupted journey.''

Usiha proved much more hospitable, and they were not only kindly welcomed, but were able to procure the food which they needed so badly. Here, however, they were once in danger from the braying of an ass.

"When in sight of their conical cotes, we dispatched one of our native guides to warn the natives that a caravan of Wangwana was approaching, and to bear messages of peace and good will. But in his absence, one of the Kinyamwezi asses set up a terrific braying, which nearly created serious trouble. It appears that on one of his former raids the terrible Mirambo possessed a Kinyamwezi ass which also brayed, and like the geese of the Roman Capitol, betrayed the foe. Hence the natives insisted, despite the energetic denial of our guide, that this ass must also belong to Mirambo, and for a short period he was in a perilous state. They seized and bound him, and would probably have dispatched him had not the village scouts returned laughing heartily at the fright the vicious ass had caused.''

VICTORIA NYANZA.

Two days after these thrilling incidents they reached the shores of Victoria Nyanza. Before them lay a vast sheet of water, which a dazzling sun transformed into silver and which stretched away across to a boundary of dark blue hills and mountains.

Crowds of savages soon surrounded them from all sides. They informed him that the lake was so large that it would take eight years to trace its shores, and that there were a people dwelling on its shores who were gifted with tails, another a tribe of cannibals, who preferred human flesh to all kinds of meat. It was almost impossible to get the superstitious natives to follow him out on the lake. Only used to paddling they were afraid of the sails and fled when they were hoisted. Finally he selected two men and with this crew set sail upon the big waters. We cannot relate all the adventures he met on this historic circumnavigation. Reaching the northeastern part of the lake they met a large canoe, propelled by forty paddlers, who when they came within fifty yards seizing their long tufted lances and shields began to sway them menacingly.

FISHING AT STANLEY FALLS.

"They edged toward us a little nearer," says Stanley, "and ended by ranging their long canoe alongside of our boat. Our tame, mild manners were in striking contrast to their bullying, overbearing and insolent demeanor. The paddlers, half of whom were intoxicated, laid their hands with familiar freedom upon everything. We still smiled, and were as mild and placable as though anger and resentment could

20

never enter our hearts. We were so courteous, indeed, that we permitted them to handle our persons with a degree of freedom which appeared to them unaccountable—unless we were so timid that we feared to give offense. If we had been so many sheep, we could not have borne a milder or more innocent aspect. Our bold friends, reeling and jostling one another in their eagerness to offend, seized their spears and shields, and began to chant in bacchanalian tones a song that was tipsily discordant. Some seized their slings and flung stones to a great distance, which we applauded. Then one of them, under the influence of wine, and spirits elated by the chant, waxed bolder, and looked as though he would aim at myself, seated observant but mute in the stern of my boat. I made a motion with my hand as though deprecating such an action. The sooty villain seemed to become at once animated by an hysteric passion, and whirled his stone over my head, a loud drunken cheer applauding his boldness.

"Perceiving that they were becoming wanton through our apparently mild demeanor, I seized my revolver and fired rapidly into the water, in the direction the stone had been flung, and the effect was painfully ludicrous. The bold, insolent bacchanals had at the first shot sprung overboard, and were swimming for dear life to Ngevi, leaving their canoe in our hands. 'Friends, come back, come back; why this fear!' cried out our interpreter; 'we simply wished to show you that we had weapons as well as yourselves. Come, take your canoe; see, we push it away for you to seize it.' We eventually won them back with smiles. We spoke to them as sweetly as before. The natives were more respectful in their demeanor. They laughed, cried out admiringly; imitated the pistol shot; 'Boom, boom, boom,' they shouted. They then presented me with a bunch of bananas. We became enthusiastic admirers of each other."

After having met many warlike tribes and successfully escaped their traps they finally arrived at Usavara, the hunting village of Kabaka, where

STANLEY MET THE MIGHTIEST MAN OF EQUATORIAL AFRICA.

But he himself must tell of his reception:

"When about two miles from Usavara, we saw what we estimated to be thousands of people arranging themselves in order on gently rising ground. When about a mile from the shore, Magassa gave the order to signal our advance with fire-arms, and was at once obeyed by his dozen musketeers. Half a mile off I saw that the people on the shore had formed themselves into two dense lines, at the ends of which

A CONCERT.

stood several finely dressed men, arrayed in crimson and black and snowy white. As we neared the beach, volleys of musketry burst out from the long lines. Magassa's canoes steered outward to right and left, while two or three hundred heavily loaded guns announced to all around that the white man, of whom Mtesa's mother had dreamed, had landed. Numerous kettles and bass drums sounded a noisy welcome, and flags, banners and bannerets waved, and the people gave a great shout. Very much amazed at all this ceremonious and pompous greeting, I strode up toward the great standard, near which stood a short young man, dressed in a crimson robe which covered an immaculately white dress of bleached cotton, before whom Magassa, who had hurried ashore, kneeled reverently, and turning to me begged me to understand that this short young man was the Katekiro. Not knowing very well who the Katekiro was, I only bowed, which, strange to say, was imitated by him, only that his bow was far more profound and stately than mine. I was perplexed, confused, embarrassed, and I believed I blushed inwardly at all this regal reception, though I hope I did not betray my embarrassment.

"A dozen well-dressed people now came forward, and grasping my hand declared in the Swahili language that I was welcome to Uganda. The Katekiro motioned with his head, and amid a perfect concourse of beaten drums, which drowned all conversation, we walked side by side, and followed by curious thousands, to a court-yard, and a circle of grass-thatched huts surrounding a larger house, which I was told were my quarters.

"The Katekiro and several of the chiefs accompanied me to my new hut, and a very sociable conversation took place. There was present a native of Zanzibar, named Tori, whom I shortly discovered to be chief drummer, engineer, and general jack-of-all-trades for the Kabaka. From this clever, ingenious man I obtained the information that the Katekiro was the prime minister, or the Kabaka's deputy. * * * Waganda, as I found subsequently, were not in the habit of remaining incurious before a stranger. Hosts of questions were fired off at me about my health, my journey and its aim, Zanzibar, Europe and its people, the seas and the heavens, sun, moon, and stars, angels and devils, doctors, priests, and craftsmen in general; in fact, as the representative of nations who 'know everything,' I was subjected to a most searching examination, and in one hour and ten minutes it was declared unanimously that I had 'passed.' Forthwith after the acclamation, the stately bearing became merged into a more friendly one, and long, thin, nervous black hands were pushed into mine enthusiastically, from which I gathered that they applauded me as if I had won the honors of a senior wrangler. Some proceeded direct to the Kabaka and informed him that the white man was a genius, knew everything, and was remarkably polite and sociable; and the Kabaka was said to have 'rubbea his hands as though he had just come into possession of a treasure.'"

After this searching examination was concluded, and reported to Mtesa, that chief dispatched refreshments for his guest. "These few things," as they were styled in the message accompanying them, were fourteen fat oxen, sixteen goats and sheep, a hundred bunches of

ROYAL HOSPITALITIES.

bananas, three dozen fowls, four wooden jars of milk, four baskets of sweet potatoes, fifty ears of green Indian corn, a basket of rice, twenty fresh eggs, and ten pots or maramba wine. When the traveler had eaten and was satisfied, the Kabaka would send for him.

Promptly at the appointed hour, two pages came to summon the traveler to the presence of the foremost man of Central Africa.

"Forthwith we issued from our courtyard, five of the boat's crew on each side of me armed with Snider rifles. We reach a short broad street, at the end of which is a hut. Here the Kabaka is seated with a number of chiefs, *Wakungu* [generals] and *Watongeleh* [colonels] ranked from the throne in two opposing kneeling or seated lines, the ends being closed in by drummers, guards, executioners, pages, etc., etc. As we approached the nearest group, it opened, and the drummers beat mighty sounds, Tori's drumming being conspicuous from its sharper beat. The foremost man of Equatorial Africa rises and advances, and all the kneeling and seated lines rise—generals, colonels, chiefs, cooks, butlers, pages, executioners, etc., etc.

"The Kabaka, a tall, clean-faced, large-eyed, nervous-looking, thin man, clad in a tarbush, black robe, with a white shirt belted with gold, shook my hands warmly and impressively, and bowing not ungracefully, invited me to be seated on an iron stool. I waited for him to show the example, and then I and all the others seated ourselves.

"He first took a deliberate survey of me, which I returned with interest, for he was as interesting to me as I was to him. His impression of me was that I was younger than Speke, not so tall, but better dressed. This I gathered from his criticisms as confided to his chiefs and favorites.

"My impression of him was that he and I would become better acquainted, that I should make a convert of him, and make him useful to Africa."

It will be remembered that Speke's description of this potentate was not a very favorable one—vain and heartless, a wholesale tyrant and murderer, delighting in fat women. It had been his custom, in receiving a visitor with honors, to have his executioners strike off the heads of several slaves or subjects on the spot. Stanley found him intelligent, and well worthy the heartiest sympathies that Europe had to give him. What was the reason for this change? Stanley answers in his journal, in the entry written at this very time:

"I see that Mtesa is a powerful emperor, with great influence over his neighbors. * * * I have witnessed with astonishment such order and law as is obtainable in semi-civilized countries. All this is the result of a poor Muslim's labor; his name is Muley bin Salim. He it was who first began teaching here the doctrines of Islam. False and contemptible as these doctrines are, they are preferable to the ruthless instincts of a savage despot, whom Speke and Grant left wallowing in the blood of women, and I honor the memory of Muley bin Salim —Muslim and slave trader though he be—the poor priest who had wrought this happy change. With a strong desire to improve still more the character of Mtesa, I shall begin building on the foundation stones laid by Muley bin Salim. I shall destroy his belief in Islam, and teach the doctrines of Jesus of Nazareth.''

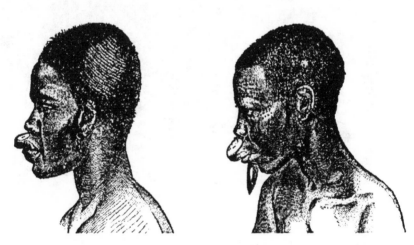

WOMEN AT MTESA'S COURT.

Two days after his arrival at Usavara, Mtesa distinguished "Stamlee" by holding what he termed a review of his fleet, forty canoes, holding some twelve hundred men. "The captain of each canoe was dressed in a white cotton shirt and a cloth head-cover, neatly folded turban fashion, while the admiral wore over his shirt a crimson jacket profusely decorated with gold braid, and on his head the red fez of Zanzibar. Each captain, as he passed us, seized shield and spear, and with the bravado of a matador addressing the Judge of the Plaza to behold his prowess, went through the performance of defense and

WOMEN BREAKING CORN.

attack by water. The admiral won the greatest applause, for he was
the Hector of the fleet, and his actions, though not remarkably graceful, were certainly remarkably extravagant. The naval review over,
Mtesa commanded one of the captains of the canoes to try and discover a crocodile or hippopotamus. After fifteen minutes he returned
with the report that there was a young crocodile asleep on a rock about
two hundred yards away.

"'Now, Stamlee,' said Mtesa, 'show my women how white men can
shoot.'

"[For the great chief was attended by a considerable number of
the women composing his harem.] To represent all the sons of Japhet
on this occasion was a great responsibility, but I am happy to say

that—whether owing to the gracious influence of some unseen divinity who has the guardianship of their interests or whether from mere luck—I nearly severed the head of the young crocodile from its body at the distance of one hundred yards with a three-ounce ball, an act which was accepted as proof that all white men are dead shots."

Three days later, the court broke up its hunting lodge and returned to the capital, Stanley following at a later hour, since it was necessary to house his boat from the sun. The road was eight feet wide, through jungle and garden and forest and field. We need not linger over the description of the beautiful scenery enjoyed during the three hours' march before they came in sight of a large cluster of tall, conical grass huts, in the center of which rose a spacious, lofty barn-like structure. The large building, they were told, was the palace, the hill, Rubaga, and the cluster of huts, the imperial capital!

The envoy of the two great newspapers had, as we have already heard from his own lips, determined to make an effort to convert Mtesa to Christianity. It was his first missionary work; for up to the period of his first journey into the interior of Africa at least, he had "cared for none of these things." The four months' intercourse with Livingstone, however, close and constant as it was, had wrought a change; it was owing to no set effort of the elder man; but the influence of his life and character taught Stanley the worth of the religion which he professed. On the evening of the day that the traveler had his first interview with Mtesa, he wrote in his diary:

"In this man I see the possible fruition of Livingstone's hopes, for with his aid the civilization of Equatorial Africa becomes feasible. I remember the ardor and love which animated Livingstone when he spoke of Sekeletu; had he seen Mtesa, his ardor and love for him had been tenfold, and his pen and tongue would have been employed in calling all good men to assist him."

At every interview between them, the white man had made some effort to turn the conversation to the subject of religion; and not in vain. Mtesa and his principal chiefs soon became so absorbingly interested in the story of the Gospel as Stanley gave it to them that little of other business was done. Of course only the bare outlines were touched upon—those essential points which are accepted by all, and which are as intelligible to the savage and the child as to doctor of divinity.

"I showed the difference in character between Him whom white men love and adore, and Mohammed, whom the Arabs revere; how Jesus endeavored to teach all mankind that we should love all men, excepting none; while Mohammed taught his followers that the slay-

THE IMPERIAL CAPITAL.

ing of the pagan and unbeliever was an act that merited Paradise. I left it to Mtesa and his chiefs to decide which was the worthier char- acter. I also sketched in brief the history of religious belief from Adam to Mohammed. I had also begun to translate to him the Ten Commandments, and Idi, the emperor's writer, trnscribed in Kiganda the words of the Law as given to him in choice Swahili by Robert

Feruzi, one of my boat's crew, and a pupil of the Universities' Mission at Zanzibar.''

But Stanley must be looking after the men whom he had left at Kagehyi, leaving the completion of his missionary work for the present. Mtesa gave him permission to depart, and ordered Magassa to have ready thirty canoes to serve as escort.

STANLEY LEAVES GREAT MONARCH. FIERCE ENCOUNTER WITH SAVAGES.

Escorted by Magassa he returned along the western coast of the lake, all the time meeting with thrilling adventures.

''As soon as we had sailed a little distance along the coast,'' he says, ''we caught sight of a few figures which broke the even and smooth outline of the grassy summit, and heard the well-known melodious war-cries employed by most of the Central African tribes: '*Hehu-a hehu u-u-u!*' loud, long-drawn, and ringing.

''The figures increased in number, and fresh voices joined in the defiant and alarming note. Still, hungry wretches as we were, environed by difficulties of all kinds, just beginning to feel warm after the cold and wet of the night before, with famine gnawing at our vitals, leagues upon leagues of sea between us and our friends at Usukuma, and nothing eatable in our boat, we were obliged to risk something reminding ourselves that 'there are no circumstances so desperate which Providence may not relieve.'

''At 9 A. M. we discovered a cove near the southeast end of the long island, and pulled slowly into it. Immediately the natives rushed down the slopes, shouting war-cries and uttering fierce ejaculations.

''The natives consulted a little while, and several—now smiling pleasantly themselves, advanced leisurely into the water until they touched the boat's prow. They stood a few seconds talking sweetly, when suddenly with a rush they ran the boat ashore, and then all the others, seizing hawser and gunwale, dragged her about twenty yards over the rocky beach high and dry, leaving us almost stupefied with astonishment!

''Then ensued a scene which beggars description. Pandemonium— all its devils armed, raged around us. A forest of spears were levelled; thirty or forty bows were drawn taut; as many barbed arrows seemed already on the wing; thick, knotty clubs waved above our heads; two hundred screaming black demons jostled with each other, and struggled for room to vent their fury, or for an opportunity to deliver one crushing blow or thrust at us.

"In the meantime, as soon as the first symptoms of this manifestation of violence had been observed, I had sprung to my feet, each hand armed with a loaded self-cocking revolver, to kill and be killed.

KING MUNZA'S HOUSE.

But the apparent hopelessness of inflicting much injury upon such a large crowd restrained me, and Safeni turned to me, almost cowed to dumbness by the loud fury around us, and pleaded with me to be patient. I complied, seeing that I should get no aid from my crew; but. while bitterly blaming myself for having yielded—against my instincts —to placing myself in the power of such savages, I vowed that if I escaped this once, my own judgment should guide my actions for the future.

"I assumed a resigned air, though I still retained my revolvers. My crew also bore the first outburst of the tempest of shrieking rage which assailed them with almost sublime imperturbability. Safeni crossed his arms with the meekness of a saint. Baraka held his hands palms outward, asking with serene benignity:

"'What, my friends, ails you? Do you fear empty hands and smiling people like us? We are friends, we come as friends to buy food, two or three bananas, a few mouthfuls of grain or potatoes, or *muhogo* (cassava), and, if you will permit it, we will depart as friends.'

"Our demeanor had a great effect. The riot and noise seemed to be subsiding, when some fifty newcomers rekindled the smouldering fury. Again the forest of spears swayed on the launch, again the knotty clubs were whirled aloft, again the bows were drawn, and again the barbed arrows seemed flying. Safeni received a push which sent him tumbling, little Kirango received a blow on the head with a spear-staff, Saramba gave a cry as a club descended on his back.

"I sprang up this time to remonstrate, with the two revolvers in my left hand. I addressed myself to an elder, who seemed to be re-straining the people from proceeding too far. I showed him beads, cloth, wire, and invoked the names of Mtesa, and Antari their king.

"The sight of the heaps of beads and cloth I exposed awakened, however, the more deliberate passions of selfishness and greed in each heart. An attempt at massacre, they began to argue, would certainly entail the loss of some of themselves. 'Guns might be seized and han-dled with terrible effect even by dying men, and who knows what those little iron things in the white man's hands are?' they seemed to be asking themselves. The elder, whatever he thought, responded with an affectation of indignation, raised his stick, and to right and left of him drove back the demoniac crew. Other prominent men now as-sisted this elder, whom we subsequently discovered to be Shekka, the king of Bumbireh.

"Shekka, then, having thus bestirred himself, beckoned to half a dozen men and walked away a few yards behind the mass. It was the '*shauri*,' dear to a free and independent African's heart, that was about to be held. Half the crowd followed the king and his council, while the other half remained to indulge their violent, vituperative tongues on us, and to continually menace us with either club or spear.

An audacious party came round the stern of the boat and, with super-latively hideous gestures, affronted me; one of them even gave a tug at my hair; thinking it was a wig. I revenged myself by seizing his hand, and suddenly bending it back, almost dislocated it, causing him to howl with pain. His comrades swayed their lances, but I smil-ingly looked at them, for all idea of self-preservation had now almost fled.

"The issue had surely arrived. There had been just one brief moment of agony when I reflected how unlovely death appears in such guise as that in which it then threatened me. What would my people think as they anxiously awaited the never-returning master? What would Pocock and Barker say when they heard of the tragedy of Bumbireh? And my friends in America and Europe! Tut, it is only a brief moment of pain, and then what can the ferocious dogs do more? It is a consolation that if anything it will be short, sharp, sudden—a gasp, and then a silence—forever and forever! And after that, I was ready for the fight and for death.

DO YOUR WORST.

" 'Now, my black friends, do your worst; anything you choose; I am ready.'

"A messenger from the king and council arrives, and beckons Sa-feni. I said to him: 'Safeni, use your wit.'

" 'Please God, master,' he replied."

The African, like all savages, is possessed by a curiosity easily aroused, and the natives followed Safeni, observing his every motion as he endeavored to make himself understood. As Mr. Stanley ob-serves, Safeni proved himself "a born diplomat." He used all the arts of the pantomime. His face was sweet and smiling; his hands made most eloquent gestures; he exhibited all the graces and elo-quence of the advocate, pleading before the jury for a client in danger for his life. In a short time he came back to his party radiant with hope, declaring it was all right, that they were safe; but that the savages insisted they should stay with them until they should hold their *shauri*, when they would sell food to the starving party. But even as he was relating this, several men came forward and suddenly grabbed all the oars. Safeni was about to resist, but Stanley called out:

" 'Let them go, Safeni!'

"A loud cheer greeted the seizure of the oars. I became convinced now that this one little act would lead to others; for man is the same

AFRICAN VILLAGE.

all over the world. Set a beggar on horseback and he will ride to the devil; give a slave an inch, and he will take an ell; if a man submit once, he must be prepared to submit again."

It was truly a desperate case, yet Stanley and his men could do nothing. The *shauri* proceeded; a messenger came demanding gifts; they were handed over without a word of protest. Noon came; and the savages, sure of their prey, withdrew to their villages for food and drink; for, as the poet asks, "Where is the man who can live without dining?" The half-starved men in the boat were visited by the women, who consoled them with the assurance of being killed very soon; if, however, they could induce Shekka to make blood-brotherhood or eat honey with one of them, peace would ensue and they would be safe.

"About 3 P. M. we heard a number of drums beaten. Safeni was told that if the natives collected again he must endeavor to induce Shekka with gifts to go through the process of blood-brotherhood.

"A long line of natives in full war costume appeared on the crest of the terrace, on which the banana grove and the village of Kajurri stood. Their faces were smeared with black and white pigments. Almost all of them bore the peculiar shields of Usongora. Their actions were such as the dullest-witted of us recognized as indicating hostilities. Even Safeni and Baraka were astounded, and their first words were:

" 'Prepare, master. Truly, this is trouble.'

" 'Never mind me,' I replied; 'I have been ready these three hours. Are you ready, your guns and revolvers loaded, and your ears open this time?'

" 'We are,' they all firmly answered.

" 'Don't be afraid; be quite cool. We will try, while they are collecting together, the women's suggestion. Go frankly and smiling, Safeni, up to Shekka, on the top of that hill, and offer him these three *fundo* of beads, and ask him to exchange blood with you.'

"Safeni proceeded readily on his errand, for there was no danger to him bodily while we were within a hundred and fifty yards, and their full number as yet unprepared. For ten minutes he conversed with them, while the drums kept beating, and numbers of men painted for war were increasing Shekka's force. Some of them entertained us by demonstrating with their spears how they fought; others whirled their clubs like tipsy Irishmen at Donnybrook fair. Their gestures were wild, their voices were shrill and fierce, they were kindling themselves into a fighting fever.

"Safeni returned. Shekka had refused the pledge of peace. The natives now mustered over three hundred. Presently fifty bold fellows

EXECUTION OF A MUTINEER IN STANLEY'S CAMP.

came rushing down, uttering a shrill cry. Without hesitation they came straight to the boat, and hissing something to us, seized our kiganda drum. It was such a small affair, we did not resist; still the manner in which it was taken completely undeceived us, if any small hope of peace remained. Loud applause greeted the act of gallantry.

"Then two men came down toward us, and began to drive some cows away that were grazing between us and the men on the hill. Safeni asked of one of them:

" 'Why do you do that?'

" 'Because we are going to begin fighting presently, and if you are men, you may begin to prepare yourselves,' he said, scornfully.

" 'Thanks, my bold friend,' I muttered to myself; 'those are the truest words we have heard today.'

"The two men were retiring up the hill.

" 'Here, Safeni,' I said, 'take these two fine red cloths in your hand; walk slowly up after them a little way, and the minute you hear my voice run back; and you, my boys, this is for life and death, mind; range yourselves on each side of the boat, lay your hands on it carelessly, but with a firm grip; and when I give the word, push it with the force of a hundred men down the hill into the water. Are you all ready, and do you think you can do it? Otherwise we might as well begin fighting where we are.'

" 'Yes, *Inshallah*, master,' they cried out with one voice.

" 'Go, Safeni!'

"I waited until he had walked fifty yards away, and saw that he acted precisely as I had instructed him.

" 'Push, my boys! Push for your lives!'

"The crew bent their heads and strained their arms. The boat began to move, and there was a hissing, grinding noise below me. I seized my double-barreled elephant rifle and shouted: 'Safeni! Safeni! Return!'

"The natives were quick-eyed. They saw the boat moving and with one accord they swept down the hill uttering the most fearful cries. My boat was at the water's edge.

" 'Shoot her into the lake, my men; never mind the water!'

"And clear of all obstructions she darted out upon the lake. Safeni stood for an instant on the water's edge, with the cloths in his hand. The foremost of a crowd of natives was about twenty yards from him. He raised his spear and balanced himself.

" 'Spring into the water, man, head first!' I cried.

"The balanced spear was about to fly, and another man was preparing his weapon for a deadly cast, when I raised my gun and the bullet ploughed through him and through the second. The bowmen halted and drew their bows. I sent two charges of duck-shot into their midst

HUNTING HIPPOPOTAMI.

with terrible effect. The natives retreated from the beach on which the boat had lately lain.

"Having checked the natives, I assisted one of my men into the boat, and ordered him to lend a hand to the others, while I reloaded my big guns, keeping my eyes on the natives. There was a point about a hundred yards in length on the east, which sheltered the cove. Some of the natives made a rush for this, but my guns commanded the exposed position, and they were obliged to retire.

"The crew seized their rifles, but I told them to leave them alone, and to tear the bottom-board out of the boat and use them as paddles; for there were two hippopotami advancing on us open-mouthed, and it seemed as if we were to be crushed in the water after such a narrow escape from the ferocious people ashore. I permitted one of the hippos to approach within ten yards, and, aiming between his eyes, perforated his skull with a three-ounce ball, and the second received such a wound that we were not molested by him.

"Meanwhile, the savages, baffled and furious at seeing their prey escape, had rushed, after a short consultation, to man two canoes that were drawn up on the beach at the northwest corner of the cove. Twice I dropped men as they were endeavoring to launch the boats; but they persisted, and finally launching them, pursued us vigorously. Two other canoes were seen coming down the coast from the eastern side of the island. Unable to escape, we stopped after he had got out of the cove and waited for them.

"My elephant rifle was loaded with explosive balls for this occasion. Four shots killed five men and sank two of the canoes. The two others retired to assist their friends out of the water. They attempted nothing further, but some of those on shore had managed to reach the point, and as we resumed our paddles, we heard a voice cry out:

" 'Go and die in the Nyanza!'

"And saw them shoot their arrows, which fell harmlessly a few yards behind us. We were saved!' "

THE VOYAGE CONTINUED.

It was five o'clock in the evening; they had had no food all day, and had only four bananas in the boat for twelve hungry men. The weak boards which they had for paddles did not answer the purpose very well, and in the dead calm which succeeded a gentle breeze, they were able to make only three-quarters of a mile an hour. A gale came up, and too weak to paddle any more they gave themselves up to the fury of the winds. It sank at last, and ordering that one of the thwarts should be chopped up, Stanley made coffee with which to refresh his half-starved companions.

They had had but little food before leaving Alice Island, on April 27; and this coffee, with the four bananas, was all that passed their lips until the afternoon of the 30th. They landed, then, on an uninhabited island; the leader shot a brace of large fat ducks; two of the men found some bananas, and two others found some luscious berries.

Continuing their voyage, they landed at the cove of Wiru May 4, and bought some food of the natives. Two days later, after a storm that brought to mind the parting words of the natives of Bumbireh, they reached Kagehyi, and were heartily welcomed by the others. There was but one white man among the shore party, and Stanley inquired where Frederick Barker was, and why he did not come to meet them.

"Because," answered Frank Pocock, his face clouding with the recollection of loss, "he died twelve days ago, and he lies there."

As he spoke, he pointed to a low mound of earth by the lake. Thus two of the four white men who had set out from Zanzibar had died on the way; and the journey was not half done.

It was Stanley's intention to return to Uganda with his full party, but the opposition of a chief whose territory lay between Kagehyi and Mtesa's country made it impossible to make the journey by land, as he wished to do. He therefore decided to make it by water, as before; but had much difficulty in obtaining canoes for the purpose. At last, after a personal visit to Lukongeh, the chief of Ukerewe, he succeeded in getting twenty-three. These were very old, and he at once set his men to work to repair them, while he began negotiations for provisions. The vessels were for the transportation of one hundred and fifty men, women and children; twelve thousand pounds of grain, five hundred pounds of rice, a hundred loads of beads, cloth and wire, and thirty cases of ammunition. Most of the last-named article was on the Lady Alice. The flotilla sailed at 9 A. M. on June 20; but before they reached the Miandereh Islands that night, five canoes had sunk, with five guns, one case of ammunition, and twelve hundred pounds of grain. Fortunately, all the people were saved; but it was only by the most strenuous efforts on the part of Stanley and his men. It is in connection with their brave behavior this night that we first hear of the two brothers, Uledi and Shumari, whose names were afterward to be more prominent in the story. The canoes were thoroughly inspected the next day, and the work of repairing them was not shirked as it had been before starting from Kagehyi.

Leaving a garrison of forty-four men at Refuge Island, which they reached June 24, Stanley returned to Kagehyi for the last time; and rejoined the other party July 11. Leaving a garrison at Miandereh again for his canoes were not numerous enough to transport the whole party at once) he went on his way toward Uganda.

TIPPOO TIB.

He must of course pass Bumbireh on his way thither; and it was necessary to give the chief of that island a lesson. The king of Iroba was captured; and being a neighbor of the chief of Bumbireh, was held as a hostage until his subjects had captured Shekka. Fortunately, they were about this time reinforced by a number of men whom Mtesa had dispatched to hunt up Stanley; so that the strength of the party now encamped on Mahyiga Island was four hundred and seventy men. This was the condition of affairs when messengers came from Antari, King of Ihangiro, the superior of Shekka, demanding the release of that chief. It was promised that when they should be released, Antari's people would sell food to the travelers. But this was a mere pretext by which Antari sought to gain the confidence of Stanley, preparatory to a trial of strength; and when some of the Waganda, deceived by the apparent friendliness, ventured to Bumbireh, they were attacked and eight of them badly wounded, six dying from the effects of their injuries after the arrival of the party in Uganda.

ANOTHER BATTLE WITH SAVAGES.

It was a question in Stanley's mind what course should be pursued. Had it been a purely military expedition there would of course have been no doubt; but for some time he hesitated about striking a blow except in direct self-defense. Finally, however, he decided that gratitude to Mtesa and his Waganda demanded that blood should atone for blood. More than this, it was dangerous to leave such a deed unavenged; for the savage cannot understand forbearance, which to him seems cowardice; patience, which is to him evidence of effeminacy. As he could not see any way to avoid the conflict, he determined to meet them on their own island, and by one decisive stroke break this overweening savage spirit. But Stanley's own words must tell of the just punishment inflicted.

"We steered straight towards the more exposed hill-slopes. The savages, imagining that we were about to effect a landing there, hurried from their coverts, between two and three thousand in number. I examined the shores carefully, to see if I could discover the canoes which had conveyed this great number of warriors from the mainland. Meanwhile we pulled slowly, to afford them time to arrange themselves.

"Arrived within a hundred yards of the land, we anchored in line, the stone anchors being dropped from midships that the broadsides might front the shore. I told Lukanjah of Ukerewe to ask the men of Bumbireh if they would make peace, whether we should be friends, or whether we should fight.

"'Nangu, nangu, nangu!' (No, no, no!) they answered loudly, while they flourished spears and shields.

"'Will they not do anything to save Shekka?'

" '*Nangu, nangu!* Keep Shekka; he is nobody. We have another M'kama' (king).

" 'Will they do nothing to save Antari's son?' [who also was held as a hostage.]

SUCKING THE POISON FROM A WOUND RECEIVED FROM A POISONED ARROW.

" '*Nangu, nangu.* Antari has many sons. We will do nothing but fight. If you had not come here, we should have come to you.'

" 'You will be sorry for it afterward.'

" 'Huh!' incredulously; 'we are ready; come on.'

Further parley was useless; so each man having taken aim was directed to fire into a group of fifty or thereabouts. The result was several killed and wounded. The savages, perceiving the disastrous effect of our fire on a compact body, scattered, and came bounding down to the water's edge, some of the boldest advancing until they were hip-deep in water; others, more cautious, sought the shelter of the cane-grass, whence they discharged many sheaves of arrows, all of which fell short of us.

"We then moved to within fifty yards of the shore, to fire at close quarters, and each man was permitted to exercise himself as he best could. The savages gallantly held the water-line for an hour, and slung their stones with better effect than they shot their arrows. The spirit which animated them proved what they might had done had they succeeded in effecting a landing at Mahyiga by night, but here, however, the spear, with which they generally fight, was quite useless.

"Perceiving that their spirit was abating, we drew the canoes together, and made a feint as though we were about to rush forward by hundreds with their spears on the launch. The canoes were then suddenly halted, and a volley was fired into the spearmen, which quite crushed their courage, causing them to retreat up the hill far away from the scene. Our work of chastisement was complete.

"The Waganda spearmen, two hundred and thirty strong, who had been, up to this time, only interested spectators, now clamored loudly to be permitted to land, and to complete the work of vengeance. M'Kwanga was fierce in his demands; the Wangwana seconded the Waganda, and in their hot ardor several of the canoes rushed on the shore; but as this extremity was not my object, I resisted them; and when, despite my refusal, they persisted in their attempts to land, I threatened to fire on the first man, Mgwana or Mganda, who set foot on the shore; and this threat restored order."

The way being thus cleared, they proceeded on their journey, and reached Dumo, in Uganda, a week later (August 12, 1875). Here they learned that Mtesa was making preparations for a war against the

Wavuma. Before they reached Ntewi, he had already marched against Usoga. Two courses were open to Stanley; either he could attempt the journey to the Albert Nyanza unaided, or he could proceed to Mtesa's camp, and thence prosecute the journey. He decided upon the latter course, believing that the delay would be made up by the shorter route which Mtesa's help would enable him to take.

THE EMPEROR OF UGANDA.

He found the emperor of Uganda and his warlike court encamped about the Ripon Falls. Mtesa received him with great cordiality, but informed him that it was not customary for strangers to proceed on their journey while the Kabaka was at war; if Stanley would but wait until he had chastised the insolent Wavuma, he should have guides to Muta Nzige. Stanley was also informed that the natives of the country lying along the route, under their chief, Kabba Rega, were at war with the whites of Kaniessa (Gondokoro), and hence that a considerable force would be required. There was nothing for it, then, but to await the end of Mtesa's war.

Mtesa attempted to end it by negotiations, but his peace party, dispatched to the Wavuma camp on Ingira Island, was massacred before his very eyes. He decided at length to give battle to the enemy daily becoming bolder and more boastful. The result was that the Wavuma were left masters of the situation. Mtesa threatened that in the next battle, the chief who behaved cowardly should be burned, while his lands should be given to the peasant who distinguished himself. Let us again quote the words of Stanley:

"The entire war-fleet of two hundred and thirty vessels rode gracefully on the calm gray waters of the channel. The line of battle, I observed, was formed by Chambarango, in command of the right flank, with fifty canoes; Sambuzi, Kukavya, Chikwata and Saruti, all subchiefs, were ranged with one hundred canoes under the command of Kauta, the imperial steward, to form the center; the left flank was in charge of the gallant Mkwenda, who had eighty canoes. Tori commanded a force of musketeers, and with his four howitzers was stationed on the causeway, which was by this time two hundred yards from the shore.

A SEA BATTLE ON NAKARANGA.

"In the above manner the fleet of vessels, containing some sixteen thousand men, moved to the attack upon Ingira. The center, defended by the flanks, which were to menace the rear of the Wavuma should they approach near the causeway, resolutely advanced to within thirty yards of Ingira, and poured in a most murderous fire among the slingers of the island, who, imagining that the Waganda meant to carry the island by storm, boldly stood exposed, resolved to fight. But they were unable to maintain that courageous behavior long. Mkwenda then moved up from the left, and attacked with his musketeers the Wavuma on the right, riddling their canoes, and making matters specially hot for them in that quarter.

"The Wavuma, seeing matters approaching a crisis, and not wishing to die tamely, manned their canoes, and a hundred and ninety-six dashed impetuously, as at first, from the rushes of Ingira with shrill loud yells, and the Waganda lines moved backward to the center of the channel, where they bravely and coolly maintained their position. As the center of the Uganda line parted in front of the causeway, and disclosed the hotly advancing enemy, Tori aimed the howitzers and fired at a group of about twenty canoes, completely shattering more than half of them, and re-loading one quickly, he discharged several bolts of iron three inches long among them with terrible effect. Before this cool bearing of the Waganda, the Wavuma retired to their island again, and we saw numbers of canoes discharging their dead and wounded; and the Waganda were summoned to the Nakaranga shore to receive the congratulations of the emperor and the applause óf the vast multitude. Mtesa went down to the water'c edge to express his satisfaction at their behavior.

" 'Go at them again,' said he, 'and show them what fighting is.'

"And the line of battle was again formed, and again the Wavuma darted from the cover of the reeds and water-cane with the swiftness of hungry sharks, beating the water into foam with their paddles, and rending the air with their fearful yells. It was one of the most exciting and animating scenes I ever beheld; but, owing to the terror of the stake with which their dread monarch had threatened them, the Wa-

ganda distinguished themselves for coolness and method, and the Wavuma, as on a former occasion, for intrepidity and desperate courage.

"A third time the Waganda were urged to the battle, and a third
time the unconquerable and desperate enemy dashed upon them, to be
smitten and wounded sore in a battle where they had not the least
chance of returning blow for blow without danger of being swept by the
cannon and muskets on the causeway.

THE RYNCHOCYON—A PECULIAR AFRICAN RAT.

"A third battle was fought a few days after between one hundred
and seventy-eight Wavuma canoes and one hundred and twenty-two
Waganda; but had the Waganda possessed the spirit and dash of their
enemies, they might have decided the war on this day; for the Wavuma were greatly dispirited. A fourth battle was fought the next
day by two hundred and fourteen Waganda canoes and two hundred
and three Wavuma canoes, after the usual delay and premonitory
provocation. The Wavuma obtained the victory most signally. * * *

The Waganda were disorganized and dispirited after the signal defeat they had experienced. * * * On inquiring into the cause of the disaster, I learned that Mtesa's gunpowder was almost exhausted, and that he had scarcely a round left for each musket."

Although Stanley was bound to Mtesa by past evidences of friendship, as well as by the hope of assistance in the future, he could not but feel strong admiration for the heroic Wavuma; and bent his energies "upon a solution of the problem how to injure none, but satisfy all." While he was considering this puzzling question, he was summoned to the council-chamber, where Mtesa was making ready to torture to death a Wavuma who had fallen into his hands. The emperor had but a few days before announced himself a Christian; and Stanley now warmly protested against such an un-Christian act. His arguments were disregarded for a long time, but finally, Mtesa listened to him. Stanley then promised to build a structure which should terrify the Wavuma, if Mtesa would but give him plenty of help.

The Waganda are timid about fighting on water, being unused to the unstable element; it was for this reason that Stanley had advised the building of a causeway from the mainland to the island, that they might thus be on a more equal footing with the seamen Wavuma; but the Waganda chiefs did not take kindly to the idea, and the causeway was not finished. Mtesa now gave orders that Stanley's directions should be minutely obeyed.

He selected three of the strongest built canoes, each seventy feet long and six and one-half feet wide; and had them drawn up four feet from each other. Tall trees were laid across them, and lashed firmly to the thwarts. Seven-foot poles were lashed to the thwarts of the outer canoes, and long poles, one inch in diameter, twisted in among these. When completed, it resembled an oblong stockade, which the spears of the enemy could not penetrate; and formed a floating fort, propelled by invisible rowers, and manned by more than two hundred men. This immense structure slowly advanced toward the island, while a voice from within asked the Wavuma if they were ready to submit to Mtesa now; if they went through the form of submission, he offered pardon to all; if they refused, this terrible thing would blow.

FIRST VIEW OF LAKE ALBERT NYANZA.

them into atoms. The Wavuma, terrified by the strange thing, which doubtless contained some powerful spirits, yielded to the demand; and the mysterious structure solemnly began its way back to the cove whence it had started. Thus the Wavuma, like the Trojans, were conquered by strategy when their determined valor defied open force.

Here ends this marvellous circumnavigation of that mysterious large lake, which no white man before had explored. Its thrilling adventurous, brisk fighting and dangerous escapades even surpass Ulysses' adventures as told by the immortal Homer and we should have to fill a whole book would we narrate them all. King Mtesa granted our heroes the desired guide and escort for his visit to Albert Nyanza, and they at once began their overland march, carrying their barge, Lady Alice, and a canoe which had been named the "Livingstone." They had to pass through warlike tribes, but their escort consisted of more than 2,000 men besides Stanley's own force of 180, so that they were not attacked by the natives.

THEY ARRIVE AT ALBERT NYANZA.

They reached the shores of the lake in January; but there was a precipice with a sheer descent of fifty feet, down which the boats must be lowered; and while they were debating about the best way to accomplish this, hostile demonstrations by the natives frightened the Waganda, who were already discontented; and the leader of that force determined to return. Stanley was advised by his captains that half of his own force would accompany the Waganda in spite of all they could do; and he was therefore compelled to return with them. With the punishment that Mtesa inflicted upon his disobedient subjects, we have nothing to do. He expressed the greatest regret to Stanley that they had not fulfilled their orders; and offered a force of a hundred thousand men for the accomplishment of the traveler's purpose, if that number should be necessary. The offer was, however, declined; and Stanley left Uganda.

Stanley next visited Rumanika, the gentle king who was subordinate to the fiery Mtesa. The dusky giant (for Rumanika was six feet six in his bare feet) received Stanley with much kindness, and praised his country, Karagwe. He claimed not only the great river, Kagera, but a more wonderful thing still, the Hot Springs of Mtagata. Under the escort of this chief, Stanley began the circumnavigation of Lake Windermere, March 8; and made several similar excursions from his camp on the Kagera.

March 11, Rumanika furnished him with an escort of thirty men and a guide for his visit to Mtagata Hot Springs, which they reached

NIAM-NIAMS (MAN AND WOMAN).

after two days' journey. These remarkable springs are six in number, the temperature varying from one hundred and seven degees Fahrenheit to one hundred and twenty-nine and one-half degrees. A sample of the water taken to London and there analyzed, showed it to be faintly alkaline, holding sodium carbonate in solution. The natives praised the waters of the springs so highly that Stanley resolved to test them in his own person; but although he remained three days there and drank an enormous quantity of the water, he experienced no good. He intimates that the benefit received in cutaneous diseases results more from the unusual cleanliness than from any virtue in the water it-self.

A great deal of information was received from Rumanika concerning the geography of the surrounding country; and his sub-chiefs added their quota. Rumanika's knowledge (not drawn from personal experience) included a race of people but two feet high, another with tails, and still another with ears so long that they touched the ground when the man stood upright, and when he lay down, formed a sleeping mat and a covering from the cold.

Having traced the extreme southern sources of the Nile, from the marshy plains and cultivated uplands where they are born, down to the mighty reservoir called the Victoria Nyanza, Stanley, on April 7, resumed his "journey in a southerly direction, and traveled five miles along a ravine, at the bottom of which murmured the infant stream Luhugati. On coming to its source we ascended a steep slope until we stood on the summit of a grassy ridge at the height of five thousand six hundred feet by aneroid. Not until we had descended a mile to the valley of Uyagoma did I recognize the importance of this ridge as the water-parting between one of the feeders of the Lake Victoria and the source of the Malagarazi, the principal affluent of Lake Tanganyika."

Descending into the basin of the Tanganyika, the expedition arrived at Serombo April 22, and here received a visit from the mighty Mirambo whose war with the Arabs was now at an end. He insisted on making blood-brotherhood with Stanley, and tried to excel the white man in the generosity of his gifts.

We need not follow them through the uneventful journey to the shore of the Tanganyika. They arrived at Ujiji May 27, 1876. Providing for the well-being of his followers during his absence, Stanley set out, June 11, with eleven men and two boy gun-bearers, to circumnavigate the lake, with the view of finding its outlet. The Lady Alice was accompanied by a canoe lent by an Arab, called the Meofu. The Arabs of Ujiji were quite convinced that these vessels would never be able to live in the Tanganyika, and predicted the most doleful things.

They arrived at the banks of the Lukuga July 16. It will be remembered that Cameron positively asserted that this river flows out of

22

Lake Tanganyika. Stanley was unable to find any current; and decided that what had been a river, the affluent of Tanganyika, was now
but a creek or inlet, above which were marshes and ooze. He explains
this by supposing that the surface of Tanganyika has been steadily
rising, until the lake is now above the mouth of the original river; and
adduces proof that the lake had actually risen considerable since the
time that he, in company with Livingstone, explored its shores. His
recollections of particular points were confirmed by Arabs resident at
Ujiji.

SMALL-POX AND FEVER.

The circumnavigation of the lake was completed July 31, after an
absence of fifty-one days from Ujiji. Stanley found the small-pox
raging in this place, and it had carried off five of his men, who had
evaded vaccination at Rosako. The fever attacked him, as it had also
attacked his lieutenant, Frank Pocock, during his absence; and to add
to their troubles, thirty-eight men deserted on the eve of their departure from Ujiji. Five more disappeared during the first stages of their
journey, one of whom was Kalulu. Stanley determined to recover these
men, for he had shortly before treated them with the greatest generosity, distributing three hundred and fifty pounds' worth of cloth among
them gratuitously. Pocock and Kacheche were sent after the deserters,
and captured seven, one of whom was Kalulu; these receiving merited
punishment, an end was put to misconduct and faithlessness for the
time.

The shores of the Luama were reached October 11; and they followed
this stream for a distance of two hundred and twenty miles, to its confluence with the greater river. The Luama here was about four hundred yards wide; the Lualaba, one thousand four hundred. "A broad
river, of a pale grey color, winding slowly from south and by east.
* * * A secret rapture filled my soul as I gazed upon the majestic
stream. The great mystery that for all these centuries Nature had kept
hidden away from the world of science, was waiting to be solved.
* * * Before me lay the superb river; my task was to follow it to the
ocean."

At the village of Mkwanga, eight miles from the confluence of these rivers, they met with Tippu Tib, otherwise Hamed bin Mohammed, a noted Arab trader with whom Cameron had had dealings; and from whom they learned how the Englishman had failed to obtain the canoes necessary for the descent of the Lualaba. The Arab endeavored to dissuade him from the attempt; and painted the difficulties of the journey in strong colors. Stanley himself saw what they were; Livingstone the Beloved had failed to overcome them by persuasion; Cameron had failed to overcome them with his forty-five Snider rifles—an argument more generally understood by the savages. Tippu-Tib would not consent to be his escort unless Stanley would return to Nyangwe with him. What should be done? Stanley took his trusty lieutenant into council, and carefully stated all the advantages and difficulties of the various alternatives that presented themselves. Both were at heart anxious to explore the Lualaba to its mouth, but neither would say so. Under these circumstances, Frank made a proposition.

" 'I say, sir, let us toss up; best two out of three to decide it.'

" 'Toss away; here is a rupee.'

" 'Heads for the north and the Lualaba; tails for the south and Katanga.'

"Frank stood up, his face beaming. He tossed the rupee high up. The coin dropped.

" 'What is it?' I asked.

" 'Tails, sir,' said Frank, with a face expressive of strong disapproval.

" 'Toss again.'

"He tossed again, and tails was again announced—and six times running tails won. We then tried straws—the short straws for the south, the long straws for the River Lualaba—and again we were disappointed, for Frank persisted in drawing out the short straws, and in leaving the long straws in my hands.

" 'It is of no use, Frank. We'll face our destiny despite the rupee and the straws. With your help, my dear fellow, I will follow the river.' "

A contract was concluded with Tippu Tib, by which the trader agreed to accompany them sixty marches, of four hours each, when, if they found the country hostile, they should return with him to Nyangwe; if they met Portuguese or Arab traders, a portion of the expedition was to continue the journey with them, and the remainder to return with Tippu Tib. This arrangement prevented desertions, as no Arab would harbor a runaway from an expedition with which one of their own countrymen was connected.

November 5, 1876, they left Nyangwe, one hundred and forty-six men comprising the expedition proper while Tippu Tib mustered seven hundred. Their road lay through the dense, almost impenetrable forest; and their progress at first was necessarily slow. So slow, indeed, that the Arab trader became disgusted, and regardless of the loss of the money, which was to be forfeited if he refused to fulfill his part of the contract, announced that he intended to return. Arguments at length persuaded him to compromise, and the expedition again took up the line of march.

In a village of Uvinza, Stanley found the principal street decorated with skulls which looked to him like those of the human species. The chief and his people, however, informed him that they were soko skulls; that the sokos stole their bananas, and were because of that hunted by his people, the flesh being used for meat. Stanley purchased two of the skulls, some of which bore the marks of the hatchet which had caused death; and on his return to England submitted them to Professor Huxley. The eminent scientist unhesitatingly pronounced them human, one being a man's, the other a woman's; thus showing that the Wavinza are cannibals.

November 19, they reached a point on the Lualaba forty-one miles north of Nyangwe, in latitude three degrees thirty-five seconds south, and twenty-five degrees, forty-nine seconds east longitude. From this point, Stanley speaks of the river as the Livingstone, claiming that as the name is changed each time it receives an affluent, it is useless to attempt to follow the native designations. Here it was, while busily planning the future journey, that Stanley suddenly saw his way clear before him. They had encamped on the banks of the river, and he had been considering the means of crossing it.

"I sprang up; told the drummer to call to muster. The people responded wearily to the call. Frank and the chiefs appeared. The Arabs and their escort came also, until a dense mass of expectant faces surrounded me. I turned to them and said:

" 'Arabs! Sons of Unyamwezi! Children of Zanzibar! Listen to words. We have seen the Mitamba of Uregga. We have tasted its bitterness, and groaned in spirit. We seek a road. We seek something by which we may travel. I seek a path that shall take me to the sea. I have found it.'

" 'Ah! A-ah-h!' and murmurs and inquiring looks at one another.

" 'Yes! *El hamd ul Illah!* I have found it. Regard this mighty river. From the beginning it has flowed on thus, as you see it flow to-day. It has flowed on in silence and darkness. Whither? To the Salt Sea, as all rivers go. By that Salt Sea, on which the great ships come and go, live my friends, and your friends, Do they not?'

"Cries of 'Yes! yes!'

" 'Yet, my people, although this river is so great, so wide and deep, no man has ever penetrated the distance lying between this spot on which we stand and our white friends who live by the Salt Sea. Why? Because it was left for us to do!'

" 'Ah, no! no! no!' and despairing shakes of the head.

" 'Yes,' I continued, raising my voice; 'I tell you, my friends, it has been left from the beginning of time until today for us to do. It is our work, and no other. It is the voice of Fate! The ONE GOD has written that this year the river shall be known throughout its length! We will have no more Mitambas; we will have no more panting and groaning by the wayside; we will have no more hideous darkness; we will take to the river, and keep to the river. To-day I shall launch my boat on that stream, and it shall never leave it until I finish my work. I swear it!'

" 'Now, you Wangwana! You who have followed me through Turu, and sailed around the great lakes with me; you have followed me like children following their father through Unyoro and down to Ujiji, and as far as this wild, wild land, will you leave me here? Shall I and my white brother go alone! Will you go back and tell my friends that you left me in this wild spot, and cast me adrift to die? Or will you, to whom I have been so kind, whom I love as I would love my children, will you bind me, and take me back by force? Speak, Arabs! Where are my young men, with hearts of lions! Speak, Wangwana, and show me those who dare follow me!'

"Uledi, the coxswain, leaped upward, and then sprang towards me, and kneeling grasped my knees and said:

" 'Look on me, my master! I am one! I will follow you to death!'

" 'And I,' Kacheche cried.

" 'And I, and I, and I,' shouted the boat's crew.

" 'It is well. I knew I had friends. You then who have cast your lot with me stand on one side, and let me count you.'

"There were thirty-eight. Ninety-five stood still and said nothing.

" 'I have enough. Even with you, my friends, I shall reach the sea. But there is plenty of time. We have not yet made our canoes. We have not yet parted with the Arabs. We have yet a long distance to travel with Tippu Tib. We may meet with good people, from whom we may buy canoes. And by the time we part I am sure that the ninety-five men now fearing to go with us will not leave their brothers, and their master and his white brother, to go down the river without them. Meantime, I give you many thanks, and shall not forget your names.' "

While Stanley was speaking to the Arabs, endeavoring to persuade them that cataracts and cannibals were dangers which he should over-come, a canoe had approached from the opposite bank, with two men in it. They demanded a thousand cowries for each man whom their tribe should set across the river; and being offered ten, withdrew, utter-ing a peculiar cry, which Stanley's interpreter declared was a war-cry. Stanley crossed the river in the Lady Alice, and entered into nego-tiations with the horde of savages that he found there. It was agreed, upon the demand of the natives, that ten men should go from each side to a certain island the next morning and make blood-brotherhood. For-, tunately the white man was on his guard; and secretly posted a reserve of twenty men in the bushes before sending off Frank and the stipulated

ATTACK ON A NEGRO VILLAGE BY SLAVE HUNTERS.

escort. The savages landed later, and although they behaved well at first
by the time that six canoes had discharged their human cargo they be
came so violent that had not Frank and his men risen with their gun
ready they would have been speared where they sat. Seeing the state o
affairs, the reserve emerged from the bushes. Stanley, who was fou
minutes' row up the stream in the Lady Alice, bade his men bend t
their oars; and the treacherous savages, seeing that their wiles ha
been foreseen, took to their canoes and paddled away.

Stanley then landed thirty men with axes on the other side of th
river; and floating down to a point opposite the Wenya village, tossed ;
small bag of beads on shore, and professed himself willing to pay for th
ferriage, explaining that it was useless for them to resist longer, a
thirty of his men were already landed in their country. A good under
standing seemed to be thus established; and the expedition was ferrie
over in safety.

But the natives seized the first opportunity to decamp; and when th
travelers went to their village the next morning, to cement the ne
friendship by means of gifts, not a soul was to be found. It was th
same in the neighboring villages; the alarm had spread from place t
place during the night.

The force was now divided, thirty-six men, including Stanley, form
ing the river party, while the remainder marched by land. The rive
party arrived November 23, at the mouth of the Ruiki, and after wait
ing until the next morning, rowed up stream to look for the others. No
finding any trace of them, the boat returned to the camp, where abou
two-thirds of this small party had been left as a garrison. It had bee
attacked during the leader's absence; but although there were severa
sheaves of iron-headed and wooden spears, besides reed arrows, in th
camp, no one of the travelers had been wounded. The land party did no
arrive until the next day; and told of having been attacked, three of thei
number being killed. They had lost the road and were thus delayed.

The rapids of Ukassa were passed the next day; not without dange
from the natives as well as from the waters; and from this point forwar
we find the two perils constantly besetting the adventurers. Nor wa
this all; such was the physical condition of the men, that "there wa

enough work in the stricken expedition for a dozen physicians. Every day we tossed two or three bodies into the deep waters of the Livingstone—poor creatures, what a life! wandering, ever wandering, in search of graves."

NEW DIFFICULTIES.

Let us follow the history of a few days more minutely than ever; to see what were the difficulties besetting them. It is December, and they have passed the island of Mpika about the middle of the month.

"While rowing down, close to the left bank, we were surprised by a

THE QUAGGA.

cry from one of the guards of the hospital canoes, and turning round saw an arrow fixed in his chest. The next instant, looking towards the bank, we saw many men in the jungle, and several arrows flew past my head in extremely unpleasant proximity.

"We sheered off, pulling hard down stream. * * * We drew in shore, and sending out ten scouts to lie in wait in the jungle, I mustered all the healthy men, about thirty in number, and proceeded to construct a fence of brushwood. Presently a shriek of agony from another of my men rang out through the jungle, followed immediately by the sharp crack of the scouts' Sniders, which again was responded to by an infernal din of war-horns and yells, while arrows flew past us from all directions. Twenty more men were at once sent into the jungle to assist the scouts, while, with might and main, we labored to surround our intended camp with tall and dense hedges of brushwood, with sheltered nooks for riflemen. After an hour's labor, the camp was deemed sufficiently tenable, and the recall was sounded. The scouts retreated on the run, shouting as they approached:

" 'Prepare! prepare! they are coming!'

"About fifty yards of ground outside of our camp had been cleared, which, upon the retreat of the scouts who had been keeping them in check, was soon filled by hundreds of savages, who pressed upon us from all sides but the river, in the full expectation that we were flying in fear. But they were mistaken, for we were at bay, and desperate in our resolve not to die without fighting. Accordingly, at such close quarters the contest became terrific. Again and again the savages hurled themselves upon our stockade, launching spear after spear with deadly force into the camp, to be each time repulsed. Sometimes the muzzles of the guns almost touched their breasts. The shrieks, cries, shouts of encouragement, the rattling volley of musketry, the booming war-horns, the yells and defiance of the combatants, the groans and screams of the women and children in the hospital camp, made together such a medley of hideous noises as can never be effaced from my memory. For two hours this desperate conflict lasted. More than once, some of the Wangwana were about to abandon the struggle and run to the canoes, but Uledi the coxswain and Frank threatened them with clubbed mus-

kets, and with the muzzles of their rifles drove them back to the stock-
ades. At dusk the enemy retreated from the vicinity of the clearing;
but the hideous alarms produced from their ivory horns, and increased
by the echoes of the dense forest, continued; and now and again a venge-
ful poison-laden arrow flew by with an ominous whiz to quiver in the
earth at our feet, or fall harmlessly into the river behind us."

A strict watch was kept during the night; but the men in the camp
were so quiet that those in the jungle thought they slept, and attacked
them. In the morning, they rowed about five hundred yards down the
river, and occupied a deserted village on the right bank.

"We were not long left unmolested. The savages recovered their
wits, and strove desperately to dislodge us, but at each end of the village,
which was about three hundred yards long, our muskets blazed inces-
santly. I also caused three or four sharp-shooters to ascend tall trees
along the river banks, which permitted them, although unseen, to over-
look the tall grasses and rear of the village, and to defend us from fire.
* * * The combat lasted till noon, when, mustering twenty-five
men, we made a sally, and succeeded in clearing the skirts of the village
for the day. * * * During the night there was a slight alarm, and
now and then the tapping on the roofs and the pattering among the
leaves informed us that our enemies were still about, though we did not
reply to them. The next morning an assault was attempted; but the
enemy retreated almost immediately into the jungle.

DESPERATE BATTLE WITH NATIVES.

"About noon, a large flotilla of canoes was observed ascending the
river close to the left bank, manned by such a dense mass of men that
any number between five hundred and eight hundred would be within the
mark. We watched them very carefully until they had ascended the
river about half a mile above us, when, taking advantage of the current, they bore down towards us, blowing their war-horns, and drumming vigorously. At the same moment, as though this were a signal
in concert with those on land, war-horns responded from the forest, and
I had scarcely time to order every man to look out when the battle-tem-
pest of arrows broke upon us from the woods. But the twenty men in the

nests at the corners of the villages proved sufficient to resist the attack from the forest side, Frank Pocock being in charge of one, and Sheikh Abdallah of the other, while I, with twenty men lining the bushes along the water line, defended the river side.

"This was a period when every man felt that he must either fight or resign himself to the only other alternative, that of being heaved a headless corpse into the river. * * * Therefore, though the notes of the war-horns were dreadful, our foes pertinacious and numerous, and evidently accustomed to victory, I failed to observe one man among my people then fighting who did not seem desirous to excel even Uledi the coxswain.

"The battle had continued half an hour with a desperate energy, only qualified by our desperate state. Ammunition we possessed in abundance, and we made use of it with deadly effect, yet what might have become of us is doubtful, had not the advanced guard of Tippu Tib and our land division arrived at this critical juncture, causing dismay to the savages in the forest, who announced the reinforcement by horns to the savages in the canoes, many of whom were making strenuous efforts to effect a landing. The river savages, upon hearing these signals, withdrew, but as they were paddling away they proclaimed their intention of preventing all escape, either up river or down river, and expressed their contempt for us by throwing water towards us with their paddles. We saw the canoe mysteriously disappear behind an island, situated about sixteen hundred yards off and opposite to our camp."

That night, Stanley and Pocock, with crews of picked men, made their way, with muffled oars, to the island, and captured thirty-eight of the enemy's canoes. This enabled them to make their own terms with the savages, who were glad enough to make blood-brotherhood with Safeni for the return of fifteen of their vessels. Stanley had lost four men killed in the contest and thirteen wounded.

Stanley now determined to dispense with his Arab escort; and since a sufficient number of canoes had been procured, to take to the river in good earnest. Food must be procured and prepared for at least twenty days; the canoes must be thoroughly overhauled, and lashed in couples, to prevent their capsizing. The vessels were named by the Zanzibaris after those which visited their native place; except half a dozen, which were christened by the two white men.

Christmas day was passed pleasantly and happily. Three days later the final farewells were spoken; the Arabs returned toward the starting-point, and the expedition sailed down the river, toward the Unknown.

For a week they journeyed through a country where the war-cry, frequently heard, was "Meat!" but fortunately they were not seriously molested, as their camp was always well guarded at night; and the fame of their prowess had evidently preceded them. On January 4, 1877, they came within hearing of the first cataract of Stanley Falls. But louder yet sounded the piercing yells of the savage Mwana Ntaba from both sides of the great river. This tribe had attacked them the previous afternoon, but had been repulsed, a huge canoe of theirs being captured by the Lady Alice. Theirs was a terrible alternative; either they must face the cannibals, collected in they knew not what numbers, or they must dare the cataracts. Possibly it was only a choice between deaths, by knives or by drowning; the latter was certain, if they chose the water route; the former left room for hope, if they chose the land route. They therefore decided to fight the way around the cataracts.

"There was only one way to resolve the problem, and that was to meet the Bakumu and dare their worst, and then to drag the canoes through the dense forest on the left bank. Accordingly, we prepared for what we felt assured would be a stubborn contest. At early dawn of the 10th of January, with quick throbbing pulses, we stole up the river for about a mile, and then with desperate haste dashed across to the shore [from the island where they had been encamped] where we became immediately engaged. We floated down to the bend just above the cataract, and there secured our boats and canoes out of the influence of the stream. Leaving Frank with eight men and sixty axes to form a stockade, I led thirty-six men in a line through the bushes, and drove the united Baswa and Bakumu backward to their villages, the first of which were situated a mile from the river. Here a most determined stand was made by them, for they had piled up heaps of brushwood, and cut down great trees to form defenses, leaving only a few men in front. We crept through the jungle on the south side and succeeded in forcing an entrance and driving them out. We had thus won peace for this day, and retreated to our camp. We then divided the expedition into two parties, or relays, one to work by night, the other by day, after which I took a picked body of pioneers with axes and guns and cut a narrow path three miles in length, blazing the trees as a guide, and forming rude camps at intervals of half a mile. * * *

"We were not further disturbed during this day. In the evening Frank began his work with fifty axemen, and ten men as scouts, deployed in the bushes in front of the working party. Before dawn we were all awakened, and making a rush with the canoes, succeeded in safely reaching our first camp by 9 A. M., with all canoes and baggage. During the passage of the rear-guard the Bakumu made their presence known to us by a startling and sudden outburst of cries; but the scouts immediately replied to them with their rifles, and maintained their position until they were supported by the other armed men, who were now led forward as on the day before. We chased the savages two miles inland, to other villages which we had not hitherto seen; and these also we compelled them to abandon."

PASSING THE CATARACTS.

Thus the work of passing the cataracts went on, night and day, and after seventy-eight hours' immense exertions, the canoes were launched once more. But their difficulties were not yet at an end. Three cataracts had been passed in safety; how many remained below? But perhaps an extract from Stanley's journal will give a more vivid picture of the occurrences the day after the third cataract was safely passed than any other words could do:

"January 14.—As soon as we reached the river we began to float the canoes down to a two-mile stretch of rapids to a camp opposite the south end of Ntunduru Island. Six canoes were taken down safely by the gallant boat's crew. The seventh canoe was manned by Muscati, Uledi Muscati, and Zaidi, a chief. Muscati, the steersman, lost his presence of mind, and soon upset his canoe in a piece of bad water. Muscati and his friend Uledi swam down the furious stream to Ntunduru Island, whence they were saved by the eighth canoe, manned by stout-hearted Manwa Sera and Uledi, the coxswain of the Lady Alice; but poor Zaidi, the chief, paralyzed by the roar of the stream, unfortunately thought his safety was assured by clinging to his canoe, which was soon swept past our new camp, in full view of those who had been deputed with Frank to form it, to what seemed inevitable death. But a kindly Providence, which he has himself gratefully acknowledged, saved him even on the brink of eternity. The great fall at the north end of Ntunduru Island happens to be disparted by a single pointed rock, and on this the canoe was driven, and, borne down by the weight of the waters, was soon split in two, one side of which got jammed below, the other tilted upward. To this the almost drowned man clung, while perched on the rocky point, with his ankles washed by the stream. To his left, as he faced up stream, there was a stretch of fifty yards of falling water; to his right were nearly fifty yards of leaping brown waves, while close behind him the water fell down sheer to six or eight feet, through a gap ten yards wide, between the rocky point on which he was perched and a rocky islet three hundred yards long.

"When called to the scene by his weeping friends from my labors up river, I could scarcely believe my eyes, or realize the strange chance which placed him there; and certainly a more critical position than the poor fellow was in cannot be imagined. * * * The solitary man on that narrow pointed rock was apparently calmer than any of us; though we could approach within fifty yards, he could not hear a word we said; he could see us, and feel assured that we sympathized with him in his terrible position.

"We then, after collecting our faculties, began to prepare means to save him. After sending men to collect rattans, we formed a cable, by which we attempted to lower a small canoe, but the instant it seemed to reach him the force of the current hurrying to the fall was so great that the cable snapped like packthread, and the canoe swept by him like an arrow, and was engulfed, shattered, split, and pounded into fragments. Then we endeavored to toss toward him poles tied with creepers, but the vagaries of the current and its convulsive heaving made it impossible to reach him with them, while the man dared not move a hand, but sat silent, watching our futile efforts, while the conviction gradually settled on our minds that his doom, though protracted, was certain.

"Then, after anxious deliberation with myself, I called for another canoe, and lashed to the bow of it a cable consisting of three one-inch rattans twisted together and strengthened by all the tent ropes. A similar cable was lashed to the side, and a third was fastened to the stern, each of these cables being ninety yards in length. A shorter cable, thirty yards in length, was lashed to the stern of the canoe, which was to be guided within reach of him by a man in the canoe.

"Two volunteers were called for. No one would step forward. I offered rewards. Still no one·would respond. But when I began to speak to them, asking them how they would like to be in such a position without a single friend offering to assist in saving them, Uledi the coxswain came forward and said:

" 'Enough, master, I will go. *Mambu Kwa Mungu'*—My fate is in the hands of God.

"And immediately he began preparing himself by binding his loin-cloth firmly about his waist. Then Marzouk, a boat-boy, said:

" 'Since Uledi goes, I will go too.'

"Other boat-boys, young Shumari and Aaywa, offered their services, but I checked them, and said:

" 'You surely are not tired of me, are you, that you all wish to die? If all my brave boat-boys are lost, what shall we do?' "

RESCUE OF ZAIDI.

"Uledi and his friend Marzouk stepped into the canoe with the air of gladiators, and we applauded them heartily, but enjoined on them to be careful. Then I turned to the crowd on the shore who were manning the cables, and bade them beware of the least carelessness, as the lives of the three young men depended on their attention to the orders that would be given.

"The two young volunteers were requested to paddle across the river, so that the stern might be guided by those on shore. The bow and side cables were slackened until the canoe was within twenty yards of the

HIPPOPOTAMI THAT MR. ROOSEVELT WAS VERY SUCCESSFUL IN SHOOTING.

roaring falls, and Uledi endeavored to guide the cable to Zaidi, but the
convulsive heaving of the river swept the canoe constantly to one side,
where it hovered over the steep slope and brown waves of the left
branch, from the swirl of which we were compelled to draw it. Five
times the attempt was made, but at last, the sixth time, encouraged by
the safety of the cables, we lowered the canoe until it was within ten
yards of Zaidi, and Uledi lifted the short cable and threw it over to him
and struck his arm. He had just time to grasp it before he was carried over into the chasm below. For thirty seconds we saw nothing of
him, and thought him lost, when his head rose above the edge of the falling waters. Instantly the word was given to haul away, but at the first
pull the bow and side cables parted, and the canoe began to glide down
the left branch with my two boat-boys on board! The stern cable next
parted, and, horrified at the result, we stood muttering: "*La il Allah, il
Allah,*' watching the canoe severed from us drifting to certain destruction, when we suddenly observed it halted. Zaidi, in the channel clinging
to his cable was acting as a kedge-anchor, which swept the canoe against
the rocky islet. Uledi and Marzouk sprang out of the canoe, and lean-
ing over assisted Zaidi out of the falls, and the three, working with desperate energy, succeeded in securing the canoe on the islet.

"But though we hurrahed and were exceedingly rejoiced, their position was still but a short reprieve from death. There were fifty yards
of wild waves, and a resistless rush of water, between them and safety,
and to the right of them was a fall three hundred yards in width, and
below was a mile of falls and rapids, and great whirlpools, and waves
rising like little hills in the middle of the terrible stream, and below
these were the fell cannibals of Wane-Mukwa and Asama.

"How to reach the island was a question which now perplexed me.
We tied a stone to about a hundred yards of whipcord, and after the
twentieth attempt they managed to catch it. To the end of the whipcord
they tied the tent rope which had parted before, and drawing it to our
side we tied the stout rattan creeper, which they drew across taut and
fastened to a rock, by which we thought we had begun to bridge the
stream. But night drawing nigh, we said to them that we would defer
further experiment till morning.

"Meantime the ninth canoe, whose steersman was a supernumerary of the boat, had likewise got upset, and he out of six men was drowned, to our regret, but the canoe was saved. All other vessels were brought down safely, but so long as my poor faithful Uledi and his friends are on the islet, and still in the arms of death, the night finds us gloomy, sorrowing, and anxious.

"January 15.—My first duty this morning was to send greetings to the three brave lads on the islet, and to assure them that they should be saved before they were many hours older. Thirty men with guns were sent to protect thirty other men searching for rattans in the forest, and by nine o'clock we possessed sixty strong canes, besides other long climbers, and as fast as we were able to twist them together they were drawn across by Uledi and his friends. Besides, we sent light cables to be lashed round the waist of each man, after which we felt trebly assured that all accidents were guarded against. Then hailing them I motioned to Uledi to begin, while ten men seized the cable, one end of which he had fastened around his waist. Uledi was seen to lift up his hands to heaven, and waving his hands to us as he leaped into the wild flood, seizing the bridge cable as he fell into the depths. Soon he rose, hauling himself hand over hand, the waves brushing his face, and sometimes rising over his head, until it seemed as if he scarcely would be able to breathe; but by jerking his body occasionally upward with a desperate effort, he so managed to survive the waves and to approach us, where a dozen willing hands were stretched out to snatch the half-smothered man. Zaidi next followed, but after the tremendous proofs he had given of his courage and tenacious hold we did not much fear for his safety, and he also landed, to be warmly congratulated for his double escape from death. Marzouk, the youngest was the last, and we held our breath while the gallant boy was struggling out of the fierce grasp of death. While yet midway the pressure of water was so great that he lost his hold of two cables, at which the men screamed in terror lest he should relax his hold altogether from despair; but I shouted harshly to him:

" 'Pull away, you fool. Be a man.'

"At which with three hauls he approached within reach of our willing hands, to be embraced and applauded by all. The cheers we gave were so loud and hearty that the cannibal Wane-Mukwa must have known, despite the roar of the waters, that we had passed through a great and thrilling scene.''

SHOUTS OF DEFIANCE AND THREATS.

We need not follow them through their almost daily encounters with the hostile natives, many of whom were cannibals; some of them were driven off, others were glad to make friends with the white men and their followers. They arrived at the mouth of the Aruwimi, February 1. At this point in the river, they had seen many canoes. Stanley continues:

"We heard shouts of defiance or threats, we knew not which—we had become indifferent to the incessant noise and continued fury. • • • As soon as we have fairly entered the waters [of the Aruwimi] we see a great concourse of canoes hovering about some islets which stud the middle of the stream. The canoe-men, standing up, give a loud shout as they discern us, and blow their horns louder than ever. We pull briskly on to gain the right bank, and come in view of the right branch of the affluent, when, looking up stream, we see a sight that sends the blood tingling through every nerve and fiber of the body, arouses not only our lively interest, but also our most lively apprehensions—a flotilla of gigantic canoes bearing down upon us, which both in size and numbers eclipse anything encountered hitherto! Instead of aiming for the right bank, we form in line, and keep straight down the river, the boat taking position behind. Yet after a moment's reflection, as I note the numbers of the savages, and the daring manner of the pursuit, and the apparent desire of our canoes to abandon the steady compact line, I give the order to drop anchor. Four of our canoes affect not to listen, until I chase them, and threaten them with my guns. This compelled them to return to the line, which is formed of eleven double canoes, anchored ten yards apart. The boat moves up to the front, and takes position fifty yards above them. The shields are next lifted by the non-combatants, men, women, and children in the bows, and along the outer lines, as well as astern, and from behind these the muskets and rifles are aimed.

"We have sufficient time to take a view of the mighty force bearing down on us, and to count the number of the war-vessels which have been collected from the Livingstone and its great affluent. There are fifty-four of them! A monster canoe leads the way, with two rows of up-standing paddles, forty men on a side, their bodies bending and swaying in unison as with a swelling barbarous chorus they drive her down toward us. In the bow, standing on what appears to be a platform, are ten prime young warriors, their heads gay with feathers of the parrot crimson and gray; at the stern, eight men with long paddles whose tops are decorated with ivory balls, guide the monster vessel; and dancing up and down from stem to stern are eight men who appear to be chiefs. All the paddles are headed with ivory balls, every head bears a feather crown, every arm shows gleaming white armlets. From the bow of the canoe streams a thick fringe of the long white fiber of the Hyphene palm. The crashing sound of large drums, a hundred blasts from ivory horns, and a thrilling chant from two thousand human throats, do not tend to soothe our nerves or to increase our confidence. However, it is neck or nothing. We have no time to pray, or to take a sentimental look at the savage world, or even to breathe a sad farewell to it. So many other things have to be done speedily and well.

"As the foremost canoe comes rushing down, and the consorts on either side beating the water into foam, and raising their jets of water with their sharp prows, I turn to take a last look at our people, and say to them:

"'Boys, be firm as iron; wait until you see the first spear, and then take aim. Don't fire all at once, keep aiming until you are sure of your man. Don't think of running away, for only your guns can save you.'

"Frank is with the Ocean on the right flank, and has a choice crew, and a good bulwark of black wooden shields. Manwa Sera has the London Town—which he has taken charge of instead of the Glasgow—on the left flank, the sides of the canoe bristling with guns, in the hands of tolerably steady men

A MONSTER CANOE MANNED WITH WARRIORS.

"The monster canoe aims straight for my boat, as though it would run us down; but when within fifty yards swerves aside, and when nearly opposite, the warriors above the manned prow let fly their spears, and on either side there is a noise of rushing bodies. But every sound is soon lost in the ripping and crackling of musketry. For five minutes we are so absorbed in firing that we can take note of nothing else; but at the end of that time we are made aware that the enemy is re-forming about two hundred yards above us.

"Our blood is now up. It is a murderous world, and we feel for the first time that we hate the filthy, vulturous ghouls that inhabit it. We therefore lift our anchors, and pursue them up stream along the right bank, until rounding a point we see their villages. We make straight for the banks, and continue the fight in the village streets with those who have landed, hunt them out into the woods, and there only sound the retreat, having returned the daring cannibals the compliment of a visit."

Still floating down the river, they came to the country of the Bangala February 14. Stanley had some hopes of conciliating this tribe by means of gifts, as they were somewhat accustomed to the visits of the traders; for the travelers were now indeed approaching the portion of the river which was known to the merchants. Let us see how these efforts to make friends succeeded:

"We had left Observation Island about half a mile behind us when the prows of many canoes were seen to emerge out of the creek. I stood up and edged toward them, holding a long piece of red cloth in one hand and a coil of brass wire in another. We rested on our oars, and the men quietly placed their paddles in the canoe, and sat up, watchful, and ready for contingencies. As we floated down, numbers of canoes advanced.

"I hailed the natives, who were the most brilliantly decorated of any that I had seen. * * * The natives returned no answer to my hail; still I persisted. I observed three or four canoes approaching Frank's vessel with a most suspicious air about them, and several of their canoes menacing him, at which Frank stood up and menaced them with his weapon. I thought the act premature, and ordered him to sit down and look away from them. I again raised the crimson cloth and wire, and by pantomime offered to give it to those in front, whom

I was previously addressing; but almost immediately those natives who had threatened Frank fired into my boat, wounding three of my young crew, and two more natives fired into Frank's canoe, wounding two. The missiles fired into us were jagged pieces of iron and coppor precisely similar to those which the Ashantees employed. After this murderous

THE BUSH HOG.

outrage there was no effort made to secure peace. The shields were lifted, and proved capital defenses against the hail of slugs. Boats, shields and canoes were pitted, but only a few shields were perforated.

"The conflict began in earnest, and lasted so long that ammunition had to be redistributed. We perceived that, as the conflict continued, every village sent out its quota. * * * At three o'clock, I counted sixty-three canoes opposed to us. * * * And, allowing five guns on an average to each of the sixty-three canoes, there were three hundred and fifteen muskets opposed to our forty-four. Their mistake was in supposing their slugs to have the same penetrative power and long range as our missiles had. * * * After the departure of the wounded chief to the shore, the firing became desultory, and at 5:30 P. M. our antagonists retired, leaving us to attend to our wounded, and to give three hearty cheers at our success. This was our thirty-first fight on the terrible river—that last but one—and certainly the most determined conflict that we had endured.''

STANLEY'S THIRTY-SECOND FIGHT WITH SAVAGES.

The thirty-second fight took place March 9, a band of savages attacking them just as they were preparing breakfast; fourteen men were wounded before the savages were repulsed, but none were killed.

March 11, they arrived at a widening of the river into a lake-like expanse, which the leader, at the suggestion of his lieutenant, named Stanley Pool. Although their struggles with the natives were now at an end, having reached a point where they were more accessible to trade, the travelers found that they were by no means safe from dangers by river. Just below that expansion of the stream which was thus christened, are the cataracts now known as Livingstone Falls; and here new trials awaited them.

Passing several bad pieces of river, they had reached a point just below the Cauldron, and Stanley was superintending arrangements for a camp on the hard white sand of the river-bank. Glancing up, to his horror he caw the Crocodile, one of the canoes, in mid-river, far below the point which they had rounded, gliding with the speed of an arrow toward the falls over the treacherous calm water. Human strength availed nothing; he could but watch the vessel as she darted over the fall, bearing with her his boy Kalulu and four others. They saw it whirled round three or four times, then plunged down into the depths; out of which the stern presently emerged pointed upward; and then they knew that Kalulu and his canoe-mates were no more.

A second canoe darted by the horrified spectators, but almost by a miracle shot over the falls, and was brought to land below, the two men in its escaping harm. A third canoe darted past them, having but one man in it; but was less fortunate than the others, and was whirled down to instant death.

In remembrance of the victim who had been most intimately connected with the leader, his body-servant Kalulu, the cataract was named Kalulu Falls. But Stanley himself was not to escape danger from the violence of the river. He had devised a means of descending the river in safety even in the midst of rapids, by means of cables of cane; but the impediments were greater at this point than they had ever been before, and by a careless slacking of the stern cable, the current swept the boat from the hands of that portion of the crew whose duty it was to lower her cautiously down the fall, to the narrow line of ebb-flood below the rocky projection. It was useless to direct the men; for the human voice was drowned in the roar of the mad waters; oars were only useful to assist the helm, for they were flying with terrific speed past the series of boulders which strangled the river.

"After two miles we were abreast of the bay or indentation at which we had hoped to camp, but the strong river mocked our efforts to gain it. The flood was resolved we should taste the bitterness of death. A sudden rumbling noise, like the deadened sound of an earthquake, caused us to look below, and we saw the river heaved bodily upward, as though a volcano was about to belch around us. Up to the summit of this watery mound we were impelled; and then divining what was about to take place, I shouted out:

"'Pull, men, for your lives!'

"A few frantic strokes drove us to the lower side of the mound, and before it had finished subsiding, and had begun its usual fatal circling, we·were precipitated over a small fall, and sweeping down toward the inlet into which the Nkenke cataract tumbled, below the lowest line of the Lady Alice rapids. Once or twice we were flung scornfully aside, and spun around contemptuously, as though we were to insignificant to be wrecked; then availing ourselves of a calm moment, we resumed our oars, and soon entering the ebb-tide, rowed up river and reached the sandy beach at the junction of the Nkenke with the Livingstone.''

FRANK POCOCK'S DEATH.

June 3, Stanley left the camp at Mowa to proceed to Zinga, in order to establish a camp at the latter place; the boats were then to be transported overland, since the river would not allow of a voyage between these two points. Frank Pocock was left behind, for the time, until the leader should send men back with a hammock to carry him forward, for he was suffering so much with ulcers on both feet that he was quite lame. The shoes of both had given out, though Stanley managed to keep his, tattered and slit as they were, upon his feet; and the slightest wound from the roughness of the road is liable in that climate to be poisoned by the bite of the insects. But Pocock was impatient, and insisted upon being taken in a canoe which Uledi had been ordered to proceed with. In vain the faithful servitor argued that it was not safe for them to go by river; the young Englishman, a waterman by training, laughed at his fears, and declared it was but cowardice which made him and his comrades hesitate. The boatmen were at last goaded by these taunts to undertake that which their better judgment told them was simply fool-hardy.

"In a few seconds they had entered the river; and in obedience to Frank, Uledi steered his craft for the left side of the river. But it soon became clear that they could not reach it. There was a greasy slipperiness about the water that was delusive, and it was irresistibly bearing them broadside over the falls; and observing this, Uledi turned the prow, and boldly bore down for the center. Roused from his seat by the increasing thunder of the fearful waters, Frank rose to his feet, and looked over the heads of those in front, and now the full danger of his situation burst upon him. But too late! They had reached the fall, and plunged headlong amid the waves and spray. The angry waters rose, and leaped into their vessel, spun them round as though on a pivot, and so down over the curling, dancing, leaping crests they were borne, to the whirlpools that yawned below. Ah! then came the moment of anguish, regret and terror!

THE DOG-HEADED THYLOEINUS.

" 'Hold on to the canoe, my men; seize a rope, each one,' said he, while tearing his flannel shirt away. Before he could prepare himself, the canoe was drawn down into the abyss, and the whirling, flying waters closed over all. When the vacuum was filled, a great body of water was belched upward, and the canoe was disgorged into the bright sunlight, with several gasping men clinging to it. When they had drifted a little distance away from the scene, and had collected their faculties, they found that there were only eight of them alive; and alas for us who were left to bewail his sudden doom, there was no white face among them. But presently, close to them another commotion, another heaving and belching of waters, and out of them the insensible form of the 'little master' appeared, and they heard a loud moan from him. Then Uledi, forgetting his late escape from the whirling pit, flung out his arms and struck gallantly toward him, but another pool sucked them both in, and the waves closed over him before he could reach him; and for the second time the brave coxswain emerged, faint and weary—but Frank Pocock was seen no more.''

This was not the last of Stanley's troubles; many of his men, seeing no apparent hope of reaching smoother waters or a less difficult road, declared that they would go no further; and more than thirty of them actually set out on their journey back. They were, however, persuaded to return; not only by those who remained faithful to him, but by the determination of the natives to help none of those who had deserted their white master.

He had thought it slow traveling when, from the 16th of March to the 21st of April inclusive, a period of thirty-seven days, the expedition had made but thirty-four miles' progress; but it required thirty days to transport the expedition from Mowa to Zinga, a distance of three miles; and four men had been drowned during that time.

Late in July they reached the Yellala. Here the boats were abandoned, even the Lady Alice being left to bleach and rot on the shores of the mighty river; and everything not absolutely necessary being given to the men to buy food, the worn and weary and sadly diminished expedition set out on the way to the coast, five or six days off.

STARVATION AND SICKNESS.

They were literally starving men, for the food which they were able to obtain from the natives was small in quantity and poor in quality. Nearly forty of them were sick, with dysentery, ulcers, or scurvy; they had no fear of death left, and no hope of life; they dragged themselves wearily onward, not knowing who would be the next to fall, only sure that none of them would again reach their home.

And what of the leader? He had shared all their trials; he was hungry and weary and footsore and heartsore as they were; he had seen the last companion of his own race swept away by the remorseless Congo, it was on him that the responsibility of the whole expedition rested; but the indomitable spirit which was lacking in the "untutored mind" of the black men bore him up and gave him strength to utter words of encouragement to them.

They arrived at the village of Nsanda August 4; the chief seemed kindly and pleasant. He informed the new-comer that he had frequently been to Boma, that he carried ground-nuts there and exchanged them for rum. Suddenly Stanley asked him if he would carry a letter to Boma, and allow three men of the expedition to accompany him. He promised to send two of his young men, and Stanley wrote his letter—an appeal "To any Gentleman who speaks English at Embomma" for such help as was needed—food for immediate use, and cloth with which to purchase further supplies. Uledi, Kacheche, and two others, one of whom was a pupil of the Universities' Mission at Zanzibar, and was to act as interpreter, volunteered for the journey; and two guides were furnished by the chief.

The expedition marched on more slowly, finding it impossible to procure food where they were; "Wait for the market days," they were told. Two days later, while they were encamped near Banza Mbuko, and Stanley was thoroughly sick at heart because of the distress of his starving people, the messengers returned, bringing with them rice, sweet potatoes and fish in generous quantities for all hands, and rum and tobacco in smaller quantities, to be dealt out by the master; with such luxuries as wheaten bread, butter, tea, coffee, loaf-sugar, jam, sardines, salmon, plum-pudding, ale, sherry, port and champagne for the white man who had left all these behind him three years before.

GREETING THE VAN OF CIVILIZATION.

Messengers were dispatched bearing the hearty thanks of the now well-fed men, and then the main body again took up the line of march. August 9, 1877, they prepared to greet the "van of civilization," the 999th day after their departure from Zanzibar. Of the welcome which there awaited him at the hands of those who had so promptly and generously responded to his appeal, we need not speak; our story draws to a close as the gaunt and way-worn men descend the slope toward the white town of Boma, and start with surprise as they see a steamer anchored in the broad brown river.

Here they remained two days; and then proceeded down the river on this steamer to Kabinda. The sickness of many members of the expedition detained Stanley here for some time, as he was anxious to see all his men off to Zanzibar before sailing for Europe; but at last he was free to return, and though he chose to accompany the members of the expedition as far as the Cape of Good Hope on their return journey, he was still eagerly looking forward to the home-coming. Yet even at this time he was not unmindful of the feelings of his followers; he saw that they were sorrowful, and guessed the reason; they acknowledged that it was so, that they hearts were heavy because he was about to leave them while they were still far from their homes; and he resolved to accompany them on the voyage from Cape Town to Zanzibar. November 26, they arrived at the end of their return journey; and December 13, having paid-off all his men and also what was due to the surviving relatives of those who had not returned, Stanley embarked for England. A journey through the Dark Continent, was, for the first time in the history of the world, an accomplished fact.

CHAPTER XXII.

WONDERFUL TROPICAL SCENERY IN AFRICA.

The Sources of the Nile Still Undiscovered—Immense Mountain Ranges—Endless Primeval Forests— A Grand Spectacle—Great Variety of Tropical Trees—Beautiful Lakes and Fascinating Landscapes—Africa Still the Field for Ambitious Discoverers—Early Explorations.

LARGE areas of the Dark Continent, where Roosevelt now is adding new laurels to his glorious career, are still never seen by any white man. And wonderful enough the sources of the famous river Nile, Egypt's fertilizer, which has been known and navigated for thousands of years, are still undiscovered. Many bold and enterprising travelers have from time to time attempted to solve this interesting problem, but like the North Pole the Nile has eluded their efforts and still is hiding his hoary head somewhere in the sands of unapproachable deserts; or may be in some cave of the mysterious and weird rocks so vividly described by Rider Haggard in his grotesque novel "She."

While many recent explorers have sailed far up the Nile and thus been approaching what may be called its sources, still neither Americans, nor Englishmen, nor Germans nor Belgians have succeeded to quench their thirst in its remotest source somewhere in the Moon mountains.

This is, so to say, the last problem in African geography which is yet unsolved. The continent has been traversed from south to north and from east to west and in all possible directions; two tribes of Pygmies have reached Europe and America from their fabulous haunts in the endless forests; the mountain peaks Kilimanjaro, Kenia and Ruwenzori have been scaled; the large primeval forest has been traversed; the last great inland lake is found; but no one has as yet cleared up the mystery of the Nile. It still remains as stubborn as the

mute Sphinx on its sandy shores. Who is going to solve this problem?
Is Roosevelt going to have something to say about it? Who knows?

There are four main routes along which the Nile's sources might
be reached. One is the route from Cairo to the lake. It is a magnificent route, leading through a marvellous tropical country, but it is too

THE PECCARY.

long and slow as the traveler has to proceed by steamboat on the Nile.
Then there is another route in the opposite direction from the lake to
Cairo, less slow but not so full of adventures and game. The route
through Mataeri and the mouth of the Congo river is also slow and
tedious, as it takes several months to reach the interior of the country
along this gigantic river.

The best route is no doubt through the Suez Canal to Mombasa, then along the Uganda Railway to Nairobi and the great lakes, where Roosevelt began his hunting expedition, then farther down along the Aruwimi to the Stanley Falls and down the Congo river to the Atlantic. This is no doubt the shortest and most convenient route, as the traveler can go by rail or steamboat the greater part of the way, with the ex-

EMIN PASHA (DR. E. SCHNOTZER).

ception of 700 miles, and will be brought within a distance of only 200 miles from the upper Nile.

Along this route you can cross Africa from ocean to ocean in four months spending one month in hunting, one month on the Nile and Lake Tanganyika, and the two remaining months on the journey from coast to coast. This gives the traveler a fair idea of African colonization, for he passes through both British and German East Africa, Rhodesia, French and Belgian Congo and Portuguese West Africa. By no other

24

route can you get a chance to visit so many European colonies in so short a time. There you also meet the richest hunting grounds in the world. Vegetation in this part of Africa is extraordinary luxuriant and varying from the fertile coast at Mombasa and Bangala to the snow-clad peaks of Ruwenzori, you pass through landscapes of wonderful beauty and a peculiar character.

Another advantage in taking this route is the insight it gives into the commercial and industrial resources of Africa. You get an opportunity to study the rubber and ivory trade at close range, and to get an idea of the immense and untold wealth hidden in the large tropical forests and the endless prairies and mountains.

You sail through the straits of Babelmandeb to Zanzibar. This was the starting point for two of Stanley's great expeditions, and here the third one ended. Here Emin Pasha fell from a window and came pretty near breaking his neck after having emptied too many champagne bottles at Major Wissmann's dinner. Here the slave-trade flourished for a thousand years. And from Mombasa Roosevelt started out on his famous hunting and scientific expedition, which has enriched our store of knowledge of tropical Africa more than any previous exploration.

We have already described the wonderful tropical scenery, the marvellous plant and animal world along the Uganda Railway up to Victoria Nyanza. The lake lies 3,000 feet above the level of the sea. The rainfall in this tropical region is 47 inches a year. On the other side of the lake the route is continued across undulating highlands and mountains, which form the very backbone of the great continent as far as the Albert Nyanza. Then the traveler has before him a wild and difficult road to the sources of Aruwimi and then follows this river 400 miles until it joins with the Congo. From this point it is still 1,000 miles to Stanley Pool, where the majestic Crystal Mountains tower high up above the clouds. Here you can take the railroad for 350 miles to Miadi, where the ocean steamers land, 150 miles from the mouth of the river.

In giving these distances we have not taken in consideration the many windings of the river and the road, and when the traveler arrives at the coast he will surely have covered not less than 3,000 miles, though in a straight line it would be 400 miles less.

The highest point on the route is Ruwenzori, about 20,000 feet above the level of the sea. The highlands which extend from the eastern slope of the mountain ranges to the Aruwimi prairies are about 700 miles wide. This mountain range is a continuation of the immense chain of mountains which extends from the northeastern corner of Europe to the Cape. It begins with the Ural or Caucasus, continues through Asia Minor, with Mount Ararat, Lebanon and Sinai, through Abyssinia and south through Central Africa to the Cape, where it meets the southern branch of the western mountain chain.

The Crystal mountains again are a continuation of the gigantic chain of mountains which begins in the Scandinavian peninsula and stretches southward through Germany over the Alps and Apennines. It again appears in the Atlas and Congo mountains and at last ends in the Cape. These huge mountain chains form a gigantic V on the surface of the earth with the angle in the Cape and the wings in the northern corners of Europe.

Through Central Africa along the Equator runs an immense unbroken and continuous primeval forest large enough to cover California and full of interesting objects for the student of natural history. Among the trees growing here are the acacia, the mahogany, several varieties of palms, mimosas, laurels. Here we find the convolvulus, an immense parasite which climbs the giant trunks and kills them in its treacherous embrace. Here grow many varieties of the bamboo, and other gigantic reeds, and the bottomless marshes are overgrown with water-lilies and orchids.

The vegetation is most luxurious during the rainy season, but the scenery varies much less than in the temperate zones. Between the giant trees are groves of bushes and clustering undergrowth broken by fields of grass or impenetrable shrubbery. The fan palms are clustered together in groves and in the marshes grows the prickly date. There are also the fig trees, among whom the sycamores are the most remarkable, and the large-leaved tamarinds. In the interior of these primeval forests temple-like corridors lie veiled in eternal shadow and are spanned by dense roofs of foliage, rising vault above vault, the galleries appearing like an impenetrable wall of vari-colored foliage, through which the avenues open out in every direction, while the murmuring voice of springs and running streams fills the air. The average height of the leafy roof measures from 75 to 100 feet, but seen from without the galleries by no means make the imposing impression we would expect for the elevation or depression of the ground takes away some of the effect. Gigantic tree trunks, thickly overgrown with wild pepper, rise from the depths and support wide-spreading branches draped with lichens and vines, while other tree stems, long since dead and decaying, serve as supports for colossal vines and form impenetrable bowers, large as houses, within whose walls reigns a perpetual darkness. The thick greenery, interwoven with the climbing parasites, the tangled shrubbery, and the moss-covered mouldering trunks, make the advance through these waves of massive vegetation anything but easy, while the heavy humid atmosphere, reminding us of our greenhouses, and the constant moisture, produced by the exhalations of the woods itself makes the traveler gasp for breath and wish-himself out on the plains again.

Ants, mosquitoes, the tsetse and other poisonous flies, swarm over the ground and fill the air with their buzzing music, while thousands of summerbirds chase each other and sport among the branches, and the Colibris chase the insects. There are huge Goliashbills, wonderful insects resembling blocks of wood, fishes who dig themselves down deep in the mud and can live there for months. Among the birds we note the Pepperbirds, the Cherrybirds, the Heron, the Flamingo, the Crane and the Ibis.

In this forest we also find the Gorilla and the Chimpanzee, the highest developed and most intelligent of all animals, and also Pygmies, the least developed of all men. These dwarfs occupy a considerable district lying on both sides of the Aruwimi, and nearly midway between Yambuga and Albert Nyanza. Their average height is certainly not more, perhaps less, than three feet in height, while there are as many of the exceptionally short that scarcely exceed two feet; a majority of them are slightly under three feet. But though short of stature they are uncommonly muscular and are also very ingenious, peculiarly in working iron. Their chief weapons are bows and arrows, the former being occasionally made of steel and the latter invariably tipped with metal. The Pygmies are fishers and hunters and pursue both callings with great success. In hunting the largest game they go in consider-

THE OBYX.

able bodies, surrounding such animals as the elephant and literally worrying him to death by persistent pursuit and the shooting of hundreds of arrows into it, reminding one of the Lilliputians in Gulliver's travels. They possess considerable quantities of ivory as trophies of the hunt, and they manifest no small ingenuity in carving it into fantastic designs for bracelets, anklets, armlets and even necklaces. They wear no beards, have woolly hair, black eyes, thick lips, flat noses and large mouths. There is not wanting evidence of their being cannibals. Human skulls have often been seen by travelers on poles about their villages and in a single instance a fairly well-cured human arm was seen hanging to the outside wall of a hut. It bore the appearance of having been smoked for a considerable time, but none of the villagers could be induced to talk about any of their habits. Even on the lowest step of barbarism man seems to be ashamed of his low habits. Still traces of a higher instinct are not lacking among them. The domestic ties are evidently very strong and there is no evidence of polygamy. During a short stay at one of the villages a child of one of the natives died and Stanley saw the evidences of intense grief which the event caused. The mother appeared to be crazed by her sorrow and had to be restrained by her friends from committing some desperate act. Another woman, probably the grandmother, took the dead body upon her lap and poured out a libation of tears and wailings that was deeply affecting to behold. Another tribe wears a cow-tail hanging from the belt behind, which led to the belief among travelers that they had natural tails.

The fauna of this forest comprises the largest animals such as the elephant and the giraffe. The most melodious of all singing birds, the nightingale, spends his winters here. Here also we find the redbreasted and gray parrot and some of the most poisonous and largest snakes as the python. It is a land of wonder and surprise.

Some peculiarities of this fauna deserve to be noticed. The gorilla is found only in the western part of this territory, along the Atlantic coast, but has never yet been seen south of the Congo River; the giraffe is never seen west of Loulaba, hardly west of the whole mountain range from Ruwenzori; the rhinoceros lives mostly in south and east Africa; the zebra does not appear west of Loulaba. It looks as if many of the central-African beasts were confined within certain boundaries, outside of which they never venture. A plausible reason for this is that once an immense lake has covered the present Congo valley, Sudan and very likely also Sahara. This lake formed an unsurmountable dividing line between east and west Africa, thus preventing the animals on both sides to mix and cross. Not until the lake was drained began the crossing process, which is still going on and will gradually change the African animal world, unless European and American hunters prevent it by exterminating it. This explanation, however, is not entirely satisfactory. It does not explain why the gorilla dwells in west Africa while the Chimpanzee is spread all over eastern Africa and so on.

FACE OF THE GORILLA.

The traveler through these regions will often be reminded of many dramatic incidents in modern history. Most of the great African explorers have made Zanzibar their starting point. Burton and Speke started from there on their journey to Tanganyika and Victoria Nyanza, and to Zanzibar the body of David Livingstone was taken, when the heroic discoverer had died. And then there is the road from Victoria to Albert Nyanza, along which Stanley undertook his celebrated expedition for the relief of Enim Pasha. And then the long voyage down the river. But where Stanley and his followers once had to cut their way through the impenetrable forests and fight with desperate savages for months we now pass in a few days on a comfortable steamer or by railroad.

The most tempting diversions during this long journey are hunting elephants in the vicinity of Kilimanjaro, or antelopes and other big game around the sources of Athia in Kikuegu, or lions near Tanganyika, or champanzees in the forests along Aruwimi or Congo. Along Aruwimi one will meet with the Pygmies.

One of the most necessary reforms in Africa is protection of its big game. There are laws enough enacted for this purpose, but they cannot be enforced and the process of extermination is ruthlessly going on, and in a not far distant future this wonderful animal world will have passed into history, and be seen only in our museums and zoological gardens. And the Dark Continent is yet crying for other still more pressing reforms. Nominally the slave trade is abolished, and the shameful export of human beings is stopped. But in Africa itself this nefarious traffic is just as flourishing as ever. The Africans themselves keep slaves. And to liberate these bondsmen is no easy task.

The expenses for a journey through the vast territory we have described are of course considerable. It is estimated that five white men with one hundred porters and helpers can accomplish it for $10,-000, if it does not take longer than six months.

BRUCE IN SEARCH OF THE SOURCE OF THE NILE.

Among the early explorers who more than a century ago risked their lives in vain attempts to solve the mystery of the Nile, James Bruce takes a conspicuous place. He was an Englishman of scholarly attainments, bold and enterprising.

The rumor that war was about to be declared between Great Britain and Spain induced Bruce to offer his services upon an expedition of some danger. The offer was under consideration for some time, but was not accepted. It paved the way, however, for other missions, of not much less danger, and of much greater importance to the world. Lord Halifax desired him to go to Barbary, to study the ruins of architectural beauty which travelers reported to exist there, and make public the infomation so obtained. In the course of the interviews between them, the subject of exploring the Nile was broached; and Bruce afterward declared that at this instant of his life his heart suggested to him "that this great discovery should either be achieved by me, or remain, as it had done for the last two thousand years, a defiance to all travelers, and an opprobrium to geography."

Shortly after the conversation which prompted this resolve, Bruce was appointed British consul at Algiers. Here he remained for two years, the intervals between the duties of his troublous office being fully occupied by studies. He learned here, from a venerable Greek

LONGHORNED GOAT.

priest, the modern Greek language, which was afterward of great use to him in Abyssinia. He also acquired much valuable knowledge of surgery.

Finally succeeding in effecting a recall, for his life at Algiers had by no means been all that his fancy had painted it before starting, Bruce began the work which the prime minister had suggested—visiting and taking views of the ruins of Barbary. With this end in view, he traveled through the greater part of northern Africa; and it was three years after he left his consulate before he sailed from Cyprus for Egypt, to seek the sources of the Nile.

Arrived at Cairo, he was fortunately mistaken for a skilled astrologer by the all-powerful Coptic secretary of Ali Bey, who was at the head of the government. This reputation, together with his skill as a physician, obtained him peremptory letters of recommendation from the bey to various potentates through whose territories he must pass. Thus equipped, he set out from Cairo in December, 1768.

His progress up the Nile was marked by no misfortune. On the contrary, the same knowledge which had served him so well at Cairo again came into play at his time of greatest danger, when he was in the power of an Arab chief. The chief was ill, and Bruce relieved his pain; the Arab could not sufficiently thank him; but pronounced a solemn curse on any of his people who should molest the traveler. This chief advised him, when he admitted that his object was to reach Abyssinia, to return to Kenek, and go thence overland to Kosseir; thence to cross the Red Sea to Jiddah, near Mecca, and from that port to sail for Abyssinia. Notwithstanding this advice, Bruce continued his journey until he reached the first cataract, near Assouan; then he returned, and followed the old chief's advice, traveling across the country under the protection of a caravan of the adviser's followers.

ARRIVES AT ABYSSINIA.

Bruce spent considerable time in making a survey of the Red Sea; and it was not until September, 1769, that he finally anchored in the harbor of Massowa, the ancient port of Abyssinia. This country had been the goal of Portuguese travels in a previous century. We have already seen that rumors of a Christianized country in the heart of Africa led the early Portuguese explorers of Guinea to imagine that they had at last heard of the location of Prester John; in the sixteenth century, missionaries of this nation reached Abyssinia from a different direction. According to tradition, the Abyssinians had been converted to Judaism by their sovereign, the Queen of the South who visited Solomon; in the fourth century of our era they were converted to Christianity. The Portuguese missionaries made strenuous efforts to turn them from the Greek Catholic to the Roman Catholic form of faith, and for a time seemed to be successful; but they were finally compelled to abandon the attempt. For almost seventy years, there had been no communication whatever between this country and Europe. Abyssinia seemed almost to have been blotted from the map of the world. The immense distance, the climate in which it was situated, the deserts which nearly surrounded it, and the barbarous character of the tribes which surrounded it, were of themselves enough to deter most travelers; and the dangers of the route had not been softened in the accounts of the returned unsuccessful missionaries.

It was with considerable difficulty and after a delay of two months, that Bruce escaped the naybe of Massowa, who demanded handsome presents in addition to those which the traveler had voluntarily bestowed upon him. But having left Massowa, and thus escaped the importunities of the naybe, his delays and difficulties were not by any means at an end. The favor of a relative of the naybe warned him against taking the easier road, since it might be dangerous; and the rough and mountainous pathway which was thus recommended as safer was the scene of suffering. But by great address, Bruce succeeded in winning the favor of the natives with whom he came in contact; and after a journey which occupied ninety-five days, he came in sight of Gondar, the capital of Abyssinia, about four hundred miles from Massowa.

Here he had the good fortune to effect a cure of several persons who were suffering with smallpox; among them was a child of Ras Michael, the real ruler of the kingdom; for the power of the king was but nominal. Much to the dismay of Bruce, the gratitude of these persons whose friends he had cured took the form of securing for him official appointments about the person of the king; however high the honor which they intended to bestow, this proceeding would have put an end to his attempts at discovery as effectually as their most determined enmity could have done.

The country was disturbed at the time by the revolt of Fasil; and the royal army marched from the capital against the rebel. Bruce of course accompanied it, though not always with the main body of the troops; and it was while on this expedition that he obtained his first sight of the Nile, and of one of its magnificent cataracts. This was the one which is known as the sixth (in ascending the river) and is about sixty miles north of the modern Khartoom.

Fasil, alarmed by the strength of the army which had pursued him, gave his allegiance to the king; and does not seem to have met with any punishment for his rebellion. The royal army returned to Gondar, Bruce of course accompanying it. His desire to find the fountains of

THE MALAYAN TAPIR.

the Nile had only been whetted by the sight of the river; and he was more determined than ever to proceed upon his quest.

Fasil's embassadors had heard of the fame of the physician from the far country, and besought him for something which would cure a cancer on the lip, with which Fasil's principal general was afflicted. They declared that Fasil would be better pleased with a medicine which would restore his favorite to health, than with the magnificent appointments which the king lavished upon the repentant rebel. Hearing this assertion, Bruce requested that the king would give him the village of Geesh, and the source of the Nile; evidently supposing that the latter was not far from Gondar. Indeed he asserts distinctly that he had

THE IBEX.

been within fifty miles of the head of the river when obliged to return, with the rest of the king's army, to the capital. The request was granted, and ratified by a solemn oath from the king; while Fasil's embassadors undertook that their master should act as his guide.

But the truce between the king and this powerful rebel was of short duration; the very morning after this promise was made, certain provinces which had suffered severely from the devastations of the royal army on its late march rose against the king; or rather, against his chief adviser. It was not for several months, therefore, that Bruce was enabled to set out on his journey.

October 28, 1770, he and his party began the undertaking. His instruments required six men for their transportation, relieving each other at stated intervals. His difficulties, however, were now all in his own cause; he was no longer exposed to danger through the quarrels of others; he was at last engaged in the actual work of exploration.

Proceeding on their journey from Lake Tsana, they turned southward; for it must be remembered that the traveler was in search of the source of the Blue Nile, which is sometimes considered the main river. They found many peasants flying before Fasil's army, which had been put in motion for some reason with which the explorer was not acquainted. Fasil was at Bamba, a small village of miserable huts; and thither Bruce went, knowing well that the rebel chieftain could forward him in his object. Perhaps it would be well to let Bruce tell the story of their first interview in his own words:

"After announcing myself, I waited about a quarter of an hour before I was admitted. Fasil was sitting upon a cushion, with a lion's skin upon it, and another stretched like a carpet before his feet. He had a cotton cloth, something like a dirty towel, wrapped about his head; his upper cloak or garment was drawn tight about him over his neck and shoulders, so as to cover his hands. I bowed, and went forward to kiss one of them, but it was so entangled in the cloth that I was obliged to kiss the cloth instead of the hand. This was done, either as not expecting I should pay him that compliment (as I certainly should not have done, being one of the king's servants, if the king had been at Gondar) or else it was intended for a mark of disrespect, which was very much of a piece with the rest of his behavior afterward.

"There was no carpet or cushions in the tent, and only a little straw, as if accidentally, thrown thinly about it. I sat down upon the ground, thinking him sick, not knowing what all this meant. He looked steadfastly at me, saying, half under his breath:

"'Endet nawi? bogo nawi?'

THE MANKEOOR.

"Which in Amharic, is:

" 'How do you do? Are you very well?'

"I made the usual answer:

" 'Well, thank God.'

"He again stopped, as for me to speak. There was only one old man present, who was sitting on the floor mending a mule's bridle. I took him at first for an attendant; but, observing that a servant, uncovered, held a candle to him, I thought he was one of his Galla; but then I saw a blue silk thread which he had about his neck, which is a badge of Christianity all over Abyssinia, and which a Galla would not wear. What he was I could not make out; he seemed, however, to be a very bad cobbler, and took no notice of us.

" 'I am come,' said I, 'by your invitation and the king's leave, to pay my respects to you in your own government, begging that you would favor my curiosity so far as to allow me to see the country of the Agows and the source of the Abay (or Nile), part of which I have seen in Egypt.'

" 'The source of the Abay!' exclaimed he, with a pretended surprise; 'do you know what you are saying? Why, it is God knows where, in the country of the Galla, wild, terrible people. The source of the Abay! Are you raving?' he repeats again; 'are you to get there, do you think, in a twelvemonth or more, or when?'

" 'Sir,' said I, 'the king told me it was near Sacala, and still nearer Geesh; both villages of the Agows, and both in your government.'

" 'And so you know Sacala and Geesh?' says he, whistling and half angry.

" 'I can repeat the names that I hear,' said I: 'all Abyssinia knows the head of the Nile.'

" 'Aye,' says he, imitating my voice and manner, 'but all Abyssinia won't carry you there, that I promise you.'

" 'If you are resolved to the contrary,' said I, 'they will not. I wish you had told the king so in time, then I should not have attempted it; it was relying upon you alone that I came so far—confident, that if all the rest of Abyssinia could not protect me there, that your word singly could do it.'

"He now put on a look of more complacency.

" 'Look you, Yagoube,' says he [Bruce had assumed the name of Yagoube, the Arabic form of his own Christian name]; 'it is true I can do it, and, for the king's sake, who recommended it to me, I would do it; but the chief priest, Abba Salama, has sent to me to desire me not to let you pass farther; he says it is against the law of the land to permit Franks like you to go about the country, and that he has dreamed something ill will befall me if you go into Maitsha.'

"I was as much irritated as I thought it possible for me to be.

" 'So, so,' said I, 'the time of priests, prophets, and dreamers is coming on again.'

THE SAIGA.

" 'I understand you,' says he, laughing for the first time; 'I care as little for priests as Michael does, and for prophets too; but I would have you consider the men of this country are not like yours; a boy of these Galla would think nothing of killing a man of your country. You white people are all effeminate; you are like so many women; you are not fit for going into a province where all is war, and inhabited by men, warriors from their cradle.'

25

"I saw he intended to provoke me; and he had succeeded so effectually that I should have died, I believe, if I had not, as impudent as it was, told him my mind in reply.

" 'Sir,' said I, 'I have passed through many of the most barbarous nations in the world; all of them, excepting this clan of yours, have some great men among them above using a defenseless stranger ill. But the worst and lowest individual among the most uncivilized people never treated me as you have done today under your own roof, where I have come so far for protection.'

" 'How?' he asked.

" 'You have, in the first place,' said I, 'publicly called me Frank, the most odious name in this country, and sufficient to occasion me to be stoned to death, without farther ceremony, by any set of men, wherever I may present myself. By a Frank you mean one of the Romish religion, to which my nation is as adverse as yours; and again, without having ever seen any of my countrymen but myself, you have discovered, from that specimen, that we are all cowards and effeminate people, like or inferior to your boys and women. Look you, sir: you never heard that I gave myself out as more than an ordinary man in my own country, far less to be a pattern of what is excellent in it. I am no soldier, though I know enough of war to see yours are poor proficients in that trade. But there are soldiers, friends and countrymen of mine, who would not think it an action to vaunt of that, with five hundred men, they had trampled all your naked savages into dust.'

"On this, Fasil made a feigned laugh, and seemed rather to take my freedom amiss. It was, doubtless, a passionate and rash speech.

" 'As to myself,' continued I, 'unskilled in war as I am, could it be now without any farther consequence, let me be but armed in my own country-fashion, on horseback as I was yesterday, I should, without thinking myself overmatched, fight the two best horsemen you shall choose from this your army of famous men, who are warriors from their cradle; and if, when the king arrives, you are not returned to your duty, and we meet again as we did at Limjour, I will pledge myself, with his permission, to put you in mind of this promise, and leave the choice of men to your option.'

"This did not make things better. He repeated the word duty after me, and would have replied, but my nose burst out in a stream of blood and that instant a servant took hold of me by the shoulder to hurry me out of the tent. Fasil seemed to be a good deal concerned, for the blood streamed out upon my clothes. I returned, then, to my tent, and the blood was soon stanched by washing my face with cold water. I sat down to recollect myself, and the more I calmed, the more I was dissatisfied

THE BULOU.

at being put off my guard; but it is impossible to conceive the provocation without having proved it. I have felt but too often how much the love of our native soil increases by our absence from it; and how jealous we are of comparisons made to the disadvantage of our countrymen by people who, all proper allowances being made, are generally not their equals, when they would boast themselves their superiors. I will confess farther, in gratification to my critics, that I was from my infancy of a sanguine, passionate disposition; very sensible of injuries which I had neither provoked nor deserved; but much reflection from very early life, continued habits of suffering in long and dangerous travels, where nothing but patience would do, had, I flattered myself, abundantly, subdued my natural proneness to feel offences which common sense might teach me I could only revenge upon myself.

"However, upon farther consulting my own breast, I found there was another cause that had co-operated strongly with the former in making me lose my temper at that time, which, upon much greater provocation, I had never done before. I found now, as I thought, that it was decreed decisively that my hopes of arriving at the source of the Nile were forever ended; all my trouble, all my expense, all my time, and all my sufferings for so many years were thrown away, from no greater obstacles than the whimsies of one barbarian, whose good inclinations I thought I had long before sufficiently secured; and, what was worse, I was now got within less than forty miles of the place I wished so much to see; and my hopes were shipwrecked upon the last, as well as upon the most unexpected, difficulty, I had to encounter."

AN UNTAMED HORSE.

But Bruce's fears were without foundation. That night, Fasil sent him two lean sheep, and a guard of men to protect him during the night. The next morning, twelve horses, saddled and bridled, were brought to him by Fasil's servant, who asked him which he would ride. Bruce left the man to select a quiet horse for him, and forthwith mounted the one which was offered to him. The animal proved to be wholly untamed; but Bruce managed to keep his seat, and finally sent him back to Fasil as an entirely safe horse to ride. He then mounted his own horse, and showed the admiring natives something of his marksmanship.

Fasil was witness, not only of his shooting, but of his riding; although he protested that he had not sent the wild horse himself; he had none, he said, fit for the saddle, except the one which he himself rode; but any of his horses, driven before the party, would ensure their safety from the attacks of surrounding savages. He again protested that he was innocent of any desire to injure the traveler, and assured him that the groom who had taken him such a horse was in irons, and would be put to death within a few hours.

" 'Sir,' replied Bruce, ''as this man has attempted my life, it is I that should name the punishment.'

" 'It is very true,' replied Fasil; 'take him, Yagoube, and cut him in a thousand pieces, if you please, and give his body to the kites.'

" 'Are you really sincere in what you say?' said Bruce; 'and will you have no after excuses?' ''

THE BALL ARMADILLO.

He swore solemnly that he would not.

" 'Then,' returned the traveler, 'I am a Christian; the way my religion teaches me to punish my enemies is by doing good for evil; and therefore I keep you to the oath which you have sworn, and desire you to set the man at liberty, and put him in the place he held before; for he has not been undutiful to you.' ''

One of the attendants, turning to Fasil, said, while a murmur of approbation ran through the assemblage:

"Did I not tell you what my brother said about this man? He was just the same all through Tigre."

Fasil replied in a low tone, which Bruce's ears barely caught:

"A man that behaves as he does may go through any country."

In an interview which Bruce afterward had with Fasil, the latter promised a guide who was thoroughly acquainted with the country through which they were to pass, and who had the additional recommen dation of being well known as an attendant of Fasil's, so that the stranger's safety would be by this means secured. He then invested Bruce with the government of Geesh, in accordance with the king's grant. He also swore seven Galla chiefs to defend Bruce to the utmost if he should be attacked, and to see that he wanted for nothing which their stores could supply.

October 31, the party set out. Bruce notes that the Galla chiefs paid but little attention to him, although they lavished every possible mark of respect upon the saddle horse which Fasil had given him, to be led in advance of the party. On the third day after they left the camp of Fasil, they came in sight of the mountain of Geesh. The long-sought fountains of the Nile were just beyond it.

But the winding stream must be followed for no little distance before they could reach this elevation. Nor would the inhabitants permit them, when it was necessary to cross the river, to ride across on their horses or mules. They insisted that Bruce and his party should take off their shoes, and even signified that they would stone those who attempted to wash the dirt from their clothes. Patiently forbearing any protest against these superstitious notions, older than the Christianity which they nominally professed, Bruce endeavored to comply with their demands, and restrained his servants who would have returned rudeness for rudeness.

While the sight of Fasil's horse prevented any of these half-savage natives from attacking the party, it was of disadvantage to them in another way. Seeing the sign of the chief's protection, the inhabitants concluded that the party had been sent out for the purpose of collecting taxes. The human mind appears to have a natural prejudice against the collector of taxes; and in oriental countries, this feeling is not lessened by the enormity of the imposts exacted. The natives accordingly fled from their homes and hid themselves and their portable property; so that Bruce was at some trouble to obtain the necessary provisions.

Following the windings of the constantly lessening stream, they

THE CAPE ANT EATER.

journeyed until a little after noon of the fourth day. They had then arrived at the summit of a mountain, from which they had a distinct view of all the remaining territory of Sacala, the mountain of Geesh, and immediately beneath them, the Nile itself, strangely diminished in size, and now only a brook that had scarcely water enough to turn a mill. The mighty river at this point and at this season was not four yards wide, and barely four inches deep. It ran swiftly over a bottom of small stones, with hard black rock appearing among them. A little below the point at which Bruce saw it at this time, it is full of inconsiderable falls; but at this point, it was easy enough to pass. The guide pointed out to the traveler the position of the two hillocks of green sod where the fountains of the Nile were to be found; and Bruce ran down the hill toward the point.

BRUCE REACHES SUPPOSED SOURCE OF THE NILE.

He had been cautioned to remove his shoes when approaching the spot, since the people about this place were even more bigoted in their reverence for the river than those whom the party had before encountered; it was then in the guise of a reverent worshiper that he approached the spot toward which, for many years, his thoughts had been directed. But let him tell his own story of the feeling which in this hour of success possessed him:

"I came to the altar of green turf, which was in the form of an altar, apparently the work of art, and I stood in rapture over the principal fountain, which rises in the middle of it.

"It is easier to guess than to describe the situation of my mind at that moment—standing in that spot which had baffled the genius, industry, and inquiry of both ancients and moderns for the course of near three thousand years! Kings had attempted this discovery at the head of armies, and each expedition was distinguished from the last only by the difference of the numbers that had perished, and agreed alone in the disappointment which had uniformly and without exception followed them all. Fame, riches, and honor had been held out for a series of ages to every individual of these myriads these princes commanded, without having produced one man capable of gratifying the curiosity of his sovereign, or wiping off this stain upon the enterprise and abilities of mankind, or adding this desideratum for the encouragement of geography. Though a mere private Briton, I triumphed here, in my own mind, over kings and their armies; and every comparison was leading nearer and nearer to presumption, when the place itself where I stood, the object of my vainglory, suggested what depressed my short-lived triumph. I was but a few minutes arrived at the sources of the Nile, through numberless dangers and sufferings, the least of which would have overwhelmed me but for the continual goodness and protection of Providence. I was then, however, but half through my journey, and all those dangers which I had al-

THE GREAT ARMADILLO.

ready passed awaited me again on my return; I found a despondency gaining ground fast upon me, and blasting the crown of laurels I had too rashly woven for myself.''

He soon recovered from this feeling of despondency, in outward appearance at least; and drank to the health of the king (George III.) in the waters of the newly discovered fountain. He remained at Geesh four days, making various surveys and astronomical observations.   The result of about forty observations made at this time places the head-waters of the Blue Nile in north latitude 10 degrees, 59 minutes, 25 seconds, and 36 degrees, 55 minutes, 30 seconds east longitude; the barometer indicating an elevation of something more than two miles above the level of the sea.

Some slight description of the scene which he had come through such difficulties and dangers to behold may not be out of place here.   The hillock of green sod, which he compares in form to an altar, even if it had not been purposely fashioned in that shape, is in the midst of a small marsh, about twelve feet in diameter, surrounded by a wall of sod, at the foot of which is a shallow trench which collects the water.   In the center of this hillock there is a hole, filled with water, which appears perfectly still; there is no appearance whatever of ebul-lition upon its surface, such as is usual in springs; this hole the traveler found by measurement to be about three feet in diameter and six feet deep.   At the distance of ten feet from this hillock, there is a second fountain, eleven inches in diameter and eight feet deep; and at twenty feet there is a third fountain, two feet in diameter and six feet deep. Both these smaller fountains are surrounded by walls of sod and trenches similar to the embankment about the first which the traveler saw.   The water from all these unites in one stream which, the dis-coverer calculated, would fill a two-inch pipe.

In regard to the importance of Bruce's discovery, there have been many things said by those who would wish to lessen his fame.   It is urged, first, that he was not the first European who had discovered the source of the Nile.   It is true that the Portuguese Jesuits who, shortly after the foundation of their order, went as missionaries to the Greek Catholics of Abyssinia, explored the surrounding country with more or less thoroughness; one of their number, Paez, had actually visited and described in writing this spot, one hundred and fifty years before it was seen by Bruce.   But this description, which had been written originally in Portuguese, had been published only in a Latin translation; more than this, it contained such a number of incredible statements that the friends of Paez were not anxious that it should be read, lest it cast discredit upon his reputation for veracity. Thus the knowledge was doubly locked up; the intelligence may be said never to have reached the ear of the public; and certainly the question where the Nile has its source was regarded as one which had never been satisfactorily answered.

NOT THE REAL SOURCE.

It is also said that the source of the Blue Nile is not the source of the Nile; that the White Nile is the larger river, the main stream; and that therefore the head-waters of this river should be regarded as the true fountains of the Nile. Bruce himself admits that this is true; more than this, that were it not for the constantly flowing stream of the White, fed by the tropic rains, the waters of the Blue Nile would be lost in the desert before they reached Egypt. But, he urges, and others have supported this opinion, the usage of the surrounding tribes shows that the Blue is regarded as the Nile, equally at least with the White. But while it cannot be denied that Bruce solved only the easier of the two problems, and left the more difficult for a later generation, it must be admitted that the fact of his being the pioneer in this portion of the continent (if we except the Portuguese, whose history had caused the natives to look with enmity upon all white men) gives him equal honor with those who have solved the more intricate and difficult question of the source of the White Nile. A recent authority, surveying the field of African discovery from the vantage-ground of modern knowledge of the Dark Continent, declares that Bruce's journey forms an epoch in the annals of discovery.

The discoverer's return through Abyssinia was considerably delayed by the disturbed state of the country, where, as during the past year, intestinal wars were raging. He was further alarmed by the fear that the old rule would be enforced, which forbade a stranger to leave the country. He could only secure the king's permission to depart by promising to return, as soon as his shattered health would permit, with as many of his family as possible, and a full supply of horses and arms. As a recognition of the soldierly service which he had rendered, the king presented him with a gold chain of one hundred and eighty links, weighing about three pounds and a quarter, a weight equivalent to that of $500 and over in gold.

Notwithstanding this apparent willingness to have him leave the country, the king threw many trifling difficulties in the way of his doing so; and these circumstances, combined with the troubled state of the country to which reference has above been made, prevented his departure for more than a year after the actual discovery of the sources of the Nile. Late in December, 1771, he left Gondar, his route lying through Sennaar. The journey thence to Assouan occupied more than eleven months; and was performed only by incredible exertions through a country heated by the nearly direct rays of the sun, and covered with heat-reflecting sand. It was more than a year after leaving Gondar that he reached Cairo, whence his route home was mere child's play to the journey which had preceded.

BARBAROUS CUSTOMS OF THE ABYSSINIANS.

Bruce horrified his countrymen by his description of the barbarous customs of the Abyssinians, and got roundly scoffed at, for instance, for his stories of cutting off steaks from a live cow. Nevertheless, at the present day, raw meat feasts are none the less practiced than then. When all the guests are assembled, the animals are slaughtered, and within three minutes the choicest morsels of raw meat, of the fattest, are brought in palpitating for the chief and those of high rank. Long knives are handed round to all, and each cuts himself a large piece from the part offered him.

Bruce also described the Abyssinians as never making a new law, as with their usual superstition and obstinacy they ascribe to their ancient statutes a Divine or sacred authority. Thus, when a case is before the judges, they say: "Let us hear what the *Fitha Negust* (their law-book) says." It is opened solemnly, and the first passage which can be found bearing at all on the subject, is read and acted upon, all other considerations being disregarded. On the occasion of a lawsuit, both parties, accuser and accused, must find security or be fastened together during the continuance of the suit; and afterwards the loser must again give security on all the points for which he may be condemned. Also he must hand over a certain amount, according to the importance of the case, to the judges, who get no other pay beyond the numerous presents which they receive on all hands.

Returned home Bruce was enthusiastically received not only in England but in France and Italy as well. His statements, however, were received with incredulity, which wounded his sensitive spirit to such an

THE RUFFED LEMUR.

extent that he retired to his paternal seat and lived in retirement for twelve years, busy with publishing and illustrating his travels. He died at the age of sixty-four.

MUNGO PARK.

Other early explorers were Sparrman, a Swede, and Le Vailland, a Frenchman, who traveled under the auspices of "The African Society," which was formed in 1788 by a number of Englishmen interested in the advancement of geographical science. The most successful of these early explorers was Mungo Park, a young Scotchman, who had been educated as a physician and spent two years in preparing himself specially for the work.

He sailed in May, 1795; and reached the mouth of the Gambia in the next month. He intended to ascend the Gambia as far as practicable, then strike across the country until he should reach the Niger. He was attended only by a few negro servants when, early in December, he set forth on his quest for the Dark Waters, as the natives still call this long-sought river. The first native king whom he met admired his coat so much, that it was impossible to avoid offering it as a present; since the failure to do so would probably have been the forerunner of a robbery; the second, under pretense that he had paid no duties on entering the territory, stripped him of all goods which he did not contrive to hide before the arrival of the customs officials; the third, under the excuse of acting as his guide and guard through a wild country, compelled him to give, as nominal presents, half of the little that remained to him. Truly had it been said, by a yet earlier traveler, that the beggars of Europe may learn much, in point of unblushing voracity, from the higher classes of savage Africa.

For a time, the traveler did not meet with any more beggars; perhaps because he had but little left which could tempt them. He received information from a chief who appeared to be friendly, that it would be impossible for him to take the direct route to Timbuctoo, as the country was then the scene of war. His only alternative was to go by way of the Moorish kingdom of Ludamar, a perilous route, which had already proved fatal to one explorer, his predecessor, Major Houghton.

He feared much from the bigotry and barbarity of the Moors; but after some delay, succeeded in obtaining a safe conduct to Goombo, a place on the frontier of Bambarra. After this he progressed slowly, finding the negroes kind and hospitable, the Moors insulting and thievish. Finally, having arrived at Sami, early in March, he was commanded to await the coming of a Moorish prince's favorite wife, who was anxious to see what a Christian looked like.

SUSPICIONS AND INDIGNITIES.

Transported to the capital, Benown, he was compelled to submit to many indignities; for the Moors could not be persuaded that a European was neither a locksmith nor a barber by nature. He suffered, also,

THE AFRICAN WILD BOAR.

from lack of food and water; for the dry season was on, and his jailers feared the supply of drink would run short if they indulged their prisoner too freely.

Thus refreshed, he journeyed on, mounted on the back of the horse whose fleetness had enabled him to escape from the Moors. After several repulses from the villages where he tried to obtain food, he reached a point where he considered himself safe from the Moors; and determined to rest there for two or three days.

Pushing onward, his horse soon became so completely worn out that he was obliged to lead, instead of riding it; and his own clothes were in such a miserable plight, his shoes being entirely gone, that he was the subject of jibes from all whom he met. At length, however, he saw rising before him the smoke of Sego, a town which he knew was on the Joliba or Niger River. Spurred on to new exertions by the prospect of such near success, he overtook some former fellow-travelers, who had, a little while before, distanced him.

DISCOVERY OF THE NIGER.

"See the water!" said one of them, shortly afterward, pointing. "Looking forward, I saw," said he, "with infinite pleasure, the great object of my mission, the long sought for majestic Niger, glittering in the morning sun, as broad as the Thames at Westminster, and flowing slowly to the eastward. I hastened to the brink, and having drunk of the water, lifted up my fervent thanks in prayer to the Great Ruler of all things, for having thus far crowned my endeavors with success."

Having been robbed of all his possessions by the Moors, Park had no presents with which to conciliate the court of Sego, and hence met with a very cool reception. He was kindly treated, however, by an old woman from whom he asked a night's shelter; and the king finally gave him a bag of cowries, of value sufficient to maintain him and his horse for fifty days, and sent him on his way.

The traveler continued to descend the Niger, halting at Sansanding. Here the natives insisted that he should perform his evening devotions publicly, and partake of a meal of eggs. The first of these propositions he declined, but accepted the second. They brought him a number of raw eggs, which they imagined would best please him; but finding that he would not eat them in that condition, his host killed a sheep and prepared him a plentiful supper. On so slight a thread does the explorer's chance of a satisfying meal sometimes hang.

Park had proceeded but a short distance from Sansanding, when his faithful horse gave out; and he was obliged to proceed by some other means. Covered with blisters, and suffering severely from the stings of insects, he resolved to hire a boat and descend the river to Silla. Here

TREE-CLIMBING MONKEY.

he was received very coldly; and learned that at Jenne, the next large town, the power was really in the hands of the Moors, whose influence would increase as he journeyed eastward. He was told, by many of the negroes, that the Moors of that portion of the country were fanatical

26

and bigoted in the extreme; one of them related that he had entered a public inn of that country, when the landlord had spread a mat on the floor, saying to him:

"If you are a Mussulman, you are my friend, sit down on this mat; if not, you are my slave, and with this rope will ⊐ lead you to market."

Alone, without influence or other means of conciliating these people, from whose milder brethren he had already suffered much, Park concluded that it would be his wisest course to return, and make known to his countrymen the measure of success which he had achieved. This was not small; for up to this time, the direction of the Niger had been a subject of dispute. It seems that every possible theory had been advanced by those who had heard that there was a great river in this part of Africa. The ancients believed that it flowed into the Nile; the people of the middle ages, as we have seen, were under the impression that it flowed into the Atlantic Ocean; and their immediate successors, the earliest Portuguese and English explorers, identified it with the Senegal or with the Gambia; later writers have confused it with the Congo. Park was the first European who followed its course for any considerable distance, and thus determined that its direction was eastward, and not westward.

NEW MISFORTUNES.

Not all his misfortunes had beset him on his journey toward the Niger; some awaited him on his return. He proceeded without more than ordinary adventures until he reached the mountainous country west of Bammakou; here he was set upon by two men, and robbed of the very clothes which he wore; his worst shirt, a pair of trousers and his hat being all that was left to him. It was particularly fortunate that the robbers did not carry off the last-named article, as he carried his memoranda in the crown of it.

The articles of which he had been robbed were recovered by the exertions of a chief to whom Park appealed; but this was only after a delay of two weeks; and unfortunately, his pocket-compass was broken when it was returned to him. On the remainder of his way, he was, on the whole, hospitably treated; although the people who were on his route were suffering, to some extent, from famine. He had the good fortune to fall in with a caravan, the leader of which assured him it was impossible to traverse the country at that season; but offered to support him in the meantime, and when the proper time for the journey arrived, to conduct him in safety to the settlements. This offer was accepted, and the bargain concluded; his guide, on their arrival at Pisania, on the Gambia, receiving double the stipulated price. They reached this point in June, 1797, just two years after Park had arrived in Africa. The

THE BROWN CAPUCHIN.

traveler was so hindered by various circumstances that it was not until Christmas day that he reached London, where he was received by his friends as one risen from the dead; for fairly well authenticated proofs of his death had actually reached them many months before his return, and had never been contradicted.

But the explorer was not content to rest upon his laurels. He was ready, at the first intimation that his services were required, to set out again. But it had been seen, by this time, that the enterprise of private individuals, or even of associations, was not sufficient for the success of such great undertakings; nothing could do so well as a government expedition. The second expedition of Park was, therefore, undertaken under the auspices of the British government, and was intended to have sailed in 1801. But the war with France, and the consequent agitation of the public mind, delayed the proceedings, so that it was not until the latter part of January, 1805, that the party actually set out.

HIS SECOND EXPEDITION.

Forty-three white men accompanied Park upon this expedition, which was provided with a native guide. The leader provided the whole party with asses at the Cape Verde Islands; the breed of these animals being excellent, and they being well fitted for traversing the rugged hills that form the watershed between the Niger and the rivers that empty into the Atlantic by a westward course.

When they were ready to set out from the western coast, it was evident that the rainy season could not be far distant; and at this portion of the year, travel was beset with many dangers for Europeans. It would have been prudent to have remained near the coast until the rains were over; but inaction was impossible to Park in his enthusiastic state of mind. He insisted on proceeding on his way; and accordingly set out from Pisania early in May.

The party was so strong, that it was not dependent upon the protection of the petty kings through whose territories they must pass; but they no longer had any claim upon the hospitality of these chiefs; and were considered as fair prey for the depredations of many who had received Park well, when he was alone and friendless. With much exertion the party reached Sansanding. They had traveled by water a great part of the way since reaching the Niger, and had therefore avoided some of the fatigue which a journey overland would have occasioned. But there was a danger inseparable from the country at that season; the heat and moisture combined proved fatal to nearly all the party. Before they reached Sansanding, thirty-nine of the party had perished; Park writes that not one of these had died from any accident, nor had they had any contest with the natives. One of the five survivors was deranged by the terrible experiences through which they had passed.

But the indomitable spirit of the explorer would not yield, even when his companions fell thick around him. When his brother-in-law died, he wrote: "I then felt myself as if left a second time lonely and friendless amid the wilds of Africa." Nevertheless in the same dispatches in which he communicates the lessening of his party, he expresses his determination to press onward at all costs; and speaks of the journey down the Niger as a journey homeward. He adds: "Though all the Europeans who are with me should die, and though I myself were half-dead, I would still persevere."

TRAGIC DEATH OF MUNGO PARK.

The party purchased three slaves, so that, with the guide, their number was nine. It would appear that they passed rapidly down the river, which was now, in consequence of the heavy rains, in a very favorable state for their enterprise. But the king of Yaour, or Yauri, a city more than half way between Timbuctoo and the sea, became much offended because the white men passed his residence without offering suitable presents. He sent a party to pursue them. This party went by land and took possession of a pass where rocks hemmed in the river, so that there was but a narrow channel. When Park arrived at this place, he thought to force his way past the obstruction; but they assailed him with darts, stones, pikes, and arrows. He defended himself a long time; two of the slaves were killed; the crew threw everything they had into the river, and fired constantly at the savage enemy. At last, overcome by numbers and fatigue, unable to keep the canoe against the strength of the current, Park seized one of his companions, and jumped overboard. What words were uttered, if any, we know not; but one after another of the three survivors followed the example set by these two, and all were drowned. The only soul remaining, a slave, stood up in the boat and cried for mercy. They took him and the boat to the king; and savage revenge was gratified.

The story is told by the guide, who was found and induced to seek for information of those who had seen the party after his own contract had been fulfilled, and he had left them to return to the settlements. As thus told, it was confirmed by what later travelers heard; for the

THE SQUIRREL MONKEY.

journeys of Mungo Park excited almost as much interest in Africa as in his own country, and long remained a favorite topic with those through whose country he traveled. The very spot where he perished has been identified.

The African Society made several other attempts to explore the interior of Africa; but was uniformly unfortunate. That venture which came nearest to being successful was made by Frederic Hornemann in 1797-1803. This young man, who was a student of Göttingen University, offered his services to the Society and had them accepted as soon as his character was known to them. He proceeded to Egypt, where he was detained some time by the hostility to Europeans which had been excited by Bonaparte's landing in that country. When the great French general reached Cairo, he was liberated; and he joined a caravan which was setting out for Mourzouk, the capital of Fezzan.

HUNTING SCENE IN EAST AFRICA.

The interest which the British government felt in the exploration of Africa was not allowed to languish because the first expedition sent out had resulted fatally to all concerned. In 1816, two parties were sent out, the one to explore the Niger from the westward, as Park had already done, the other to ascend the great river which empties into the Atlantic Ocean about six degees south of the equator. We know this as the Congo; but although it was called by that name in 1816, it was a well understood thing that this was merely a sectional name; that the same stream which the natives inhabiting the country around its mouth called the Congo, the people living near its headwaters knew as the Joliba or Niger. In short, the British government sent out these two expeditions, that one might descend the Niger, and the other ascend the Congo, and meet each other.

The African Society may be considered to have accomplished its object, not indeed by securing for the world a more accurate knowledge of the geography of the great southern continent but in having awakened the interest of the public, and particularly of the representative of public opinion, the king's government. Accordingly, we find it now attracting much less notice than at first; and finally, some forty years after its organization, it was merged in the Royal Geographical Society.

BARTH AND HIS COMPANIONS.

Another expedition set out, in 1849, under the leadership of James Richardson. Other members of the party were Drs. H. Barth and Overweg. Through marshes, jungles and countries inhabited by treacherous natives with barbarous habits they had to fight their way across an unknown and unhealthy territory. Such pleasing little incidents as the sight of a snake more than eighteen feet long, and nearly six inches in diameter, hanging from a tree across their path, apparently ready to seize upon the first prey that presented itself, need scarcely be noted. Whatever the white men thought about it, the natives regarded it as a god-send, for when it had been shot, they cut it open and took out the fat, which they pronounced excellent.

These expeditions opened a glimpse into the richly watered zone of the equatorial regions and by reaching Timbuctoo made known a vast territory, thus rendering the opening of a regular intercourse between Europe and these remote regions possible.

ANDERSON AND MAGYAR IN SOUTH AFRICA.

C. J. Anderson, a Swede, and F. Galton, an Englishman, are two other explorers, whose thrilling adventures in South Africa, about the middle of the last century held the world spellbound. They partly traversed the same territory as Livingstone. Arrived at Ondango they found the country of their tribe such an Elysium as their dreams had pictured. "Instead of the eternal jungles, where every moment we were in danger of being dragged out of our saddles by the merciless thorns, the landscape now presented an apparently boundless field of yellow corn, dotted with numerous peaceful homesteads, and bathed in

GABBETT'S GALOGO.

the soft light of a declining tropical sun. Here and there rose gigantic, wide-spreading, and dark-foliaged timber and fruit-trees, while innumerable fan-like palms, either singly or in groups, completed the picture."

The Ovambos form a marked contrast to some other African tribes in being strictly honest; without permission, the natives would not touch anything; and the travelers could leave their camp entirely unwatched.

Nor are they idle; work begins at sunrise and ends at sunset for all. There is no pauperism among them, and the aged and helpless are carefully tended; in marked contrast to the Damaras, who have a pleasant little way of knocking their old people on the head or carrying them away into the desert to starve.

But although exempt from some of the vices of their neighbors, the Ovambos are not altogether paragons. Polygamy is practiced to a

THE GNU.

great extent, each man having as many wives as he can afford to buy. It is interesting to note the quotations in this article of merchandise: a poor man could purchase a wife for two oxen and one cow; a rich man would be required to pay three oxen and two cows. We are not told whether the difference in price was occasioned solely by the difference in the circumstances of the purchaser, or whether the rich man paid for first choice. The king alone was not required to buy his wives; and one hundred and six families had considered the honor of the alliance sufficient value received for their daughters.

Mr. Galton returned to England after three years' adventures in the wildernesses. But Anderson was not yet ready to give it up.

One of his adventures at a fountain where they halted for a night deserves to be here recorded; and who can tell the story as well as Anderson himself?

"Hearing that elephants and rhinoceroses still continued to resort to Abeghan, I forthwith proceeded there on the night in question. Somewhat incautiously I took up my position—alone, as usual—on a narrow neck of land dividing two small pools, the space on either side of my skarm [a shallow pit with a barrier of stones in front] being only sufficient for a large animal to stand between me and the water. I was provided with a blanket and two or three spare guns.

"It was one of those magnificent tropical moonlight nights when an indescribable soft and enchanting light is shed over the slumbering landscape; the moon was so bright and clear that I could discern even a small animal at a considerable distance. I had just completed my arrangements, when a noise that I can liken only to the passage of a train of artillery broke the stillness of the air; it evidently came from the direction of one of the numerous stony paths, or rather tracks, leading to the water, and I imagined that it was caused by some wagons that might have crossed the Kalahari. Raising myself partially from my recumbent position, I fixed my eyes steadily on the part of the bush whence the strange sounds proceeded, but for some time I was unable to make out the cause. All at once, however, the mystery was explained by the appearance of an immense elephant, immediately followed by others, amounting to eighteen. Their towering forms told me at a glance that they were all males. It was a splendid sight to see so many huge creatures approaching with a free, sweeping, unsuspecting and stately step. The somewhat elevated ground whence they emerged, and which gradually sloped toward the water, together with the misty night air, gave an increased appearance of bulk and mightiness to their naturally giant structures.

"Crouching down as low as possible in the skarm, I waited with a beating heart and ready rifle the approach of the leading male, who, unconscious of peril, was making straight for my hiding-place. The position of his body, however, was unfavorable for a shot; and knowing from experience that I had little chance of obtaining more than a single good one, I waited for an opportunity to fire at his shoulder, which is

THE COUXIO.

preferable to any other part when shooting at night. But this chance, unfortunately, was not afforded till his enormous bulk towered above my head. The consequence was, that while in the act of raising the muzzle of my rifle over the skarm, my body caught his eye, and, before I could place the piece to my shoulder, he swung himself round, and, with trunk elevated and ears spread, desperately charged me. It was now too late to think of flight, much less of slaying the savage beast. My own life was in imminent jeopardy; and seeing that if I remained partially erect, he would inevitably seize me with his proboscis, I threw myself back with some violence, in which position, and without shouldering the rifle, I fired upward at random toward his chest, uttering at the same time the most piercing shouts and cries. The change of position, in all human probability, saved my life; for at the same instant the trunk of the enraged animal descended precisely on the spot where I had been previously crouched, sweeping away the stones, many of them of a large size, that formed the forepart of my skarm, like so many pebbles. In another moment his broad fore feet passed directly over my face.

"I now expected nothing short of being crushed to death. But imagine my relief when, instead of renewing the charge he swerved to the left, and moved off with considerable rapidity, most happily without my having received any other injuries than a few bruises, occasioned by the falling of the stones. Immediately after the elephant had left me I was on my legs, and snatching up a spare rifle lying at hand, I pointed at him as he was retreating, and pulled the trigger; but to my intense mortification the piece missed fire. It was a matter of thankfulness to me, however, that a similar mishap had not occurred when the animal charged; for had my gun not then exploded, nothing, as I conceive, could have saved me from destruction.

"While pondering over my late wonderful escape, I observed, at a little distance, a huge white rhinoceros protrude his ponderous and misshapen head through the bushes, and presently afterward he approached to within a dozen paces of my ambuscade. His broadside was then fully exposed to view, and notwithstanding I still felt a little nervous from my conflict with the elephant, I lost no time in firing. The beast did not at once fall to the ground, but from appearances I had every reason to believe that he would not live very long. Scarcely had I reloaded when a black rhinoceros of the species Keitlea (a female, as it proved), stood drinking at the water; but her position, as with the elephant in the first instance, was unfavorable for a good shot. As however, she was very near me, I thought I was pretty sure of breaking her leg and thereby disabling her, and in this I succeeded. My fire

SCENE IN AN EAST AFRICAN FOREST.

seemed to madden her; she rushed wildly forward on three legs, when I gave a second shot, though apparently with little or no effect. I felt sorry at not being able to end her sufferings at once; but as I was too well acquainted with the habits of rhinoceroses to venture on pursuing her under the circumstances, I determined to wait patiently for daylight, and then destroy her with the aid of my dogs. But it was not to be.

"As no more elephants or other large game appeared, I thought, after a time, it might be as well to go in search of the white rhinoceros previously wounded; I was not long in finding his carcass; for my ball, as I supposed, had caused his almost immediate death.

"In heading back to my skarm, I accidentally took a turn in the direction pursued by the black rhinoceros, and by ill-luck, as the event proved, at once encountered her. She was still on her legs, but her position, as before, was unfavorable. Hoping, however, to make her change it for a better, and thus enable me to destroy her at once, I took up a stone, and hurled it at her with all my force, when snorting horribly, erecting her tail, keeping her head close to the ground, and raising clouds of dust by her feet, she rushed at me with fearful fury. I had only just time to level my rifle and fire before she was upon me; and the next instant, while instinctively turning round for the purpose of retreating, she laid me prostrate. The shock was so violent as to send my rifle, powder-flask, and ball-pouch, as also my cap, spinning in the air; the gun, indeed, as ascertained, to a distance of fully ten feet. On the beast charging me, it crossed my mind that, unless gored at once by her horn, her impetus would be such (after knocking me down, which I took for granted would be the case) as to carry her beyond me, and I might thus be afforded a chance of escape. So, indeed, it happened; for having tumbled me over (in doing which her head and the forepart of her body, owing to the violence of the charge, was half buried in the sand), and trampled on me with great violence, her forequarter passed over my body. Struggling for life, I seized my opportunity, and as she was recovering herself for a renewal of the charge, I scrambled out from between her hind legs.

"But the enraged beast had not yet done with me. Scarcely had

I regained my feet before she struck me down a second time, and with her horn ripped up my right thigh (though not very deeply) from near the knee to the hip; with her forefeet, moreover, she hit me a terrific

THE DIADEM INDRIS AND THE WOOLLY INDRIS.

blow on the left shoulder, near the back of the neck. My ribs bent under the enormous weight and pressure, and for a moment I must, as I believe, have lost consciousness—I have, at least, very indistinct notions of what afterward took place. All I remember is, that when I raised my head I heard furious snorting and plunging among the neighboring bushes. I now arose, though with great difficulty, and made my way, in the best manner I was able, toward a large tree near at hand for shelter; but this precaution was needless; the beast, for the time at least, showed no inclination further to molest me. Either in the melee, or owing to the confusion caused by her wounds, she had lost sight of me, or she felt satisfied with the revenge she had taken. Be that as it may, I escaped with life, though sadly wounded and severely bruised, in which disabled state I had great difficulty in getting back to my skarm."

Anderson had sent one of his men, escorted by bushmen, to make known his approach to the natives living on the shores of the lake. This messenger shortly afterward returned, accompanied by two guides, belonging to the Betoana tribe; and the party proceeded through the almost impenetrable thorn-forest. On the third day after leaving the fountain which had been the scene of the adventure with the elephant and the rhinoceros, about noon, the cry of "Ngami! Ngami!" was raised by the men at the head of the caravan; and the explorer, looking before him, saw glimmering in the sunshine, a sheet of water bounded only by the horizon.

The lake was at that season at its lowest stage, and was very shallow at the point where it was first seen. Its banks were overgrown with a multitude of reeds and rushes, so that, after the first excitement of catching a glimpse of it was once over, it was far from seeming an object of much admiration. The muddy stretches whence the water had receded prevented their approaching very nearly to the lake itself; and the water, a little of which was obtained by considerable exertion, was very bitter and disagreeable.

Anderson returned to Europe in 1854; he afterwards made several other expeditions to Africa and finally settled down as a farmer near Indongo, where he died, in 1866.

CHAPTER XXIII.

ROOSEVELT'S THRILLING EXPERIENCES.

How Col. Roosevelt Hunted Lions—Exciting Adventures with Elephants, Rhinoceri, Hippopotami, Lions, Etc.—Hunting Big Game Hard, Strenuous Work—The Colonel a Mighty Hunter—Saved from Death in the Nick of Time—Kermit a Good Shot—What the Small-pox Scare Revealed—Loring and Mearns Climb Mount Kenia—Col. Roosevelt Discovers New Animal—Last Stage of the Hunting Trip—Smithsonian Institute Receives Greatest Collection of Specimens in the World.

By J. T. THOMPSON.

In hunting lions Col. Roosevelt took with him a great many natives armed with bows and arrows who beat the bush, raise a noise and drive the lion from his lair. Dogs formed the vanguard of the shooting party which was accompanied by gunbearers, for the lion is so quick in attack that even an expert hunter has no time to reload his gun after a shot. Col. Roosevelt shot his lions at a distance of from 60 to 150 yards. His habit was to put three bullets into it, one in the chest as he faced him, one in the withers as he turned to run and one in the back to break the vertebrae. The order of the shots depended upon the lion's attitude.

Many of the Colonel's first shots broke the lion's backs, although as many as five shots were necessary to dispatch one huge brute, the additional two shots being fired, one each by Sir Alfred Pease and Kermit Roosevelt.

One of the interesting bits about the distinguished Colonel's lion shooting in the Kapiti Country was that Lady Pease accompanied the party on all its lion hunts and saw the ex-President shoot all his lions and never flinched during the critical moments of the hunt, which are many, and sorely try even experienced hunters.

Elephant hunting is the most fascinating of all Big Game pursuits because of the element of danger in connection with it. It is considered, that everything being equal, the chances are about even for the hunter and the hunted. It is not a pleasure trip, nor is it a task for any but the most seasoned and nervy hunters. The hunter must be in the saddle at dawn and ride to the feeding grounds of this animal, when a herd is sighted the real work begins as one must creep, sometimes for a mile until they get to within twenty or thirty feet of them, or even nearer, and of course, if they get the wind or hear the hunter, the chances of escape are small. An elephant charging a hunter at so short a distance covers the ground quickly and to elude it one must be very quick and shoot straight and true. Col. Roosevelt secured his first elephant in the Kenia District, he was anxious to do this so that there would be better chances of preserving the skin in good condition in this cooler climate. There are larger and better elephants in the Nile Country of Uganda but the Colonel thought it unwise to wait until then when there was a good chance to get one in the Kenia District.

ROOSEVELT CHARGED BY INFURIATED ELEPHANT.

Col. Roosevelt accompanied by Mr. Cunninghame the big game hunter and guide crawled into a herd of elephants about thirty feet from a big bull he wanted to kill. He killed the elephant at the second shot. Suddenly before the Colonel could reload another bull charged him at close range from the herd. Both hunters quickly dodged behind trees, and Mr. Cunninghame fired and turned the bull from Mr. Roosevelt just in time to save his life. It was a close shave.

IN A TIGHT PLACE.

One of the Roosevelt party while in the Mweru District had an experience that would test the ability and mettle of any hunter in the world and came off victorious. He was out hunting with only a native gun bearer when he encountered a charging man-eating lion. He had just fired and killed the lion when there came charging at him a large rhinoceros. A good shot killed the rhino when to his amazement a huge bull elephant came thundering towards him which he also shot dead. The whole three of these animals had charged him within a space of twenty paces.

Many strange things happen while hunting in Africa. When Mr. Selous and Mr. McMillan, two of the Roosevelt party were out in the Nyeri District accompanied by Mr. Judd, the professional hunter, they were after lions one day and Judd was following Mr. Selous on a mule.

The grass was long and they did not see a big lion until the mule nearly stepped on it. The mule swerved suddenly and Judd fired from his hip with his rifle and almost simultaneously the mule bucked him off and he landed almost touching the lion.

He thought his last hour had come and braced himself to make the fight of his life but to his surprise the lion didn't move. After waiting for a few minutes for the attack he suddenly realized that the lion was dead. He inspected the lion carefully and found that his shot had entered the eye and killed it instantly without leaving a mark on the skin.

That there are plenty of lions in the district where Col. Roosevelt hunted is shown by the fact that prior to his visit man-eating lions had been playing havoc with the Government's safaris and traders' safaris, so that the Government at last was forced to close the road to traffic. It is estimated that over one hundred native men, woman and children have lost their lives to these man-eaters in the past year.

LETTERS FROM AMERICA.

Immediately following Col. Roosevelt's arrival in Africa hundreds of letters from the United States arrived for him on every steamer. These letters contained all kinds of requests including requests for live wild animals for zoological gardens, skins of dead animals, snakes, birds' eggs, teeth, claws of lions and tigers (the writer evidently not knowing that there were no tigers in Africa and that it would utterly spoil the value of any specimen to mutilate it by taking out the claws and teeth). There were also requests for plants, picture post cards, and for all kinds of objects including pickled meat and dried meat of game. Of course it was impossible for such requests to be granted and also impossible for Col. Roosevelt even to attempt to answer the letters, as his time was fully taken up hunting and writing for a magazine.

ROOSEVELT GETS THE ITCH.

Shortly after the expedition reached the Althi River Country Col. Roosevelt got the "Nairobi itch." This particular form of itch consists of little red spots all over the body and hands and face, and looks very bad but it is really no worse than common American hives.

A PRESENT FOR MISS ALICE.

Two baby antelopes sent by Col. Roosevelt to his daughter Alice (Mrs. Nicholas Longworth), arrived in New York in the fall of 1909 on the steamer Vaderland from Antwerp. Captain Burman of the vessel kept the little animals on the bridge, and had them fed with milk from a bottle on the way over. The antelopes were transferred from the German East Africa steamer Admiral to the Vaderland at Antwerp.

On August 9th, 1909, Col. Roosevelt and party departed for Nyeri which is suitated in the Northwest of Kenia Province. The day before they left the second consignment of specimens was shipped to the Smithsonian Institution, via Mombasa. It contained about 2,500 specimens of all kinds including birds, mammals, snakes, plants, etc.

Nyeri is an important trade centre in British East Africa. The neighborhood is the headquarters of the Masai tribe, warlike nomads, who inhabit the plains in this district. Excellent sport was promised the expedition in this district and this proved to be true Col. Roosevelt getting many fine specimens of antelope, buffalo, etc.

LORING AND MEARNS ON AN EXPLORING TRIP.

On September 3rd, 1909, J. Alden Loring and Major Edgar A. Mearns both of the Smithsonian African Expedition in charge of Col. Theodore Roosevelt left Nairobi on an exploring trip in the Province of Kenia. They intended to scale Mount Kenia which is the highest mountain in this district, being about 17,200 feet in height. This mountain was ascended for the first time in 1899 by Mackinder. The mountain has many glaciers and its timber line is at 10,300 feet. Loring and Mearns succeeded in getting to within about 700 feet of its summit which is covered with snow the year round, although the mountain is situated very close to the equator.

These two members of the party also collected thousands of rare and valuable specimens of birds, mammals, etc., and returned to Nairobi to rejoin the Colonel and his son Kermit.

A FIGHT AGAINST ODDS.

Col. Roosevelt, attended by two native boatmen, went out on Lake Naivasha in a rowboat to shoot hippopotami. The first one encountered

was a cow. Before the hunter could shoot the beast snorted angrily.
In less than a second the water all about the boat was churned to foam
by the lashings of the other hippopotami which had answered the
cow's call.

Some of the huge beasts dove under the boat and tried to upset it
by coming up under it with their snouts and backs. Others drove
straight at the boat, with jaws distended, and endeavored to bite out
the sides.

The natives cowered in the bottom of the boat, certain their doom
was at hand, and shrieked loud prayers of suppliction to their pagan
gods.

Mr. Roosevelt, however, kept his feet in the shaking boat and with
certain aim shot the two finest specimens in the water. Then he clubbed
the others on the snouts with the butt of his rifle until they gave up
the fight.

The animals slain on that hair-raising occasion were a splendid bull
and an unusually fine cow.

A ROYAL INVITATION.

Lidj Jeassu, the Crown Prince of Abyssinia invited Theodore
Roosevelt to a great elephant hunt, promising to beat up a white elephant for him and otherwise to arrange a splendid shooting pro-
gramme.

This news was brought into Berlin by Adolf Mayer, a kinsman of
King Menelik of Abyssinia, who arrived there with a commission from
the Abyssinian Government to purchase supplies.

King Menelik sent an invitation to Mr. Roosevelt at Washington to
be his guest, but Mr. Roosevelt declined, explaining that as he had
refused the invitations of several European sovereigns, he could not
make an exception of King Menelik, however much he might desire to
do so. It was then arranged that the Crown Prince should invite Mr.
Roosevelt unofficially. Before Mayer left Abyssinia a mission had been
sent to hand this invitation to Mr. Roosevelt wherever it could find him,
and King Menelik was hopeful that the former President of the United
States would accept the invitation in its present form.

The envoys of the King were empowered to point out to Mr. Roosevelt, Mr. Mayer said, "that there is unrivalled elephant hunting in Abyssinia. The Crown Prince will send out 5,000 horsemen to encircle an immense range of prairie and drive in the elephants. Hundreds and possibly thousands of elephants could be thus assembled, and there would probably be one or two white ones among this number. These beasts are not really white, but merely animals of great vigor who have lived to be gray haired."

When it was suggested that the Crown Prince of Abyssinia was only fourteen years old, Mr. Mayer replied that Abyssinians develop young. He declared that the Prince was an expert and adventurous huntsman; that he spoke English, French and German, and that he was quite capable personally of showing Mr. Roosevelt fine hunting.

"Many stories have reached the court of King Menelik," Mr. Mayer said, in conclusion, "of Mr. Roosevelt's prowess as a horseman, a hunter, a soldier and an administrator. The King is most keen to greet him, and he probably would go to the borders of his country with a great following to receive Mr. Roosevelt."

Mr. Mayer is the son of a German engineer who married a sister of King Menelik.

WHAT THE SMALLPOX SCARE REVEALED.

Just before the expedition was leaving for the Tana River District it was reported that one of the native bearers had smallpox. This necessitated a close inspection of every one of the seventy-two bearers. They were all found to be free from any disease but Col. Roosevelt was indignant when he found that 32 out of the 72 bearers who had been carrying 60 pound boxes on their heads for hundreds of miles were women.

Col. Roosevelt, on September 17th, found good shooting in the Mweru District and he was especially pleased with a large bull elephant which he shot, the tusks of which weighed nearly 200 pounds. In response to our correspondent's question about the hunting and the expedition Col. Roosevelt said: "We are having capital fun and every member of the expedition is well."

While Col. Roosevelt hunted in the Mweru District Kermit was in the Gwaso Nyiro and was extremely successful in bagging several lions and some buffalo, but he had poor luck with elephants and his father joined him to assist Kermit in an effort to get an elephant. Kermit had killed nearly as many varieties of wild animals as his father during the trip but the elephant had proved too elusive for him. His luck changed after his father joined him for he got an elephant and a rhino in one day.

Shooting the African buffalo is one of the most hazardous tasks a hunter can undertake. They are not very plentiful nowdays and this coupled with the fact that they are a semi-water animal and live in marshes makes it hard to get at them. As a matter of fact a hunter has got to go after them in a swampy country where the advantage is all in the buffalo's favor. Col. Roosevelt had some thrilling experiences hunting this animal, which he says is incredibly strong and fast over the marshy ground. A wounded buffalo is the most to be feared of all African wild beasts and in one instance the whole Roosevelt party were in great danger but escaped unhurt.

On October 15th, 1909, the expedition arrived from the North of Guaso Nyiro all well with the exception of a native porter who was tossed by a wounded rhinoceros. On this trip Col. Roosevelt shot three more elephants which completed the group for the Smithsonian Institute at Washington. He also killed a large bull elephant for the American Museum of Natural History at New York. Much other game was shot on this trip including a rhino with excellent horns, a buffalo, a giraffe, an eland, a zebra, ostrich and oryza. Kermit killed two elephants and an exceptionally large rhinoceros.

TRIBAL HUNTERS SPEAR LION FOR COL. ROOSEVELT.

On December 11th, 1909, a long stream of porters could be seen winding across the veldt toward the station at Nairobi, looking for all the world like a string of ants. The stars and stripes were held aloft by a giant native, and the sound of horns made strange discords with the chanting of the weird and elusive safari song.

Shortly Col. Roosevelt arrived on the back of his favorite horse, Tranquillity. It was the end of his last trip in the British East African protectorate.

This safari trip, which was the fourth to be made out of Nairobi, gave Col. Roosevelt and his party an opportunity to witness an exciting hunt at A. E. Hoy's farm at Sirgoi, in the Guasu Nguisho country, the spearing of a lion by Nandi warriors.

Seventy of these spearsmen had been asked to take part in the drive, and they assented readily, for when a warrior spears a lion he becomes a leader of the fighting section of the tribe and may wear a headdress formed of the lion's mane, and walk at the head of the file of the Nandi warriors when on the march. When in these hunts the tribesmen display extraordinary courage.

SPEARMEN CORNER ANGRY LION.

The band of seventy almost naked men, with their long, sharp spears, attended by the chosen spectators, the latter being mounted, proceeded down a long valley, where the grass was thick and thorn trees lined its edges.

Soon a lion was observed, not more than 400 yards in front. Immediately the warriors gave chase, and in less than two miles they had rounded up the king of the wilderness. The horsemen then approached and it was seen that the lion at bay was a full grown, black maned one.

The spearsmen began their task of surrounding the quarry. Every man went to his allotted position, and the circle slowly closed in on the snarling beast, which swished its tail and kept up a continual roaring.

The warriors drew to within some twenty yards of the lion and the horsemen closed up to see the kill, yet remained at a sufficient distance so as not to interfere with the spearsmen's movements. Three times the lion made a savage charge at the now stationary warriors, but stopped short each time, with mane bristling, roaring in impotent rage at its tormentors.

LION IN DEATH THROES MAIMS NATIVE.

Again the attacking party advanced to within ten yards of their victim. One last desperate effort and the lion drove directly at the line, only to fall with ten spears quivering in its body. But in that brief moment it managed to drag down one of the natives, its claws sinking into the man's flesh.

The death of the king of beasts seemed to awaken all the fire in the warriors' blood. They began a dance of triumph around the body, waving their blood stained spears, some of which were bent by the force of the shock; holding their shields above their heads, and shouting forth blood curdling yells in the excess of their savage joy over the victory.

In the meantime the injured man was being given medical attention. He bore the pain of his wounds without a sign of concern. He who first had jabbed his spear through the lion joined in the dance at the start, but soon retired at a distance, where he seated himself, apparently indifferent to the antics of his fellows. He now was a leader of men, and must therefore not show sign that he had done anything out of the ordinary.

ROOSEVELT DISCOVERS A NEW ANIMAL.

A new animal was discovered in British East Africa by Col. Roosevelt. This new animal was first announced from the Smithsonian Institute, January 3rd, 1910, as having been discovered by the distinguished hunter and party, is a hitherto unknown species of Otocyon to which officials of the Scientific organization have given the specific name of "Vergatus." It is a small carnivorous animal closely resembling the fox.

"Otocyon Rooseveltus" as a name for the new animal was suggested as being appropriate, and one which would have perpetuated the name of the former President as the discoverer of the new species, but Smithsonian officials, fearing the discoverer would object decided to make the name which means "striped.'

The otocyon vergatus is generally buff in color and has been found to differ slightly from otocyon megalotis which is found farther south in Africa, especially in color and in the characteristics of its teeth and skull.

The otocyon is peculiar to Africa and is not represented in the United States but resembles in color the swifter kit fox of the western plains. The skull of this new form closely resembling that of the gray fox of our native fauna.

This discovery is of special interest for the reason that comparatively few new forms were expected from this region in Africa as that territory up to this time has been thoroughly examined by British Naturalists.

KERMIT HAS AMAZING LUCK.

The luck of Kermit Roosevelt has been amazing. While Col. Roosevelt was hunting with Lord Delamere, Kermit went off with R. B. Cole and his Wanderobo warriors. The Wanderobos are adepts at killing bongo, which are exceedingly rare and only to be found in the forests. In a short space of time the younger Roosevelt had secured a large and fine specimen of the female bongo and one of the young beasts. This was a feat that any old hunter might justly have been proud of, for no white man ever before had stalked and shot at bongo. There are only two cases on record of a white man shooting bongo with the aid of the natives and their dogs.

So pleased was one of the residents here with the success of the youth that he presented Kermit with a fine specimen of the male bongo, and so the Smithsonian Institution will have a complete family group, the only one in the world.

KERMIT IS BETTER SHOT THAN HIS FATHER.

When Col. Roosevelt was at the McMillan ranch, near Nairobi, he admitted that his son Kermit was a better shot than himself. He would not however tell this to Kermit as he was afraid it would make the young man think too much of himself. Kermit's prowess proved a valuable aid to the party both in getting animals for food and specimens for the Smithsonian Institute.

COL. ROOSEVELT IS RIVAL OF BIBLICAL NIMROD.

If you will open your Bible and turn to the tenth chapter of the book of Genesis, which gives a list of the descendants of Noah, you will find the name of Nimrod, who, it is said, "began to be a mighty one in the earth. He was a mighty hunter before the Lord," wherefore it is said "even as Nimrod the mighty hunter before the Lord."

Unfortunately there is no list of Nimrod's exploits. There was no national museum in the neighborhood of Mount Ararat. The Smithsonian Instituion did not exist in those days. Therefore we have no means of comparison, but it is perfectly safe to assert that, Theodore

Roosevelt, like Nimrod, the son of Cush, "began to be a mighty one in the earth" long before he went to Africa, and since he started in pursuit of lions, hippopotami, giraffe and other beasts of the field and the jungle, he has shown himself to be a mighty hunter before the Lord and has sent home more than 600 casks and bales of trophies and a menagerie of living things to prove it.

The serious work of preparing the Roosevelt trophies for exhibition began the first week in January, 1910. Scientific tanners of great skill and long experience are in Washington, and the atmosphere around the basement of the Smithsonian Institution was redolent of pungent odors, such as arise from the contact of acids and other chemical agencies that are employed to arrest the forces of nature. It will be more than a year before anything will be ready for exhibition. The Roosevelt trophies will be set up in the new museum building which is nearly completed and will doubtless be open to the public in the fall of 1910. But it will take at least a year to tan and stuff the hides and mount and install the other trophies which have been received from Africa. And it will be several years before the work is entirely completed because of the enormous extent and extraordinary value of the collections.

Up to January 1st, 1910, Mr. Roosevelt had already sent to the Smithsonian more than 6,000 objects of interest, including the skins and hides of the animals he has killed, hundreds of rare birds, reptiles, fishes, botanical specimens, native implements, utensils and other ethnological material of great scientific value and intense human interest. No expedition, either private or public, that was sent out for exploration ever produced such results. No expedition of the kind was ever conducted on such a large scale or enjoyed the extraordinary advantages which Colonel Roosevelt commanded. The officials of the British, Dutch and Portuguese governments, the local authorities and foreign population of Central Africa; the native chiefs and tribesmen, the missionaries and everybody who was capable of rendering any service to the modern Nimrod did their best to contribute to its success and never before have the jungles and wilderness of Africa been beaten so thoroughly for game or searched for all forms of animate and inanimate objects of interest.

The expedition is almost over and the trophies that have been received thus far included whatever was collected up to January 1st, 1910. Since that day the party has been busily engaged adding to the number and undoubtedly the shipments that are already on the way and those which may be expected in the future will more than double in number and in value those which have already been received.

The skins and hides were packed and shipped in casks of brine which will not be opened until the tanners are ready to work on them. The skeleton of every beast has been sent along in another package, and already a carload of bones have been boiled and scraped and put in order for articulation by the taxidermists. They will be exhibited separately. The skins and hides will be stuffed and mounted on manikins in lifelike attitudes.

The invoices already received show thirteen lions and lionesses shot by the ex-President himself, four giraffes of different species, two black rhinoceri, which are very rare, and a dozen others of more common varieties; several hippopotami and several elephants, seven zebras, and hyenas, leopards, cheetahs, hartebeestes, waterbucks, gazelles, impallas, wart-hogs, dik-diks, and other wild beasts, some of which were never before brought into this country; and all these are to be mounted for permanent exhibition in the new museum. There are also numerous cases of birds, including several varieties hitherto unknown, and several hundred small animals, such as rats, rabbits, moles, and mice, numerous snakes, lizards and other examples of crawling and creeping things which are not attractive to look at but have great scientific value.

It is interesting to conjecture how these examples of the animal kingdom, which are being rapidly exterminated, will look to future generations who will visit the national museum that is now approaching completion. Hundreds of thousands of people go to see the walking stick, the account books and the shoe buckles of George Washington. The field glasses and the sword of General Grant are of intense interest to everybody, while a rail that was split by Abraham Lincoln attracts as much attention as the capitol of the United States. Then what will future generations say when they stand in the presence of the hippopotami, the elephants, lions and other wild beasts that were shot and sent as trophies by another ex-President?

It is not the intention of the Smithsonian Institution to selfishly retain all of the trophies of the Roosevelt expedition. Dr. Walcott, the secretary, says that the duplicates will be used, according to the custom of the institution, for exchanges with other museums and for presentations to universities, colleges and museums of natural history throughout the country. Hence it is probable that every museum of importance may have one or more zoological specimens from the "bag" of our modern Nimrod.

MAKEUP OF THE EXPEDITION.

The expedition consists of six principals, besides several hundred assistant hunters, beaters-in, field taxidermists, porters and other servants and camp followers of various sorts. The chief men are Theodore Roosevelt, Kermit Roosevelt, Lieutenant Colonel Edgar A. Mearns of the medical corps of the United States army, Edmund Heller, naturalist; J. Loring Alden, naturalist, and R. J. Cunninghame, professional hunter and explorer, who is the executive officer and general manager. He had charge of the organization of the expedition and the purchase of the equipment and supplies and is the business man of the outfit.

Mr. Cunninghame is an Englishman, a famous rifle shot, and has probably more trophies to his credit than any other big game hunter in the world. He has spent almost his entire time in Africa for twenty years or more. He has made it his business to furnish outfits and guides for the nobility and millionaires of England, France, Germany and other countries who have gone out there to hunt big game. He has organized and conducted several expeditions for the British Museum and has had a larger experience in the mountains and jungles of Africa than any other man.

Lieutenant Colonel Mearns, who is on the retired list of the army, has been an agent of the Smithsonian Institution for many years in making collections of natural history specimens in different parts of the world, but this is his first experience in Africa. He has also done a good deal of work for the Museum of Natural History in New York, and is generally recognized as one of the most successful and competent collectors in the country. His specialty is birds, he is a botanist of note and is a member of all the great scientific societies in this and other countries. On this expedition he is the disbursing officer, the medical authority and the business representative of the Smithsonian Institution.

Edmund Heller is a young Californian, a graduate of Stanford University, 36 years old. At the time of his appointment he was assistant curator of zoology in the University of California. He was a member of the expedition sent to Africa by the Field Museum of Chicago in 1900 under Professor Carl E. Akeley and traversed a large part of the same section through which the Roosevelt party has been working. Mr. Heller, like Mr. Cunninghame, is, therefore, familiar with the topography as well as the work. He has also had considerable experience as a collector of mammals, birds, fishes and other objects of natural history in British Columbia, Mexico, Alaska and Central America.

J. Loring Alden of Owego, N. Y., is 38 years old, and for several years has been connected with the biological bureau of the Department of Agriculture at Washington. Formerly he was attached to the zoological gardens of Central Park, New York, and he has participated in several explorations in various parts of America as a collector and naturalist. He has a great reputation as a field naturalist and for his genius in catching animals and birds alive. This is his special work in connection with the Roosevelt expedition, and he has already demonstrated the wisdom of his choice. Col. Roosevelt says that he does not believe that three better men could be found for their special work than Alden, Heller and Mearns.

In addition to the 6,000 inanimate objects that have been sent home, a collection of several wild beasts have arrived safely at the zoological park in Washington, where they are now happy and contented. These include a male and a female lion, each about 2 years old, a male and two female lions, each about 18 months old, which Dr. Baker says are as fine specimens of the king of beasts as were ever brought to this country. There are also leopards, cheetahs, warthogs, gazelles, a large eagle of unusual species, a small vulture and a huge buteo.

THE LAST STAGE OF THE HUNT.

In January 1910 the "Smithsonian African Scientific Expedition" started for Wadelai in Belgian Kongo. Camp was pitched and named "Rhino Camp" as it was for the purpose of getting good specimens of the white rhinoceros that they selected this place. A few days after their arrival Col. Roosevelt succeeded in getting three good bulls and two cows of the white rhinoceros family as well as considerable lesser game. The naturalists collected many species of birds and mammals, insects as well as plants, flowers, etc.

CAMP RHINO HAS NARROW ESCAPE.

The second day at Camp Rhino furnished the party with an interesting experience which came nearly proving very disastrous. The camp on account of the number requires considerable space, and near the cooking tent a grass fire was accidently started. It burned with amazing rapidity and soon threatened the entire camp and its outfit. Col. Roosevelt's experience on the western plains of America stood him in good stead and he quickly had all hands working at beating and backfiring and clearing the grass immediately surrounding the camp, and by energetic work the camp was saved.

On February 2nd, 1910, a collection of moths that live on antelope horns was received at the Smithsonian Institution from the Former President Roosevelt. The donation came in the form of a pair of horns on which the larvæ were snugly imbedded. The authorities are taking good care of the horns, so that the larvæ may hatch.

Up to February 4th, 1910, Col. Roosevelt had the following trophies to his credit:

Lions	7	Leopard	1
Rhinoceroses	16	Hartebeest	1
Giraffes	10	Bohor	1
Wildebeests	8	Impalla	1
Thompson's gazelle	1	Waterbuck	1
Hippopotami	4	Buffaloes	7
Python	1	Elands	2
Ostrich	1	Topi	4

Elephants	9	Bushbuck	1
Zebra	1	Oribi	1
Oryx	1	Kob	1

Besides his list of Big Game Mr. Roosevelt has shot hundreds of smaller denizens of the jungle, beasts, birds and reptiles, as well as antelope, hartebeest, etc., for food for his own party and sefari.

Kermit Roosevelt has established his prowess as a nimrod up to the same date by shooting the following:

Lions	10	Buffaloes	4
Cheeta	3	Monkeys	2
Giraffes	2	Eland	1
Wildebeest	1	Topi	3
Leopard	1	Rhinoceroses	3
Hippopotamus	1	Elephants	2

On February 4, 1910, the Roosevelt expedition arrived at Nimule, Uganda Protectorate according to schedule. All the members were in excellent health and were delighted with the Congo district where they had good sport and secured splendid specimens of the white rhinoceros family complete. On February 5, 1910, the expedition left for Gondokoro which took them through the most trying part of their journey. Indeed for ten days they were isolated in a most dangerous wilderness hitherto so forbidding to the white man that it had not even been invaded by the telegraph companies.

On February 17, 1910, Col. Roosevelt and party were met sixteen miles from Gondokoro, Sudan, on the Upper Nile, by Chief Keriba and his native band of musicians and an immense number of natives. The parade to Gondokoro was amid a continuous clamor of native tom-toms, drums and bugles. The entrance into the village was rudely picturesque for nothing that British and native hospitality could suggest was lacking in the welcome. Reaching the town the band struck up the air "America" and following the musicians a native porter carried a large American flag. Then came the caravan proper, Col. Roosevelt, Kermit and the other American hunters and the large body of native porters who had an important if humble share in the work of the expedition.

Waiting on the Bar-el-Jabel river, the most southerly tributary of the Nile, was the launch of General Sir Reginald Wingate, Sirdar of the Egyptian army and from its masthead floated the Stars and Stripes. Col. Roosevelt boarded the launch at once and was taken to a brick house which had been placed at his disposal.

KERMIT ROOSEVELT (BWANAMTOTO) A HERO.

Soon after the expedition arrived at Gondokoro one of the native porters accidentally fell into the river. His fellow porters tried to rescue him but without success as they were afraid of the crocodiles which infest the stream. Kermit Roosevelt and Mr. Loring hearing of the accident hastened to the spot and heedless of the dangers from crocodiles and reptiles in the swift current, braved death by diving into the water in an effort to save porter. Kermit dived several times but failed to rescue the man but succeeded in bringing the body to shore although a crocodile came near him and nearly caught him. Scores of natives on the bank cheered Kermit as they watched his efforts which were commended by his father and the other members of the party. Kermit's efforts so exhausted him that he was given medical aid but soon recovered.

The final week of hunting was at this place. The party hunting along the banks of the river where they were successful in getting some excellent specimens of elephants, lions, etc.

On February 26, 1910, the party embarked on the Sirdar's launch for Khartoum where they arrived March 6th. Mrs. Roosevelt met her husband and son at this point, having come down from Cairo for that purpose.

CHAPTER XXIV.

RETURN OF COL. ROOSEVELT FROM THE JUNGLE.

By Peter MacQueen, F. R. G. S.

Remarkable Reputation He Made as a Man, a Hunter and a Statesman—The Eyes of the Whole World on This Great American, His Speeches and Striking Personality—What I Found Out in Travelling Over the United States—A Glimpse Into the Future.

WITH a back-ground of a thousand miles of jungle, where roam the animals of the Pleistocene Age; surrounded by hunters, poachers and cannibals; bearing the trophies of the most remarkable chase in history, the brilliant and popular ex-president of the United States emerged from darkest Africa at Gondokoro. His party had killed nearly 7,000 wild animals and birds, he had tramped and hungered and hunted in the vast forests of Uganda and the boundless plains of British East Africa. He had been a Frenchman to the French, a German to the Teuton, and an ideal English gentleman to the British subjects wherever he met them.

The picturesque and fascinating personality of Col. Theodore Roosevelt had been felt over every inch of United States territory for the whole year that he was in Africa. Whether statesmen legislated, or politicians plotted, or writers drove an itching pen, all these things were done with reference to the career and the power and influence of the great African hunter. He had been a man who could not be browbeaten or bought; and who would not crook the hinges of his knees that thrift might follow fawning. He had given to democrat and republican, to Catholic and Protestant, to southern man and northern man, to white and black, a fair show and a square deal whilst for seven years he had occupied the most exalted position in the world.

Roosevelt was looked for in Africa when I visited the British East Africa Protectorate a year before his arrival. The American ivory merchants were expecting his coming, the English and German military and civil officers were vying with each other in speaking kind words and expressing hospitable sentiments. The Frenchmen were bewailing the fact that there were no lions, leopards, elephants and rhinoceri in Madagascar, the French Colony. One day I visited the harbour of Mombasa and went on board a French steamer from Madagascar. A young French professor on the boat was reading very earnestly a big yellow book. I said, "Professor, what book is that you are reading?" and he replied in French "La Vie Intense." I asked him what that title meant in English and he replied in surprise "Vous etes Americaine," you not to know the Life Strenuous of one grand French Gentleman, le President Roosevel: Ah he is one grand man for France, Oh my France, my country, it is a ruin by the not to have of the life strenuous." I had not been five minutes in the German Club until a young German officer said to me in broken English: "Vil dot Herr President Roosenveld mit der Kaiser hier comin, Denken Zie?" And when a German officer mentions any man's name in connection with the Kaiser's you may know in what high esteem the man is held. On the other hand to the Englishmen of Central Africa Mr. Roosevelt was not a German or Frenchman but a typical English country squire. He was a university graduate, a sportsman of sportsmen and a statesman who could not be bribed or bullied—these are the three characteristics of the typical English gentleman.

And so this strange and buoyant boy, whom no amount of hard work, political grind and literary drudgery could tame or chasten, went through Africa like some magic white man. To the managers of the railway, to the missionaries in their difficult and thankless work, whose lives had grown monotonous and wearisome, to the English rulers on the frontier of empire to the black man emerging from 10,000 years of barbarism, came this gay, light-hearted boyish hunter who had deserted, for a holiday in the jungle, one of the mightiest places in the seats of the mighty.

The return of Mr. Roosevelt to civilization was dramatic, picturesque and characteristically informal. The newspaper reporters said that he appeared on board the English steamer bare footed with yellow trousers and a red shirt. But this is probably an exaggeration. The real truth seems to be that the Colonel landed at Khartoum in the khaki suit he wore upon his famous hunt. He had been away from America a year. Wonderful to say in that whole twelvemonth he had given voice to no opinion whatever upon American politics. Though his fame as a lion killer had gone into history with that of Hercules and Theseus, though the stories of his hunting had become a household word in the civilized world, he had made no remark whatever upon the work of his successor at Washington; he had raised no voice, he had made no protest against the most unpopular tariff measure ever passed by the government of the United States. His own great Republican Party and his own friend and candidate, in speeches and platforms had announced to the United States and to the world that they would revise the tariff downward. The new tariff had become law and nearly every dutiable article had been increased in price; the duty was taken off radium, and put on women's gloves. The tariff tinkers might as well have taken the duty of Halley's Comet in order to put it on Woollens.

Mr. Roosevelt while in the jungle was practically dead. He illustrates the great example that only after a man is dead do his countrymen appreciate his sterling qualities. A year after his death the ex-president appears at Khartoum and receives a welcome from his countrymen and from the world such as Gordon might have received if he had appeared in England after the fall of the Gladstone cabinet. The party to which Mr. Roosevelt belongs had become hopelessly divided. No man in the councils of the party could bring order out of chaos. No man was strong enough and brave enough and honest enough to look half the nation in the face and tell it that it lied. But there was a growing idea that the sun-browned hunter on the Nile was the one man that could save the party and perhaps the nation from very grave mistakes, and even from national calamities.

It was surprising how men who had hated and denounced Mr. Roosevelt, began to make a claim upon the people's sympathy by saying "I was the first man to adopt the Roosevelt policies." Or how opposition to Roosevelt in some quarters of the country was construed be the equivalent of treason to the republican party and even of disloyalty to the nation's best interests.

It would be an interesting study for the psychologist and the statesman to trace out just why and how this tremendous power has come to Mr. Roosevelt. The ex-president of course must be a man of unusual intellectual and moral talents. His private life has never even been questioned by his bitterest enemies. In his public career no man can point to a single instance of the slightest deviation from absolute honesty. The worst his foes could say about him was that he was rash and impetuous, or egotistic and arbitrary, but no man anywhere has dared to point a finger at Theodore Roosevelt and say that in any respect his character ever fell below the level of the highest and most courageous type of Christian manhood that our country has to-day.

I have been in sixteen states this winter lecturing on my trip across Central Africa where the Roosevelt party has hunted. I visited 120 towns and cities from Boston to Denver and from Philadelphia to Duluth and in not one place did I find the slightest opposition to Mr. Roosevelt. In the middle west nearly every man I met had already in his mind nominated and elected him for president in 1912. During my winter work there was just one discordant note. It was a letter I received from 53 Wall Street, New York City, and it said in effect: "You had no business to speak so flatteringly in a public lecture about Theodore Roosevelt, a discarded politician." This letter is sufficiently answered by the events of the last two months. At Khartoum the Roosevelt party was received by the English government with the greatest and most distinguished honor. It was noticeable that the Sirdar of the Sudan, Sir Reginald Wyngate, took Mr. Roosevelt first to the Gordon tree named after the famous Chinese Gordon whose lamentable death at Khartoum is part of the thrilling history of Egypt. The ex-president visited the battlefield of Omdurman and doubtless, in an honorable way, envied Lord Kitchener the brilliant glory of that famous victory. He doubtless showed the English officers just how he would have posted the Rough Riders at the fatal Donga where the lancers fell. The Sirdar visited, with the ex-president, the battlefield where he himself destroyed the power of the Mahdi. The Gordon College at Khartoum and the Missionary station not far away were visited. The missionaries of all denominations in Africa received high praise and great encouragement from the man who himself is earnestly religious.

One of the admirable traits in Mr. Roosevelt's character is his deep and abiding faith in revealed religion. He laid the foundation stone for a missionary building at Kijabe in the Rift Valley at the American-African Inland Mission. The Rev. Dr. Hurlburt and his wife did the hospitable honors and the ex-president in making a speech to the American missionaries (who by the way are non-denominational), gave it as his opinion that there was no better, safer or more practical work being done in the uplift of the natives than that done by missionaries. While his enthusiasm was great for religious work it did not end there, for at the banquets given him by the business men and the government officials at Nairobi he took occasion to express his great admiration for the English rule and the English pioneers in equatorial Africa. But he added a note of warning to the effect that the white men of Africa would be more successful in every line of life, if all the Caucasian race there tried to help and to understand one another. The pioneers he said should help the government, the government should try to understand the pioneers, and both should aid and sympathize with the missionary in his grand, unselfish work. Nothing impressed me more than his praise of the Catholic nuns, whom I had met in Uganda; his offer to lecture in behalf of mission work, and his estimate of Mother Paul, an American missionary at Kampala—that she was the strongest character he had met in Central Africa.

Now it has been remarkable to me that Mr. Roosevelt could talk so plainly to these men in Central Africa without giving them the slightest offence or in any way seeming to be using bad taste in discussing the internal problems of the land that was entertaining him. But such is the magnetic quality of the man that he goes right ahead and says what he thinks; and where other men might give grievous umbrage, Mr. Roosevelt's words are taken as those of a wise statesman, a kindly friend and a good fellow.

In Uganda the ex-president was equally popular. Six months before he reached that Protectorate I passed through the native capital of Kampala, the little native king Dauda Chwa, David the First, a grandson of the great Mtesa who entertained Stanley, showed me a map of Uganda he had made for the use of the hunting party. The boy king had marked the places where the biggest elephants could be found. The missionaries were asking about the coming visit and even the natives were already beginning to speak of Bwana Makuba, the Big Master; for they had heard the magic of his name and were sure he was some supernatural character that was going to appear in their country. And it is indeed wonderful, and not wanting in the element of mystery and magic, the fact that Mr. Roosevelt passed through the tsetse fly district, the fever swamps, and the lion haunted jungles without so much as a scratch, a cough, a cold or a fever. I saw him myself after the battle of Santiago when out of 450 Rough Riders only 121 reported for duty. He was gay and buoyant and when I asked him how he felt he replied,

"Oh splendidly, never felt better in my life. If I could only get food and medicine for my men, I would be absolutely happy."

At Khartoum the Egyptian students listened to a speech from Mr. Roosevelt. He told them what is an absolutely certain fact that in 12 years the Sudan, under British rule, had advanced more than any other country on the globe. He advised them to stick by the government that was doing so much to develop their country and give them all an equal chance; and to the men who came from the Christian missions, he characteristically said: "Be such a Christian that anybody who sees you will know that Christianity is a religion second to none." It was a strange historic and fascinating moment when this dynamic, kinetic and enthusiastic statesman of the west stood here beside the classic river Nile, and looked on its waters as they flowed away north to the Mediterranean. The Egyptian national party took offence at Roosevelt's warm appreciation of the English government. Nevertheless the genial and self-assured hunter went through Cairo, the centre of the Egyptian nationalist movement, and was on every side the conquering hero. This remarkable faculty of fitting in with all classes and conditions of men, even with those radically opposed to him, is such an unusual characteristic that through it Mr. Roosevelt wields a wonderful power.

In this country he is perhaps almost as popular in the democratic party, among the average voters, as he is in the republican. The Catholics tell me that no president in the history of America has treated their denomination with more eminent fairness and sanity. We have a good example of this in Mr. Roosevelt's visit to Uganda. At Kampala, Uganda there are two great missions—one of these is the Catholic mission at Nysambya. Among other workers in this mission the ex-president found a self-sacrificing and devoted woman, an American named Mother Paul, who has her rooms all draped with American flags. In his generous and enthusiastic way he at once volunteered to help her mission by giving a free lecture in America for the benefit of the institution. A few days later the hunters were invited to the Church of England mission at Namirambe. The ex-president was at the opening of a new medical missionary station there. He spoke to the assembled dignitaries of the English Church in his usual plain, frank, blunt, manly way. He told them he had just been to a Catholic mission and that the missionaries there had informed him of their deep debt to the medical doctor at the English mission He expressed his gladness at finding the Catholics and Protestants working side by side in deepest Africa and doing such a splendid work. He had heard that 500,000 of the natives are members of the Christian Church and that more than half a million of them can read and write the English language.

When Roosevelt came down the Nile to the Lado Enclave at the borders of Belgian territory, it is said that all the wild rovers, hunters and poachers in the great ivory country of the Congo, sent a delegation to him, inquiring whether he would not join an expedition and be its chief. One of the remarkable and fascinating pictures that comes to the mind in the return of Roosevelt to civilization is his trip down the Nile.

Surely no personage in history, not even excepting Napoleon Bonaparte, has ever brought to Egypt a more romantic and impressive personality. Here was a product of Harvard's best culture, a ruler who had handled problems alongside of which the granaries of Joseph, the armies of Menes and the unrivalled cavalry of Napoleon were but as children playing with toys. One might have seen besides the sculptured walls of Luxor, a brown-faced, cheerful, vigorous man of fifty, quite unspoiled by world-wide renown and universal popularity, riding a camel and laughing and chatting with his donkey boys. Yet no great king who has ever ruled the Nile, and no powerful ruler who has built pyramids and erected obelisks has ever had one-hundredth part the power or has ever known how to wield that power so well as this same laughing, cheerful, bright-faced man. To everybody he seems to have been as affable as a young college graduate. To his old guide Cunninghame at Khartoum, he gave both gifts and money. And to every one of the black untutored men who in patience and good heart had taken the white man's burden across hundreds of miles of scorching plains and gloomy forests, he gave not only a kind and hearty farewell but a substantial financial reward. No wonder that the black men went back into the forest saddened at the loss of Bwana Makuba, the Big Master, who had followed them to the hunt, who had waded the streams and threaded the forest with as much primeval joy as any native warrior ever did, and who in all his relations to them had been the fair and just master, a man who would not impose upon them and who while he was with them, would allow no man to do them wrong.

And now from the glistening sands of Egypt, from the glory of the pyramids, and the mysterious shadow of the sphinx he goes to Europe to be feted by kings and emperors, and to arouse in Europe the same enthusiasm and interest that he has aroused in Africa. The question seems to be in every man's mind, what will Mr. Roosevelt do when he returns to America? He will find a nation torn and racked by many divided councils. Thoughtful men are beginning to feel that Carlyle may have had some reason in saying that "Democracy is a self-cancelling business." It may become necessary in our age and country to elect a man like Roosevelt to the Presidency for life. The constant change in presidents seems to cause so much heartburning and produce so much ambition as to lead men away from the true purpose for which they were elected. I have never until recently believed that Macaulay might be right when he wrote the following sentence: "The day will come when in the State of New York a multitude of people, none of whom has had more than half a breakfast or expects to have more than half a dinner, will choose a legislature. Is it possible to doubt what sort of a legislature will be chosen? Either some Caesar or Napoleon will seize the reins of government with a strong hand or your republic will be as fearfully plundered and laid waste by barbarians in the twentieth century as the Roman empire was in the fifth; with this difference that the Huns and Vandals who ravaged the Roman Empire came from the outside and that your Huns and Vandals will have been engendered within your own country by your own institution."

These remarkable words by Lord Macaulay the historian may have no foundation in the facts of our country at present but there certainly have been many happenings within the last three years that give them at least significance. Probably no one will dream of electing Roosevelt to be our President during the course of his natural life. That is an extravagance in which no man at the present moment will indulge. But that some strong and firm and honest hand must lay its grasp upon our politics in the next few decades is the honest assumption of many thoughtful citizens. Otherwise we will have immense national calamities. When Roosevelt returns he will very likely sustain President Taft as long as he reasonably can. I make no doubt at all that he will go into the middle west, that he will be popular with the insurgents, that he will take strong, advanced ground on conservation of our national resources. He will doubtless be returned to the Senate or else elected speaker of the house, and he will in the opinion of many people without doubt be the next president of the United States.

The ex-president's visit to the King of Italy, the Kaiser, the President of France and the King of England, his powerful popularity with the great and strong rulers of the world will exalt him into a diplomatic place in American politics altogether and absolutely unique. His year in the wilderness of Africa has no doubt revived and refreshed him mentally and physically, and he will doubtless be a stronger man, a more virile thinker, a more sane and judicious statesman than he has ever been before. Of all the men or statesmen whom the Spanish-American war brought to the front, Roosevelt alone retains an immense popularity and universal regard. He left the country while his party was enraged at him and now his party stretches beseeching hands to him across the sea and asks him to come back and save its life. No man in our history has ever attained such popularity during his life time as Mr. Roosevelt, and this popularity I think comes from the immense appeal that his very decided and extremely American personality makes upon the average voter in our land. I have seen him in a single half hour discuss some red hot question with a senator from a red hot senate; then some question of international law with a statesman from Japan; then an interview with a professor on Birds, Beetles and Butterflies; then a discussion on Religion and Temperance; and then I have received from him myself a discourse on travel; and all that happened in one short thirty minutes.

Roosevelt to my mind is not either a republican or a democrat. He is more nearly an insurgent-socialist though he would never admit it himself, and would doubtless be very much displeased if anyone should tell him so. He entertains no fantastic dreams about the absolute equality of men. He knows and says so on every occasion, that only useful and independent men are desirable citizens. He has told me that he would never in the world take the slightest advantage of such a country as Venezuela; nor would he on the other hand allow Venezuela to repudiate its just debts to England, Germany or America. He told me he would rather have his son Kermit teaching in a mission in Charlestown than at the head of his class in the Harvard university. He said to me one day: "Mr. MacQueen, the best thing a man can give his son is not money nor the reputation of being the son of a president; the best thing a man can leave his son is an untarnished name."

Elbert Hubbard of East Aurora, who does not admire Roosevelt too much, said to me the other day: "Peter, I don't believe there is one dishonest bone in Roosevelt's body. I think he is a mediaeval man. I think he believes in an absolute hell, and in the trinity and in everything that he upholds, and he believes tremendously in himself. I think Roosevelt cares nothing for money, but he loves his career and will do nothing wrong or dishonest because greatness and honesty and power are the ideals of his life." These are good words and this is enormous praise from one who really does not love you. We have not heard the last of Theodore Roosevelt, we have scarcely yet heard the beginning.

CHAPTER XXV.

COL. ROOSEVELT'S TRIUMPHANT TRIP THROUGH EUROPE

The Ex-President Makes a Memorable Speech in Cairo, Egypt—Visits the Pyramids and Sphinx—Embarks for Italy—Feted and Dined by the King of Italy—Col. Roosevelt's Own Statement of Why He Did Not Visit the Pope.

By J. T. THOMPSON.

After leaving Luxor in Egypt the Roosevelt party, which now consisted of the Colonel, Mrs. Roosevelt, Miss Ethel and Kermit, spent several days sight-seeing at many of the more important places in Egypt. Everywhere the party stopped they were the guests of the representatives of the British Government which holds a protectorate over Egypt. The journeys consisted of camel rides to the tombs of Egypt's Ancient Kings, and ruins of cities that flourished over 3,000 years ago. With that strenuousness which has always characterized Col. Roosevelt, he entered into all of the events planned for his entertainment and early every morning was mounted on a camel or an Arabian horse or sometimes on a donkey to ride across the desert to view some of the wonders of this land of many wonders.

On March 24, 1910, the party arrived at Cairo, Egypt, which was lavishly decorated in honor of Col. Roosevelt. An enormous throng had gathered at the station and when the Colonel appeared from his car he was given a rousing ovation. There were hundreds of American Tourists in the crowds but there were also thousands of the swarthy natives and they gave the ex-President a welcome that in cordiality and enthusiasm surpassed that ever received by any other foreigner.

Abbas Hilmi, the Khedive, (Ruler of Egypt) paid Col. Roosevelt a great honor by sending the State Coach to his hotel to convey him to Abdin Palace where he was entertained. This State Coach is only used when Royalty visits the Khedive. Mrs. Roosevelt was entertained by the Khediva at the same time in another part of the palace.

In the evening the entire party left for a visit to the Pyramids. The night was wondrously clear and with a brilliant silver moon lighting up the heavens they reached the silent sentinels of the desert, three huge ghostlike Pyramids that have stood for ages. A short distance and the party found themselves face to face with the Sphinx. For upwards of 5,000 years, through ancient and modern times, from the days of Julius Cæsar, Marc Anthony, Cleopatra and Napoleon the unfathomable eyes of this wonderful image have gazed across the centuries of time. Here in the bright Egyptian moonlight, in the silence and mystery of the desert, Theodore Roosevelt stood and gazed at this stolid image just as the great men of history had done. What did he think? Every traveler says the impenetrable face of the Sphinx has a peculiar influence over all.

One of the unusual receptions given Colonel Roosevelt in Cairo was the American one. Five hundred Americans who were visiting in that city met him by appointment and had a regular American hand-shaking time. The Colonel was very pleased to meet so many of his own countrymen and women.

Shortly before leaving Egypt for Italy Col. Roosevelt made a speech to the students of the University of Cairo. This speech was looked forward to by many of the leading men of Egypt for it was known that the Colonel had made a careful study of conditions in Egypt and would probably handle the subject in his own blunt, forceful way. The Colonel told the students the principles of good citizenship and as an instance of bad citizenship he unmercifully lashed the man who had assassinated the Prime Minister of Egypt for political reasons a short time before. This speech in some native papers was condemned, but in general it was praised and it was said that it would be of lasting good to Egypt.

On April 2 the Roosevelt party arrived at Naples, Italy. Here another great crowd had gathered to see "The great American" as he was called. During the ride from the boat to the hotel Col. Roosevelt raised his hat smilingly, bowed right and left in acknowledgment of the repeated cheers.

On April 4th Mr. Roosevelt was received by King Victor Emmanuel at the Quirinal—The Royal Palace. The occasion gave an opportunity for another exhibition of the admiration of the public for the former president and the popular interest in his movements. The hour of his reception being known, a number of persons gathered to greet him on his way from the hotel to the royal palace.

As he alighted from his carriage at the Quirinal the cuirassiers forming the bodyguard of the king gave Mr. Roosevelt a military salute. A footman in blue velvet knickerbockers and red coat covered with gold lace preceded him to the antechamber of his majesty, where he was received by Rear-Admiral Garelli, aid on duty Count Tozzoni and Duke Cito, master of ceremonies.

Immediately afterward the honored guest was escorted to the door of the king's apartment, which when thrown open revealed his majesty standing with arms outstretched and with a smile on his lips. His majesty wore the uniform of a general of the Italian army. His words of welcome, spoken in excellent English, were cordial. King Victor and Mr. Roosevelt shook hands heartily, the monarch inviting the former president to sit at his side. Then the door of the apartment was closed and the two remained in private conversation about three-quarters of an hour.

COL. ROOSEVELT'S OWN REASONS FOR NOT SEEING THE POPE.

The audience which Col. Roosevelt expected to have with the Pope did not take place owing to conditions which the Vatican had imposed and which Mr. Roosevelt refused to accept.

While at Cairo, Egypt, Col. Roosevelt cabled the American Ambassador at Rome to arrange for an audience with His Holiness the Pope. He received the following reply: "The Holy Father will be delighted to grant an audience to Mr. Roosevelt, April the fifth and hopes that nothing will arise to prevent it, such as the much regretted incident which made the reception of Mr. Fairbanks impossible." (Vice President Fairbanks spoke in the pulpit of the Methodist College at Rome and his audience with the Pope was cancelled.)

Mr. Roosevelt replied:

"It would be a real pleasure to me to be presented to the Holy Father, for whom I entertain high respect, both personally and as the head of a great church. I fully recognize his entire right to receive or not receive whomsoever he chooses, for any reason that seems good to him, and if he does not receive me I shall not for a moment question the propriety of his action.

"On the other hand, I in turn must decline to make any stipulations or submit to any conditions which in any way would limit my freedom of conduct. I trust that on April 5 he will find it convenient to receive me." THEODORE ROOSEVELT

Ambassador Leishman replied:

"The audience cannot take place except on the understanding expressed in the former message."

To Ambassador Leishman, Rome, Italy.

"The proposed presentation is, of course, now impossible."

THEODORE ROOSEVELT.

LYMAN ABBOTT, *Editor of the Outlook, New York.*

"Through the Outlook I wish to make a statement to my fellow Americans regarding what has occurred in connection with the Vatican I am sure that the great majority of my fellow citizens, catholics quite as much as protestants, will feel that I acted in the only way possibl for an American to act and because of this fact I most earnestly hop that the incident will be treated in a matter of course way as merel personal, and, above all, as not warranting the slightest exhibition o rancor or bitterness.

"Among my best and closest friends are many catholics. The re spect and regard of those of my fellow Americans who are catholics ar as dear to me as the respect and regard of those who are protestants.

"On my journey through Africa I visited many catholic as well a many protestant missions. As I look forward to telling the people a home all that has been done by protestants and catholics alike, as I sa it, in the field of missionary endeavor, it would cause me a real pan to have anything said or done that would hurt or give pain to m friends, whatever their religious belief. But any merely personal con siderations are of no consequence in this matter. The important con sideration is the avoidance of harsh and bitter comment such as ma excite mistrust and anger between and among good men.

"The more an American sees of other countries the more profoun must be his feelings of gratitude that, in his own land there is not merel complete toleration, but the heartiest good will and sympathy betwee sincere and honest men of different faiths—good will and sympathy a complete that in the innumerable daily relations of our American lif catholics and protestants meet together and work together withou thought of the difference of creed being even present in their minds.

"This is a condition so vital to our national well-being that nothin should be permitted to jeopardize it. Bitter comment and criticisn acrimonious attack and defense, are not only profitless but harmfu and to seize upon such an incident as this as an occasion for controvers would be wholly indefensible and should be frowned upon by catholic and protestants alike, and by all good Americans."

THEODORE ROOSEVELT.

CPSIA information can be obtained
at www.ICGtesting.com
Printed in the USA
LVHW031543210520
656176LV00017B/1374